The Inner Journey of the Poet

The Inner Journey of the Poet

and other papers

by
KATHLEEN RAINE
Edited by
Brian Keeble

George Braziller
New York

Published in the United States in 1982 by George Braziller, Inc.

Copyright © 1982 by Kathleen Raine
Copyright © 1982 by Brian Keeble

Published simultaneously in Great Britain by George Allen & Unwin, Ltd.

For information address the publisher:
George Braziller, Inc.
One Park Avenue
New York, NY 10016

Library of Congress Catalog Card Number: 81-21675
ISBN: 0-8076-1039-9

Printed in England
First Edition

Foreword

The contents of the present volume have been chosen from among Dr Raine's occasional papers delivered, for the most part, to audiences over the last eight years. It supplements the previous collection, *Defending Ancient Springs* (Oxford, 1967), but by no means includes all such papers written in recent years. A collection of the author's essays on Yeats is in preparation.

Those readers already familiar with the essays of Kathleen Raine will know the consistency of her arguments from premises tried and tested over many years. This fact has provided the editor with his most obvious task, that of minimizing, without doing violence to the subtlety of the argument, the element of repetition that must inevitably occur in bringing together a collection of addresses originally destined for audiences somewhat removed in time and place. The second primary task has been to supply discreet references to the poetry and prose passages used in quotation. I have not endeavoured to be exhaustive in this, preferring to bear in mind that each paper (with one exception) was originally shaped to be read aloud. At the same time it seemed only proper that, where necessary, some guidance should be offered to the reader who may wish to go back to first sources for further study. In the case of the many quotations from William Blake, I have given in brackets a page number preceded by a 'K'. This obviously refers to the Oxford edition of Blake's *Complete Writings* edited by Geoffrey Keynes (1969).

The author is, of course, well known for her extensive work in Blake studies. This work is further enriched by two papers in the present volume: 'The Beautiful and the Holy' and 'Towards a Living Universe'. These, together with 'Science and Imagination in William Blake' (published in *Temenos* I, London, 1981) and 'Blake: The Poet as Prophet' (to appear in the 1982 volume of *Essays and Studies* published by the English Association, London) represent the author's last words on the subject of Blake and therefore complete a labour of love and intensive learning begun over thirty years ago.

I mentioned above one exception. 'Cecil Collins, Painter of Paradise' is the only paper in this collection not to have been delivered to an audience. It was written at my request to be included in the booklet series of Golgonooza Press to celebrate a friendship between poet and painter of nearly half a century and was first published in 1979. My regret that it appeared then without the benefit of illustrations is now tempered by the inclusion of five plates in the present volume.

'What is Man?' was originally a contribution to a conference on education at Dartington Hall in 1977. The text of the address was subsequently published by Golgonooza Press in 1980. Premises and Poetry was delivered to the now defunct Institute of Christian Studies, London, in 1975 and later published in *Sophia Perennis* (Tehran, 1977) vol. III, no. 2. 'The Inner Journey of the Poet' was originally given as a lecture to the College of Psychic Studies Conference in 1975 and published in the College journal *Light*. The lecture was then revised and delivered to the Analytical Psychology Club in 1976 and subsequently published in *Harvest*. The text of the present paper is taken from a further revision published by Golgonooza Press in 1976. 'Poetic Symbols as a Vehicle of Tradition' was first delivered at the Eranos Conference of 1968 and subsequently published as 'Poetic Symbols as a Vehicle of Tradition: The Crisis of the Present in English Poetry' in the Eranos *Jahrbuch 1968* (Zurich, Rhein-Verlag, 1970). 'Waste Land, Holy Land' formed the British Academy's 1976 Warton Lecture and was published as from the Proceedings of the Academy for 1976. 'Hopkins: Nature and Human Nature' was the third Annual Hopkins Lecture, delivered at University College, London, in 1972, and printed by the Hopkins Society in that year. 'David Jones and the Actually Loved and Known' is based on a paper originally read at a David Jones Weekend at the Royal Foundation of Saint Katherine, London, in 1977. It was later revised and read at the David Jones Society Conference at Pembroke College, Cambridge, in 1978 and published simultaneously by Golgonooza Press. 'The Chamber of Maiden Thought' was the Worshipful Society of Apothecaries' Annual Keats Lecture for 1981 and is here printed for the first time. 'The Beautiful and the Holy' was given at a symposium on the theme of Beauty and Psyche organised by the Psychology Department of Dallas University, Irving, Texas, in 1979. This paper also appears here for the first time. 'Towards a Living Universe' was first presented at a symposium sponsored by the Charles F. Kettering Foundation and Teacher's College, Columbia University, on Knowledge, Education and Human Values: 'Towards the Recovery of Wholeness', in 1980. It is to be published in *Teacher's College Record* but the text has been somewhat revised for its present publication. To the appropriate institutions and editors of the above, we wish to acknowledge our gratitude for permission to reprint material in the present book.

I wish to express my thanks to Cecil Collins, Arthur Giardelli, Paul

Hills, John Lane, the Dartington Hall Trust and the National Museum of Wales for their help in obtaining photographs.

Finally I must thank the author for her patience and fortitude in dealing with a multitude of queries.

BRIAN KEEBLE
January 1981

Contents

List of Illustrations

The Inner Journey of the Poet

1

'What is Man?'

IN considering education it is before all else necessary to ask that oldest of questions, 'What is man?' We find the question in the Book of Job, who asks, 'What is man, that thou shouldst magnify him? and that thou shouldst set thy heart upon him?' Job is quoting from a psalm which reminds us of the paradox of human littleness and human greatness:

> When I consider thy heavens, the work of thy fingers,
> the moon and the stars, which thou hast ordained;
> What is man, that thou art mindful of him? and the son
> of man, that thou visitest him?
> For thou hast made him a little lower than the angels,
> and hast crowned him with glory and honour.
> Thou madest him to have dominion over the works of thy
> hands; thou hast put all things under his feet.

This psalm is quoted in the Epistle to the Hebrews, in order to present to the Jews, familiar with the scriptures, the new concept of Jesus as the divine humanity incarnate; and all these texts look back, finally, to the first chapter of Genesis, where the creation of man is described:

> So God created man in his own image, in the image of
> God created he him.

—and the passage goes on to describe the dominion given to man over all living things on the earth.

When Job reminds God of his exaltation of man he does so in bitterness, complaining that man is a creature of dust who goes down to the grave unregarded. Nevertheless the theme which runs through the Bible, from Genesis to the Epistle to the Hebrews, is man as the image of God, bearer of the divine imprint; Jesus, as the Son of Man, is the realization of the first-created humanity, the *anthropos*, as imagined by the Creator before the Fall; which Fall is the result of Adam's 'sleep', a loss of consciousness, a 'descent', as the Greeks

1

would say, from a spiritual to a natural mode of consciousness, with a consequent self-identification not with the spiritual but with the natural body; which is, as Job complains, a thing of dust.

The Greeks too asked the question 'what is man?'—the riddle of the Sphinx: 'What is it that in the morning goes on four legs, at midday on two legs, and in the evening on three legs?'—a bitter evocation of the mortal worm who creeps from helpless infancy, through a brief and precarious prime to the helplessness of infirm age. Oedipus guessed the riddle, and, by implication, acknowledged the truth of the Sphinx's description of man.

Which is of course the widely accepted view of mankind in modern secular societies. Week in week out the evolutionists describe natural man on the mass media; the schools assume the finality of the scientific description of reality, including natural man (who dares question the infallibility of science—natural knowledge—or its pronouncements?). Thus in our secular society man the mortal worm is, paradoxically, denied the only dignity which properly belongs to us—our spiritual nature—and at the same time proclaimed as the lord of creation. Education of the mortal worm for a brief life on earth is inevitably therefore designed to fit men and women to the performance of tasks concerned with bodily life, tasks more or less skilled, but all alike directed to the production of material goods and the construction and control of machines, also utilized for material ends. Ultimately man becomes, within such an order, a replaceable spare-part in the great machine a materialist society has constructed, with a built-in obsolescence after fifty or so years of efficient functioning. The modern state is a self-perpetuating machine built to last longer than any individual life-time and we like to pretend that the state, or the world super-state, will last for ever—well, nearly for ever, and what difference is there between eternity and a very long time indeed? The world will last our time, we shall not be here at the end; at most we wonder about our grandchildren, but who cares about their own progeny six generations hence? 'They are destroyed from morning to evening: they perish for ever without any regarding it.'

This is the implicit, and sometimes explicit, view of the materialist Western society to which we belong, and it is difficult to remain totally untouched by the evolutionism of materialist science, which recognizes only a material order, with humankind as part of that order—the most complex and 'evolved' species which has produced man as the cleverest of the primates, by a process of natural selection. This process may produce cleverer primates yet and (as many hopefully believe) is bound to do so, because evolution, guided though it is by blind chance, can result only in Utopia; (Utopia, be it said, in the modern sense of the word, as a society in which all temporal mankind's aspirations and desires will be realized. The Catholic Thomas More would not have expected a society without any spiritual order to have any such result). In the modern Utopian dream every disease will be 'conquered', and so perhaps will death, and no one will go cold or hungry or unintegrated within the social structure; as for living, our machines will do that for us, thereby freeing us to enjoy this hell of spiritual meaninglessness for as long as we can endure it.

Utopians never give up their myth: the plain evidence goes to show that the English nation (to look no farther afield) simply cannot stand it, that the schoolchildren do not want to be trained for the kind of 'jobs' that the machines provide, in the technological Utopia where thinking is something computers do, where 'the brain' is synonymous with mind and thought. We have even had it claimed that a computer can write poems, and truth to say the examples given were all too like many produced by human beings who conceive themselves in terms of a mechanistic science.

Students engage in revolution, destruction making small demands in comparison with the complex programming of the university syllabus; besides satisfying some unformulated and baffled sense of frustration engendered by the secular society. The mass of mankind—the worker-ants—misled by the ever-present advertisements which tell us that Utopia is in every packet of this or that, grasp what they can, forever deceived by the trash of the machines which cheats their dreams of realization. Who can blame them that they are dissatisfied? Clever cynics who know about human dreams paint for them those desert-islands, those far shores and clear paradisal streams, unfelled trees, unbulldozed meadows, unravished Eves, that forever elude the purchasers of cigarettes and convenience foods, underwear and insurance policies, cosmetics made from slaughtered whales whose rotting carcases stink upon the real shores, and all the celestial omnibuses are driven on oil and coal and steel from Paradise Lost, and the tasteless bread and canned vegetables harvested from a waste land where the wild flowers and the bees are sprayed with poison, the rabbits, so popular on children's cot-covers, die of myxomatosis, and as the motorist fancies a tiger in his tank the real tigers of the earth are threatened with extermination. The world has never been more hideous, more uninhabitable, than the world created by an ideology which proclaims that this world is all, which gives to matter a

3

primacy, an all-importance unknown to other civilizations. Decidedly the way to Utopia is long and hard for the last of the primates.

If man is indeed what Blake calls the mortal 'worm of sixty winters' and 'seventy inches long', 'born in a night to perish in a night', what can education be? In a world of pure materialism education can only be utilitarian, a training to fit the human spare part for the function it is to perform during its few useful years; after which there is nothing to expect but death and death is the end, as birth was the beginning of life. The satisfaction of natural appetites is presumed to give the mortal worm, or naked ape, those satisfactions of which we are capable; including music, whose rhythms serve to stimulate or soothe, food and shelter, sensual pleasure, freedom from pain, hunger, cold, or the disorientation of those habits to which we are conditioned; 'programmed', as it is nowadays called. And so, 'distracted from distraction by distraction', as T. S. Eliot wrote of the dwellers in the waste land, we 'get by'. Drugs can alleviate whatever states of anxiety our souls may cause us, and there is yet another industry to cater for our inevitable dreams or day-dreams; for these are an as yet unexplained flaw in the perfect adaptation and functioning of mortal life: mankind continues to imagine quite other things.

The Utopian view of humanity is of course untrue; untrue not because the deductions of science concerning natural law are incorrect within their own terms—the great merit of the scientific method is its respect for evidence and, in that sense, for truth—but untrue because the assumption—the premise of Western science, that nothing exists other than the quantifiable natural world—is false. Consciousness—to take the most obvious thing in the world—cannot, for example, be quantified, cannot be dealt with at all in terms of weight and measure, of those extensions in space or in time which are the only terms proper to material science. Mental and physical entities are incommensurable not because science has not 'as yet' found a way of describing mental events in physical terms but because these belong to distinct orders. In measuring the brain-waves of dreamers or of meditators, scientists have not come one whit nearer to measuring the dreams themselves; nor can they ever do so within the terms of their proper field of knowledge. This is no reproach to natural science, which has its own field, and whose account of natural phenomena is impressive indeed—a field which rightly includes man's physical frame, its anatomy, physiology, and place within the natural universe.

4

But so overwhelmed are we by wave after wave of information about man's natural evolution and affinity with nature on the one side, and on the other by medical explanations of whatever concerns the psyche, that we easily forget that man is *not* merely a clever primate; we forget that the brain is *not* the mind, that consciousness is *not* a property of the sense-organs of which it makes use. We forget, in fact, that man is not a species of animal but a new kingdom, as distinct from the animal kingdom as mammals are distinct from rocks. Each kingdom, from the mineral to the vital, from the vital to the animate, from animal consciousness to the human kingdom of the Imagination, is subject to new laws proper to itself. This Teilhard de Chardin has made very clear to our generation, but he still has not clearly enough reminded us that mankind, as human (for of course we share the laws of chemistry with the mineral world, the vital physiology with plants, and our bodily senses with the animals) is an invisible kingdom whose world is a mental world, subject to laws proper to itself which do not conform to the categories of time and space, or to any of the laws of nature. Because this is in reality so, and equally so for atheists as for Christians, for Marxists as for Buddhists, the extreme picture of man as a spare part of his own machines can never altogether come about. We cannot altogether dehumanize ourselves. Whereas our opinions can make us very unhappy and raise in us all kinds of conflicts between what is so and what we opine to be so, they cannot alter the reality of what we are. We continue to be human, and insofar as we are human we are spiritual beings.

Western materialism is an unprecedented departure from human culture, as it has existed and developed from the stone age to the present time. From the oldest examples of human art we see human-kind seeking to express ideas, to discover a mental order; to explore our inner worlds in terms of pantheons of 'gods' who personify the qualities of human consciousness, our moods and modes of experience. From the earliest known human records we see humankind creating abstract patterns and forms not found in nature; gods of strange unnatural aspect—the more unnatural the more profoundly 'human'. Modern Amazonian savages asked Lévi-Strauss, that civilized Frenchman, why he and his kind did not paint their faces with abstract patterns in order (like the Amazonians) to affirm their humanity, their difference from the animals around them. They knew what Western anthropologists would seem to have forgotten, that to be human is, precisely, to live our myths, to live according to an inner order which is not natural, which is, in terms of natural law, unnatural. The distortions and deformations of the human face and body, the paintings and tatooings practised by primitives from the land of El Dorado to Borneo or the Congo are supremely, specifically human, being expressions of a mental, an inner world, affirmed in opposition to, in challenge of, a natural order. The pantheons of more advanced societies are more psychologically complex and subtle explorations of those inner regions of human consciousness. The familiar gods of Greece—still, in many respects, our own self-knowledge personified—are not mere moods and passions but intellections of great subtlety, related each to certain fields of knowledge. The Orphic theology in all its complexity of hierarchic relationship and causality is unsurpassed as an account of mankind's invisible worlds, a system no less elaborate in its structuring than the scientists' description of the kingdoms of nature. To name only one or two of the most obvious examples of the distinctness of these inner fields, Apollo is the principle of all mental clarity, knowledge of music and number, medicine, the ordering principle that belongs to the enlightened mind, to the rational; the changing moon-goddess to dark knowledge of the blood, to parturition, witchcraft, all kinds of feminine regions of experience. Dionysus is the genius of ecstatic possession by irrational states of consciousness, an exaltation unknown to the clear reason of Apollo's kingdom; while Ares takes over the warrior when, like the Irish Cuchullain, the battle-warp seizes him, his hair stands on end, his face is distorted with rage and his body filled with the berserk courage the Vikings delighted in, a transport of rage in which the warriors scarcely felt the wounds of battle. To each god his kingdom. In our own century these principles or energies of the psyche which materialist science had thought to dismiss as unrealities, or as primitive attempts by mankind to describe the 'laws of nature', have been renamed by C. G. Jung the 'archetypes' which are, as he says, self-portraits of the instincts. Jung was the tireless reminder of our forgetful age that the psyche is real; that it is also most dangerous. It is not from nature that this world stands in danger of destruction, but from the human mind which has invented hydrogen bombs and the ideologies in whose service such weapons may be used. If the most apalling apocalyptic prophecies are realized it will have been ourselves who have brought them about. The author of the Book of Revelation read only the possibilities within the inner worlds of mankind. We are inclined to read that book as a threat from an arbitrary and cruel (but fortunately, so the scientists reassure us, non-existent) God; but read that terrifying book as the story of inner events within the human psyche reflected—as our thoughts inevitably must be—in the world of history, and we must tremble, not at what 'God' might do to us, but at what we ourselves have it in us to do to ourselves and to our world. Is not that prophecy of poisoned seas and rivers, of Armageddon, of shelterless refugees, of destruction falling from the skies, already realized, not by some cosmic catastrophe or arbitrary act of 'victimization', as it is called, of innocent humankind by a demon-god, but by the demons who inhabit the human soul?

All the great religious traditions have been attempts to cultivate the human soul. But any attempt in our materialist civilisation to bring order to the inner worlds, to nourish the specifically human, has gone by default. Not altogether so, of course, for the past is still powerful and two thousand years of Christendom and all the wisdom of the Greek and the Hebrew traditions before that are still with us; or at least with the educated sections of society, who are less at the mercy of current ideologies. Pythagoras continues to impose upon the soul the order of the diatonic scale through such music as is still composed according to its laws. Christian art continues to remind us of the celestial hierarchies of angels, of the lives of saints lived in accordance with the laws not of nature but of the spirit; of the Christian myth of the birth of the Divine Principle into the world of generation, fully manifested in that sublime figure of Christ Pantocrator, the ruler of all, depicted in the dome of every Orthodox basilica; and whose suffering under the world-rulers for whom man is natural man, the armed ape and the toga'd ape, Western Catholicism, in the image of the Crucifix, has never allowed us to forget. For the struggle to rise from the natural to the human kingdom is hard and endless, and none of us has succeeded so well that we can afford to dismiss the symbol of the Crucifixion, which Utopians would like to banish from their brave new world; which is the hell of the human spirit whose kingdom, as it is said in the Christian Gospel, is 'not of this world'.

Let me remind you that we are still considering the question 'What is man?' I have suggested that man is, in truth, not a mortal worm but a spiritual being, immaterial, immeasurable, who is never born and never dies, because spirit is not bounded or contained within the categories of the material world of time and space, of duration and extension. In this sense, we are immortal, eternal, boundless within our own universe. Yet of the kingdom that is truly ours, specifically human, we have realised very little.

Nowadays the term 'human' has been inverted to the point of signifying precisely what is least human in us, our bodily appetites

7

and their gratification, and all that belongs to natural man; while the study of philosophy, for example, or the practice of some religious asceticism is considered 'inhuman'. Nothing in our 'permissive' society is held to be more 'human' than the act of sex; but Alexander the Great—Aristotle's pupil—said that man was never *less* human than in that act. He was not, of course, speaking of love, which is of the soul and has no necessary connection with the sexual instinct. Sex is an animal function, love a human experience. It is all too easy to revert to the animal which we, as humanity, must labour to transcend in order to come into even a small portion of our potential kingdom. The late Dr Schumacher, who in his book *Guide to the Perplexed* made many things so clear, liked to quote Aquinas's words, 'Even the least knowledge of things superior is of greater value than the most extensive knowledge of things inferior'.

Having, therefore, reminded ourselves that humanity, insofar as we are human, is a kingdom not in nature, 'not of this world', but an invisible inner universe, let us consider this universe a little more closely.

While every pantheon is a less or more perfect, a more or less crude and simple, or subtly complex representation of the structure of the human inner worlds, certain elements seem to recur and to represent the abiding structure of the psyche. The sphere quadrated by a six-armed cross, or the circle quadrated by a four-armed cross; fourness under many symbols—the four-faced gods of India; the four 'sons' of the Egyptian Harpocrates; Jesus Christ with the four evangelists, the four 'living creatures' of Ezekiel's fourfold Chariot of God, or the lion, eagle, ox and angel of the Book of Revelation. C. G. Jung in his *Psychological Types* has made the Four familiar as the 'functions' of the human psyche: reason, feeling, sensation and intuition. Blake, basing his symbol upon Ezekiel and St John, describes the four 'Zoas' or 'living creatures' whose conflicts and rebellions form the drama of his Prophetic Books. These Four are in every man; and Blake speaks of the Four Zoas as the four 'faces' of the Universal Man; as the four rivers of Paradise; as four 'worlds' or 'universes'—distinct worlds, each with its own mode of knowledge, distinct and incommensurable, as feeling or intuition with reason, or sensation with the other three. Blake, at the end of the eighteenth century, had already diagnosed what he calls 'the sickness of Albion'—that is, of the English national being—as the usurpation by the rational function—Urizen—of the throne and sceptre of supremacy which properly belongs to the Imagination, the 'human existence itself' and divine anthropos, made in the image of

8

God, which is above the Four. Urizen is the rational mind, basing its deductions upon what Blake calls a 'ratio of the five senses', and his creation is scientific materialism. The rational mind is aware of no form of knowledge higher than itself, calling the Imagination 'delusion and fancy'. This spiritual sickness of the English nation Blake saw typified in those culture-heroes of science, Bacon, Newton and Locke (to whose number others have since been added—Darwin, Huxley, Russell and so on), who share the false premise of all, that 'matter', a substance existing apart from the mind which perceives it, is the only ground of the 'real'. Under the rule of Urizen, feeling becomes no longer a mode of knowledge, but a selfish emotion; while intuition, refusing the rule of Urizen, rebels in vain. Although Blake was well able to argue the case against rationalism in its own terms—and did so most trenchantly—his most powerful weapon was the depiction of man the rationalist, anxious and purblind, unable ever to complete his conquest of the rebellious energies of life; a foolish travesty of God the Father.

Blake describes the 'sickness of Albion' under the usurping rule of Urizen as a 'deadly sleep', using the Platonic term, which sees unconsciousness, oblivion of the real, forgetfulness of the eternal worlds within, as the mark of the human condition described in the Jewish-Christian tradition as the Fall. Mankind is 'fallen', specifically, from a human (imaginative) into a natural mode of consciousness. Thus understood, the Fall has nothing to do with the commission of certain specific 'sinful' acts, but is a descent from a higher state of being into a lower, from the Imagination to the natural body; as symbolised, in the Biblical story, by the eating of the apple.

Every 'revealed' tradition is agreed upon the essential structure of the human psyche, of that invisible inner universe which is the properly human kingdom, from which we have 'fallen' into natural life; all holding our present state of consciousness as imperfect in relation to that which we essentially are, man as first created in the order of 'origins', by which a temporal beginning in the sense of the scientific evolutionists is not of course meant, but rather the type, pattern, archetype of the *anthropos*, 'made in the image of God', as described in the first chapter of Genesis. The 'human', according to tradition, is not, as for our own society, natural man but the archetypal perfect humanity, of whom every average man is a more or less obscured and distorted image. Our own secular society has sought to make everyone happy by taking as the norm 'fallen' man, Plato's dwellers in the Cave; but flattery of our fallen, or forgetful condition

9

can only superficially and briefly deceive us into believing that all is well, that we are all we should be, since each of us carries within ourselves, however obscured, the image of the *anthropos*.

This is a goal few have attained. The Buddhist world holds that Prince Siddhartha attained perfect enlightenment; Christians believe that Jesus was the Christ, fully incarnating the archetypal first-created Son of God. The Hindu tradition holds that there have been several revelations of the divinity in human form; that whenever the world has fallen into spiritual darkness a new revelation of the divine Person has again made known to us our own forgotten reality. All traditions are agreed that the divine humanity, although the type of all humanity, has scarcely ever been realised: for the Christian world, once only; for the Jews, not yet but someday; no religious tradition flatters us, as do the Utopians, by allowing us to believe that we can come within reach, or barely within apprehension, of that which we essentially are. Few attain enlightenment, few are saints. One of the most deplorable features of the secular West is the universal complacency of a mankind often barely human at all, in properly human terms. Many 'primitive' races—many American Indians, or the illiterate country people still to be found here and there in the West of Ireland or of Scotland, live upon a higher and more properly human level than the sophisticated products of our technological culture. I do not doubt that many powerful commissars could learn much of the real nature of humanity from village grandmothers with shawls over their heads and a corner of icons; icons which are, by definition, depictions of invisible spiritual essences. You find their depictions in the interior of any Orthodox church—in the Mother of God, the Pantocrator, angels, saints; or in Italy's pre-renaissance basilicas—in the Church of Saint Francis at Assisi, where the episodes of the saint's life Giotto has depicted are all of them spiritual events—dreams, visions, the casting out of demons, the beholding of the eternal Christ. In the secular world the facts that make up our news — the events narrated as biography or as fiction—are all of the natural order; how few belong to this human order, which we of the West have so deeply betrayed.

If, then, in order to 'educate' a human being it is first necessary to answer that old question 'What is man?' are we to process, to condition, to 'form', to 'brainwash' natural mankind to fit human beings for a longer or shorter lifespan in the natural world and the performance of more or less skilled tasks in the great mechanism? Or ought we not rather to consider man's invisible kingdom, the boundless interior regions we inhabit, the almost unguessed, undiscerned spiritual regions within us, so close to childhood, but later only to be attained through aspirations and disciplines which have little to do with the amassing of facts or the learning of technical skills which passes for education in our secular society?

Blake called the Divine Humanity, the imprinted archetype, the Imagination. Imagination, he said, is 'the true man', the unifying life of which the Four are the faculties, the instruments. Whereas the soul, with its fourfold universe, is individual, the Imagination is universal—the universal Self alike in all. The word 'Imagination' suggests, in common parlance, the arts; and insofar as, in a normal society, music, painting, poetry and architecture are depictions of mankind's inner worlds, the proper language of the soul, this is true; for, whereas science measures the natural world, the arts alone can depict the inner worlds. Blake called music, painting and poetry 'man's three ways of conversing with Paradise which the Flood did not sweep away'—the 'flood of the five senses' in which materialism drowns and submerges the world of Imagination.

But while it is true that the arts are the proper expression of the inner worlds, of mankind's imaginative self-knowledge, from the caves of Ajanta or Lascaux to Santa Sophia and Chartres, we must remember that not all that goes by the name of art is an embodiment of inner reality. Plato condemned naturalism in art, the mere imitation of natural behaviour. If the soul and its world—and, above that, the universal Imagination and its order—is not known, how can it be expressed? And that we live in an age of spiritual ignorance is everywhere evident in our art-forms, which are for the most part self-portraits of states of ignorance not of knowledge. Imitative, naturalistic art of the kind fashionable in the nineteenth century was not always without some vision, some reflection of Paradise seen in the forms of nature; we think of Samuel Palmer, of Calvert, Constable, Turner, for whom nature is itself the glass in which Imagination beholds itself; but, for many more, realistic depiction is mere trick photography of natural appearances; as is the 'social realism' of Marxist materialism.

The newer fashions, from abstract impressionism to the present, proclaim art as 'self-expression', sometimes glorified by the name 'creativity'; American universities have classes in so-called 'creative writing', and in our own schools there is endless talk of teaching children to express themselves 'creatively'. But self-expression is, unfortunately, very far from being an expression of imaginative vision

11

and imaginative knowledge. The final result of this century's guiding principle in the arts of 'breaking with the restrictions of the past' in order to be totally 'original' has been a school of scribbles whose total originality expresses only the ignorance of its authors; expresses nothing at all. The only 'originality' that has any value is a return to the origin, the lost knowledge of the Imagination.

The art of a secular society has suffered fatally from the identification of 'knowledge' with natural science. It has been forgotten that there can be 'knowledge', in any precise or universal sense, of the invisible worlds; knowledge no less exact than science's knowledge of the natural universe. Therefore, whereas we know very well that in order to be a mathematician or a chemist we must study the laws of mathematics or of chemistry, we have forgotten that there is knowledge proper to the soul. It is true that the mathematical and chemical laws of nature are everywhere expressed in the world about us, but we do not for that reason expect our schoolchildren to go and find them out for themselves by observation or to practise 'free expression' in chemistry, or to 'liberate themselves' from traditional mathematics in order to become original astronomers or physicists. We have far too much respect for science to turn it, as we have turned the arts, into a children's playground. We cannot expect our children, our 'young' poets and painters to discover for themselves the abiding order of the invisible worlds. Just as those who study mathematics or chemistry or plant morphology respond with recognition to what they are taught, so, far from inhibiting talent and 'creativity', knowledge of higher things can only awaken a similar response and widen the field of the individual imagination. But we have denied or forgotten that the invisible worlds can be fields of knowledge which can be taught and learned and transmitted and communicated. Other civilizations have taken this to be so as a matter of course. From Indian metaphysics, Platonic theology, Christian doctrine, down to the religiously pre-served sacred stories of the most primitive tribes, every race has preserved its own embodiments of a 'revealed' tradition concerning the inner nature of things, the order of the soul. These theologies, theogonies, sacred rites and tribal myths are not pastimes or self-expression, they are the self-knowledge of the human psyche upon which alone a culture can be based, be that culture simple as that of the Bushman or metaphysically rich as Vendanta. It is we who are the barbarians—spiritual barbarians, that is—who lack this collective language, this shared knowledge, upon which the goldsmiths of Byzantium, the builders of Chartres, the musicians of the diatonic

12

scale, the painters of Florence, down to Yeats and the poets of the Irish renaissance, drew.

My conclusion, then, is that our materialist secular society, well though it may educate in the natural sciences, altogether fails to educate the human soul, the invisible humanity which is, in Plato's words as well as Blake's, 'the true man'. We are simply not educated in these things which above all make us human. Those who inherit—who have not yet lost, under the cancerous impact of Western ideologies—some metaphysical, religious and iconographic tradition, some language of symbolic images built up throughout a civilization, are fortunate indeed. For the rest of us, all is to be remade; not altogether as if it had never been, for in the relics, the survivals of the past, we can rediscover lost knowledge, piece by piece reconstructing something, perhaps, which will serve a broken culture without a tradition of its own. Reality is always and everywhere itself; but who shall say whether we can use the language of Christendom, of the Far East, of Islam (the last prophetic revelation), of Jungian psychology, of Cabbala, of the American Indians? In all the arts there is a confusion of tongues. Blake knew everything except how to find symbolic or linguistic terms to communicate what he knew; he was eclectic in his symbols but orthodox in his Christian theology. Yeats's lifelong labour was to test, to discard or to retain, a great range of symbols and terms drawn from many traditions, Rosicrucian, neo-Platonic, Far Eastern. To recreate a common language for the communication of knowledge of spiritual realities, and of the invisible order of the psyche, is the problem now for any serious artist or poet, as it should be for educators. Yet the problem of language would resolve itself once these worlds were re-opened to our experience for the knowledge itself is primary, the terms—symbols—secondary. This rediscovery, re-learning, is a long hard task—a lifelong task for those who undertake it; yet the most rewarding of all tasks, since it is a work of self-discovery which is at the same time a universal knowledge, 'knowledge absolute' as the Vedas claim. So-called 'creativity' and 'self-expression' will not get us very far. The Grecian goldsmith, the Gothic sculptor, the painter of churches or elaborator of Islamic geometric patterns in a mosque were none of them 'expressing themselves' in the modern sense of the term; far less breaking with the past, or being 'revolutionary'. They were making use of the shared knowledge of a spiritual tradition that illuminates their work, as it illuminated the inner lives of those who participated in its unity of culture.

13

2

Premises and Poetry

ALTHOUGH in this paper scholarship would be inappropriate the conclusions I shall suggest have been reached through much reading, though of books not generally considered necessary to the understanding of 'English Literature' as taught in the universities. But I claim poetic licence—and poetic precedent—for the unorthodoxy of my studies. The poets do not read the same books as the academics, or even the same kind of books; or if the same books, read them in a different way. Thomas Taylor the Platonist, whom Emerson called the best 'feeder of poets since Shakespeare', for example, was veritably persecuted by the reviewers of the end of the eighteenth century and the early nineteenth century because he read Plato, Plotinus and Proclus for the truths they taught and not for the sake of mere erudition (which Taylor himself castigated in no uncertain terms). 'Feeder of poets' is true of 'the modern Plethon', as Taylor called himself; for it was through his translations and commentaries of the neo-Platonists and Plato himself that the Romantic poets learned their Plotinian aesthetics and their symbolic language of mythology, their doctrine of imagination and the soul. Blake and Flaxman were among his friends, Shelley's intimate friend Thomas Love Peacock (who put Taylor in his novel *Melincourt*) his admiring follower. Coleridge had read his works while still at school, and we may trace Wordsworth's mind and Keats's also, I believe, travelling over the pages of his paraphrase translation of Plotinus's *Concerning the Beautiful* (*Ennead* I, book VI), which went into a second edition and was most obviously a source book among the Romantics. Samuel Palmer in Italy planned to read Plato on his return to London; presumably in Taylor's translation, since there was no other at the time. Emerson and Bronson Alcott made of Taylor's works (scorned by the dons of Oxford) the foundation of the American Transcendentalist movement. His translation of Porphyry's *De Antro Nympharum* was early known to Yeats, doubtless through the Theosophical Society and John M. Watkins, the theosophical publisher and bookseller who reissued Porphyry's *Cave of the Nymphs*. AE called him 'the uncrowned

14

king'. And for all this, his very name, until recently, was not to be found in academic works on the Romantic poets. His books, even the few reprinted by the Theosophical Society and by John M. Watkins (and one or two in America), are extremely rare and to be found on no university syllabus, so far as I know. But I name Taylor as an example—though a central one—to illustrate my argument that there is a great field of excluded knowledge which the schools, dominated by the materialist climate of the time, do not recognize.

I was fortunate in not reading English Literature at the university (I read Natural Sciences). I did not do so because I saw no reason why educated people cannot read for themselves the literature of our own language. But from my own point of vantage (or disadvantage) I saw something of the revolution in the reading of poetry, whose beginnings lie outside the universities, in larger social changes; and whose consequences likewise go far beyond the English schools. I was spectator, but never participator in this cultural revolution; which may conceivably mark the beginning of a new civilization but assuredly marks the end of what C. S. Lewis has called 'old western' culture; of which (so he told Cambridge in his inaugural lecture as Regius Professor in the mid-1950s) he was among the last examples. But, as a student of natural sciences, I did come under the influence of the materialist ideology, and have, over the intervening years, piece by piece and with much toil and some pain re-structured my thought. I do not know how many of my own generation have shared my experience; when I meet old Cambridge contemporaries I find most of them still of the party I deserted. It is in a younger generation that I see a questioning of the materialist premises of the kind which led me to discover the excluded knowledge; which indeed is not far to seek when once we know what we are looking for.

What I saw happening (and indeed I attended several of Dr I. A. Richards's open lectures on Practical Criticism, delivered in—I think—1925 or '26) was, as I now see it, a brilliant exercise in the reading of a whole body of English poetry—almost, though not quite, of the whole body of English poetry—in the context of a culture not only unlike, but in its fundamental premises opposed to, that which had produced the literature of 'old western' culture. The method is now well known to all who have taught English in the universities; a poem is taken, preferably one unknown to the students. The exercise of dating and ascription is a secondary one, and the real purpose of Richards's now famous method is to see the poem in itself and precisely 'out of context'. This way of reading a poem works best

15

(works only, perhaps) when the culture of the student is, in general, the same as that of the poet. Only then does the answer to the question 'What does the poem mean to me?' approximate to what the poem meant to its author.

It was never Richards's intention that his 'scientific' criticism should replace the reading of poems in the context of the poet's whole work and thought, or poets in the context of their culture. But what he had designed as a teaching method, a way of focusing vague minds upon the text before them, happened to coincide with that social change which was sending for the first time to the universities students from classes hitherto uneducated. In this cultural revolution it was Leavis who made of Richards's teaching method a weapon. For it was an excellent way of encouraging such students, burdened with the sense of their own ignorance, to say 'Never mind the past, or the poet, read the poem word by word and register your own responses'. The poem was, as it presently became fashionable to say, 'the words on the page'. Add to this Leavis's performances in the art of demolishing some trifling poem by an obscure poet (with an occasional hit-and-run on the great Milton, or Shelley) and his popularity in the decades of the 'inferiority complex' is understandable. But again, Leavis, and his magazine *Scrutiny* (how well the word expresses the attitude, carried over from that phase of the natural sciences that murdered to dissect), rose on the tide of a world revolution with a new religion—scientific materialism. In this situation it could be said that the new 'scientific' criticism was an attempt to save for the new age the literature of the older culture by demonstrating how much remains to be admired and understood even when the system of thought of which it is an expression is discarded and replaced by another, whose answer to the question 'What is Man?' is so radically different. Recently, to the English television audience (popular culture in the early 1970s having overtaken Cambridge undergraduate culture of the mid-1920s) Dr Bronowski, another Cambridge contemporary, interpreted the cathedral of Rheims in terms of its construction. The vision of God and his Mother, the theology of Aquinas, the aspiration of worshipping multitudes, might never have existed. Of course Gothic architecture is, as Bronowski demonstrated, a marvel of engineering; but can it be explained in terms of the curiosity of the mastermasons about the stresses and strains in stone? Is Michelangelo's statue in the marble to be understood in so literal a way? Bronowski too was clearly concerned to save the bare ruined choirs for the post-revolutionary world in which it is supposed that

16

materialism must prevail even in those countries where Marxism as yet does not. Why the same passion for engineering has in our own time produced not Rheims or Chartres but Megalopolis Dr Bronowski did not say; or did he see no significant difference in meaning between a Gothic cathedral and one of New York's temples of commerce?

Plotinus in *Concerning the Beautiful* takes architecture as his example in illustrating a very different thesis. For him the building is not a 'construction in space' (to use a phrase popular among modern sculptors) but an idea in the artist's mind. Architectural harmony is a matter not of engineering but of intellect. (I quote Taylor's paraphrase translation of 1787.)

> But how can that which is inherent in body accord with that which is above body? Let us reply by asking how the architect pronounces the building beautiful, by accommodating the external structure to the fabric in his soul? Perhaps, because the outward building, when entirely deprived of the stones, is no other than the intrinsic form, divided by the external mass of matter, but indivisibly existing, though appearing in the many. When, therefore, sense beholds the form in bodies, at strife with matter binding and vanquishing its contrary nature, and sees form gracefully shining forth in other forms, it collects together the scattered whole, and introduces it to itself, and to the indivisible form within; and renders it consonant, congruous and friendly to its own intimate form.

For Plotinus, a building is beautiful insofar as it expresses a triumph of mind over matter's innate formlessness. Matter 'is base, and separate from the divine reason, the great fountain of forms; and whatever is entirely remote from this immortal source, is perfectly base, and deformed. And such is matter, which by its nature is ever averse from the supervening irradiations of form.' The principle of form, which Bronowski (speaking for his time and place) found in matter, Plotinus finds in mind. The 'construction in space' is redeemed from being that conglomerate heap of stones that works so named very often appear to be, by the organizing form of the idea. A circle is a circle whether it be drawn in ink or chalk or inscribed on the stone of New Grange or the turf of Stonehenge; and is neither 'the ink on the page' nor the 'construction in space'.

The poem as the 'words on the page' is the literary equivalent of Bronowski's view of architecture. The student of literature begins with the words on the page; the poet with an idea which does not yet exist in words but which does exist as an idea, a mood, an intuition;

17

even as a wordless form, somewhat like music. My own experience as a poet is that, like Plotinus's builder, one attempts to match words to an idea, the poem in the mind; or, rather, hovering just beyond the reach of the conscious mind. But our success in communication (in this the poet is less fortunate than architect or musician) is dependent upon the reader's knowledge of words, his range of literary associations. For words mean nothing in themselves; they are only a currency supported by meanings; the gold is in the bank, as it were, and the paper currency has more or less value against the reader's own equivalence in the realms of gold. The poet's too, of course; which in the present literary situation is very often more meagre than his reader's. When the reader's field of association, which alone gives meaning to words, is very different from that of the poet, he will not be reading, through 'the words on the page', the same poem as the poet wrote. He 'speaks a different language', though the words he uses may be the same on the page. But they do not carry the same meaning.

In my own lifetime I have seen—indeed experienced—the sleight of hand by which the central canon of English poetry has come to be read in a context of thought, and according to premises alien to the poets themselves. Poets of the imagination write of the soul, of intellectual beauty, of the living spirit of the world. What does such work communicate to readers who do not believe in the soul, in the spirit of life, or in anything that can be (unless the physically desirable) called 'the beautiful'? For in René Guénon's 'reign of quantity' such terms of quality become, as the linguistic philosophers would say, 'meaningless', because there is nothing for which they stand.

This is only in part a matter of period; far more it is a matter of culture; for not all who are contemporary share the same culture. Take Hopkins, who can be said to have been I. A. Richards's great discovery. Two of his pupils—William Empson and E. E. Phare—wrote on poems by Hopkins using the method of Richards's 'scientific' criticism. William Empson in his book *Seven Types of Ambiguity* wrote on *The Windhover*; as brilliant a misreading of 'the words on the page' as could be found. I remember he made much play with the key word, 'buckle':

> Brute beauty and valour and act, oh, air, pride, plume, here
> Buckle! AND the fire that breaks from thee then. . . .

'Buckle', William Empson argues, could mean that the priest will

18

'buckle' these virtues on (like St Paul's 'whole armour of God') in the life he has chosen; or that these virtues 'buckle like a bicycle wheel'; and he draws from that crumpling of the wheel those conclusions about the Jesuit's life which we should expect from the Cambridge of Russell and Wittgenstein in the heyday of Freud; who so conveniently permits the critic to argue that the poet knew not what he wrote; the dire ambiguity is there on the page. Father Arthur Thomas, S. J., has surely settled the matter once and for all by his discovery that 'buckle' is a term of falconry, and that Hopkins knew the term.

I remember secretly and rather sadly contrasting with the brilliant game my Cambridge friends were playing my own first acquaintance with Hopkins; in another world altogether, as it then seemed, in which I had, as a child, imagined I loved poetry for quite other reasons than for the barbed pleasure of picking the prickles from a hedgehog. I first heard poems by Hopkins recited by a young musician, then hovering on the brink of a monastic vocation, who had recited to me (as though in the words of the poem his own tormented aspiration found expression) those early poems Hopkins wrote in a mood of religion (or religiosity) which to many of his own generation and a few even of mine (though not in Cambridge) was a living reality. Which had read the poems more truly? Hopkins indeed was interested, as Empson was, in what could be done with words. In some ways their minds are alike, highly literate products of the classical education of the English public schools. They might have greatly enjoyed an exchange of letters; just as the freemasons of Rheims would have found much in common with Mies van der Rohe. The 'how' of construction—the quantifiable part of knowledge—they would have shared; but as to the 'what'—the qualitative—they would have spoken different languages. The materialist scientific mentality supposes the 'how' to be the 'what', the meaning of a building to be no other than its engineering.

Yeats, whose thought and whose poetry are related to a world-order totally other than the atheist humanism of his time, has suffered from radical misreading by the critics. John Wain, in an essay, 'Among Schoolchildren', dismissed Yeats's own allusion to Porphyry as of no account, and, for the 'drug' Lethe that brings forgetfulness to the generating soul, substituted the chloroform of a modern maternity ward. Clearly he had no thought of injuring Yeats's reputation—on the contrary, his misreading of the poem is an attempt to save Yeats from himself and reshape his image in a way more congenial to his own society. And Mr Wain is by no means alone in his attempt to cover up the great poet's supposedly ridiculous beliefs and discreditable studies. We are not so much concerned with 'period' (though of course the premises of societies do change) but with the changes, the losses of meaning that come about when the reader's premises are not those of the poet, when they are in the most literal sense living in different worlds.

What can be saved from a culture whose premises are of a spiritual order in an iron age peopled by Plato's 'men of clay' (the human primate of the scientist) is the quantifiable; the mechanics of construction, in whatever art. And the engineering element in the making of a poem is negligible in comparison with that of that most impressive and typical work of the reign of quantity, the space-ship. What meaning is there, in materialist terms, to the word 'poet'; or the essence—the 'poetry'—and the quality—the 'poetic'—of works of art? The adjective 'poetic' carries a certain contempt as the critics use it, and the 'poetic' element (as we use the word of the music of Schubert or Chopin, the painting of Claude or Palmer) is avoided by those typical of the 'modern movement'. Proust and even Balzac called themselves 'poets', indicating by the word at least the intention of giving expression to precisely this intangible quality that used to be called the 'poetry' of life. The preferred word in the modern movement is 'the artist'—placing the emphasis on the execution rather than the informing idea. A sculpture is a 'construction in space', a musical work a 'construction in time'. The 'work of art' is no longer an embodiment, but a body.

Beyond the question of how much a materialist present can understand, in its own terms, of the art and poetry of a spiritual past, there is the question of the kind of art—the kind of poetry—the reign of quantity can produce. The modern megalopolis, for all our understanding of the stresses and strains (in ferroconcrete if not in the soul of man), is not encouraging. It has yet to be demonstrated that, once a materialist society has exhausted the excitement of sacking the treasuries of the past in such 'revolutionary' anti-art movements as surrealism and 'pop' art, spent its nostalgia for tastes and manners inherited from a rejected culture (whose values these manners reflect), it can, or will even wish to, include poetry or 'the poetic' in its way of life.

A new culture, a new civilization, is born of a change of premises. At the height of Roman power the seed of Christianity began to germinate among slaves and social outcasts. In the age of apparent triumph of materialism, is there a comparable process already at work among a younger generation who reject the materialist Utopia?

Knowledge, in any culture, is only an agreed area of the known and the knowable; 'Let X equal knowledge' is premised and the proofs follow. Every X can of course yield its results. But there is always an excluded knowledge; and as the crude beginnings of science were the excluded knowledge of pre-Renaissance Christendom, so theology and all the wisdom of the spirit is the excluded knowledge of a materialist society. As R. P. Blackmur (apropos Eliot and Yeats) wrote in 1957, 'the supernatural is simply not part of our mental furniture'. But reality does not change its nature because we are unaware of it; a fact which the scientists themselves would not deny.

Just as science has its *gnosis* within its own terms (the quantifiable) so there is a *gnosis* of mind, which has been known and formulated in every civilization. Coomaraswamy wrote of a universal language of which the several theologies, mythologies and arts are dialectical variations. If mind is premised—is the 'X' of knowledge—the same truths will always be rediscovered. Plotinus, who wrote that 'there is nothing higher than the truth', was not a scientist; though only from scientists, in our society, is that appeal recognized. This gnosis (implicitly or explicitly) is the ground of all works of imagination. A work of art is precisely an expression in words of some intuition of imaginative reality. Poets may or may not have been religious men (who knows if Shakespeare was?) but all poetry of the imagination is the language of spiritual intuition and spiritual knowledge.

This is not the place to give chapter and verse in support of what is not after all a particularly original view, that our European variation of 'the universal and unanimous tradition' has been, with variations and accretions, neo-Platonism. Christian theology has itself its roots in Greek philosophy, and differs in no essential first principles from Platonic (or Aristotelean) metaphysics. From the point of view of religion neo-Platonism might seem a dead language; the Mysteries of Hellenic civilization no longer exist as religious cults with places of worship, rituals, a priesthood and so on. From the standpoint of the poets this very freedom has perhaps made the Platonic theology more amenable to poetic purposes than the Christian religion with its involvement in history and its other worldly ramifications. Cult belongs to time and place; and this aspect of the Christian Church itself is now assailed by inevitable change. But the first principles themselves, from which have sprung many cults and their various rituals, are defined in the Platonic theology, which is itself an embodiment of tradition. Religion is, after all, a collective art embodying a vision shared by a nation or an age. The essence of reality cannot be captured or held in any of the forms, however wonderful, which may at some time embody it. Involvement with a cult may be as dangerous to the poet as involvement in politics; however sincere, such involvement is, for the imagination, at best a symbol and at worst an irrelevance. But, as a symbolic description of the nature of things, all myths whose origin is in the imagination are unageing and may live again in poetry (as Hyperion in Keats, Prometheus in Shelley or the Greek gods in Hölderlin) after centuries. 'Religious' poetry is only a small category (unless we beg the question by calling all profoundly imaginative poetry 'religious') and often a somewhat uneasy one, since the self-searchings or conflicts of the poet as a personality often obscure and impede the imaginative vision, which comes from a deeper and impersonal source; from the Collective Unconscious, the Muse, the *anima mundi*, the Holy Spirit, the God. The name varies, the experience is constant. It is not the religion (if any) of the poet, in the personal and moral sense, that is in question. Even among poets professing the Christian religion (in forms so various to include Dante and Spenser, Milton and Vaughan, Blake and Edwin Muir) their metaphysics—their spiritual geometry —commonly proves to be neo-Platonic in essence. Coleridge, a Christian in his prose, is a neo-Platonist in his poems.

Obviously every poet's field of culture is different; but in my own detailed study of Blake's sources I have been astonished to discover how many of these he shared with the poets named, and with Yeats, Shelley, Wordsworth and others not professing the Christian faith. The canon of the learning of the imagination is constant. Such knowledge does not, like the discarded hypotheses of science, become obsolete; for it is not cumulative but a priori; or as poets and metaphysicians alike would say, not amassed by experiment but 'revealed' by inspiration; or as Plato says, by 'recollection'—*anamnesis*. To our European canon the present century has added many texts from the spiritual literature of the world without changing the essence of the knowledge or the intelligibility of its language. Such additions are no confusion, but an enrichment which in no way alters or weakens the structure. Yeats, typical of the eclectic modern situation, through theosophy, and later through his teacher Shri Purohit Swami, learned from Hindu philosophy. Early in his intellectual life he had read Swedenborg; studied Christian Cabala; the Buddhism of the Japanese *No* plays, besides Spiritualism, the folklore of Ireland and the primitive beliefs of the whole world, formed, for him, together with Plato

22

and Plotinus, the Gnostic texts and the Hermetica, a body of imaginative learning as self-consistent as (within its own terms, as an account of the phenomenal world) modern science. This structure, within which human consciousness finds its ultimate orientation, stands the test not only of intellectual analysis but of experience; opening ways that materialism can but close. I believe that this knowledge (whether intuitive or learned, or, as is usually the case, more or less of both), is no less essential to the production of works of imagination than is knowledge of, and respect for, the 'laws of nature' essential to those who launch space-missiles. Certain experiences are not otherwise attainable than by exploring regions of experience whose very existence is destroyed by the materialist philosophy which denies access to them. For if the supernatural be 'no part of our mental furniture' how can we discover those modes of being, experience our own nature, or know

> What Worlds, or what vast Regions hold
> The immortal mind that hath forsook
> Her mansion in this fleshly nook:
> And of those *Daemons* that are found
> In fire, air, flood, or under ground?

The imagination opens, now as always, into heavens and hells of the mind, beyond which lies boundless mystery.

The scientists seek in vain to quantify such knowledge; whereas, conversely, nature itself, for the imagination, becomes a living image, reflection, expression, incarnation, and language of spiritual realities, 'higher' in that they are causes of the phenomena of nature; which is 'lower' only insofar as it is the world of the effects of these causes. To the scientists themselves the Berkeleyan argument—that mind, or spirit is the only substantial reality—must, in terms of modern physics, seem unanswerable as an account of all that we actually see, hear and touch, and call a world; *maya*, as the Eastern philosophies have always understood. To the imagination everything in nature speaks of the mind which it reflects; of qualities; of 'the beautiful', that highest concept of Greek philosophy. *Nihil vacuum neque sine signum apud deum*. Without this implicit doctrine of the *signatura rerum*, the 'signatures' and 'correspondences' of things earthly to things heavenly, poetry cannot operate, being precisely the language of such correspondences. Such discourse, whether the poem be the *Divina Commedia* or Yeats's 'little song about a rose' is, I would

23

say, what poetry simply is, if it is anything at all. It is a sacred language because it speaks of qualities; and behind qualities, and sustaining them, mysteries, meanings; the holy ground of the soul's country.

Poetry, God knows, does not deal in certainties so much as in the glimpses of that country seen at certain moments by that eternal exile Psyche. The Russian Metropolitan Archbishop Anthony Bloom reproved me when I said to him that atheism could probably have no poetry. No, he said, 'poetry is the language of longing'; only when the soul is dead can there no longer be poetry. But what can the atheist (the materialist, that is, not the a-theist of Buddhism, who in no way denies the spirit) long for, unless that things should be otherwise than he believes?

What if all traditional sources were to be lost and the learning of the spirit forgotten? This of course cannot happen; since virtually the whole human inheritance of the arts, all the literature of wisdom, proclaims the 'universal and unanimous tradition' which forms the structure of all possible experience. But if—unimaginably—this were to be so; or—and this is the actual situation of innumerable people in the modern world—a generation were to grow up in ignorance of traditional spiritual teaching, yet the nature of the soul must reaffirm itself. Jung has described the 'individuation process' by which, through our own dreams and intuitions, the ego discovers its hidden and holy 'ground'. Or truth may come, as Yeats heard it spoken, 'out of a medium's mouth'. Reality being always such as it is, it must be discovered and re-experienced countless times and in various ways. And those who discover the matter will soon discover the books of knowledge and works of art which bear witness to such experience; for our own enlightenment makes accessible all that tells of what we have ourselves perceived. As Plato says, we can learn only what we already know, but do not yet know we know. The learning of the imagination can remain an excluded knowledge only so long as the premises of material science remain unquestioned and their exclusions unde-tected.

3

The Inner Journey of the Poet

OF all those great contemporaries in whose times I have lived, C. G. Jung is one of the two or perhaps three minds to whom I am most indebted. Nevertheless I am not a Jungian. In two senses this is so. First, of course, I am not a trained psychologist, and although I have read most of Jung's published writings with pleasure and profit I have never attempted to master his terms in the exact sense required by professional rigour. In the second place I suspect—though with Jung one can never be sure, for he is himself often deliberately ambiguous, or evasive—that in some important matters I would not share his point of view. What, for example, in *Answer to Job*, does he mean by the 'God-image'? Does he mean that 'God' is a psychic image, amongst others? Or does he mean that man bears in his psyche the image of God? Since I unambiguously adhere to the traditional teaching that man is made in the image of God, it may be that here I part company with many Jungians, if not with Jung himself; and probably in other contexts where metaphysical questions are involved—though Jung disclaims metaphysics and a poet would also be wise to do so; poetry, like psychology, being in essence the language not of intellect but of the soul.

I have been persuaded by a fellow lecturer at a weekend conference on The Inner Journey to talk upon that subject: not because of my knowledge of Jungian psychology but as an example of what that lecturer called 'a natural Jungian'; though we poets might equally say that Jung is a 'natural' poet, thinking in terms of myths and symbols long current in the language of the poets. The inner journey is certainly a theme poets and psychologists have in common; one might almost say that journey has, one way or another, been the theme of most of the imaginative poetry of mankind. And since there is not one of us who must not sooner or later set out upon that journey we may expect to learn from the poets some of the stages on the way all must travel. For, as Blake wrote, 'these States Exist now. Man Passes on, but States remain for Ever; he passes thro' them like a traveller who may as well suppose that the places he has passed thro' exist no more, as a Man may suppose that the States he has pass'd thro' Exist no more.' (K606)

In the middle of the road of life Dante, supreme poet of Christendom, came to himself (*mi ritrovai*)—literally 'found myself again'—to discover that he had lost his way and was in the middle of a dark forest. How he came to be there he did not know because, as he tells us, he was 'full of sleep' when he missed his way. The great *Divina Commedia* is an allegory; and yet the opening scene has upon us the impact of a dream we might ourselves have dreamed. Dante's fear, when he finds himself entangled in natural life, in 'the forests of affliction', the 'forests of the night' as Blake was later to call that place, communicates itself to us because the symbol evokes in us a resonance at a far deeper level than mere allegory. There Blake met his Tyger; and Dante too met a beast, 'burning bright'; not a Tyger but a fierce creature at once leopard, lion and wolf. He allegorizes the beast; and yet the encounter has the quality of some dream or vision in which forest and beast alike arose from the unconscious mind which creates such encounters for us. The encounter was, in any case, the determining moment of his inner life, the starting-point of his own interior journey.

As the poet fled bewildered by the forest and terrified by the beast, there came towards him one of those figures we meet on the road of life at the moment of need; sometimes in dream, sometimes in the person of a human being: the poet Virgil, an Italian like himself who, more than twelve hundred years before, had made (in the person of the hero of his epic poem, Aeneas) his own descent into Hades. Virgil is said to signify, in Dante's poem, human wisdom and tradition, and on one level this may well be so; yet in terms of the psyche and its symbolic figures, Virgil is recognizable as the archetype Jung has described as 'the wise old man' who counsels many a dreamer, or whose knowledge we project onto some teacher or master. Virgil becomes Dante's protector, companion and guide; and the two poets, Virgil, the shade, and Dante, the living man, set out upon an inward journey into 'an eternal place'; the same that Aeneas had entered, guided by the sibyl of Nemi. For those who have so 'found themselves' there can be no going back; the beast, when once we have discovered it in ourselves, forbids return; we must flee, literally for our lives, in the hope of escaping the monster we have discovered within. But the first stage of the journey takes us, not to Paradise as we might hope, or at all events to some better and safer place or state, but into the hells.

To the ancient world those shadowy regions of alienation were

26

thought of as external to ourselves; regions not of memory or of fantasy but the real habitations of discarnate spirits both human and non-human. So the descent into Hades is presented by Virgil, whose Aeneas there met the discarnate spirits of many he had known in life: his father, happy in the Elysian fields; Dido, whom he had deserted, who turned away in silence, still unforgiving. Virgil's Hades is in its turn based upon the still more primitive account given in the *Odyssey* of Ulysses' visit to a temple (which some have thought to be Stonehenge) in a dim northern land there to consult the spirit of the wise Nestor, who in life had advised the Greek heroes, on how he should get home to Ithaca. There he met his former companions— Ajax, and Achilles, still striding in his wrath—who bitterly said that it were better to be the meanest labourer on earth than a hero among the dead. We are in a world of primitive necromancy, the kind of consultation with the ancestors to be met with in all primitive tribes. If the journey is inwards those who make it are not aware that this is so.

I must here say that I hold it, on the evidence, as probable that in our inner journey we do encounter such discarnate beings as Homer, Virgil and Dante describe; our own dead, and whatever spirits besides may inhabit the unexplored regions of mind on which our own consciousness impinges. Here again I may well hold a view Jung himself may not have shared; yet he was at one time a physical researcher and in his *Septem Sermones ad Mortuos* he is nearer to Virgil (whom he so often quotes) than to Freud.

Dante's inward journey stands midway between the ancient and the modern world. In his hells, his heavens and his purgatories he did indeed meet, like Aeneas and like Odysseus, many he had known in life, besides persons who had lived in former times. But the *Commedia* is also something else: it is an exploration of the psyche, of the inner worlds and states of the poet himself. And 'the lost traveller's dream under the hill'—as Blake was later to describe that journey through the hells—begins with a descent into the depths under the mountain of Purgatory on whose summit is Paradise. Every pilgrimage must begin in the same way: if Freud did nothing else at least he made us aware that these regions are in each of us, and that the only way out is through; the way that Dante took into the dark regions of human souls.

His journey follows a descending course through ever-narrowing circles, each representing some one of the sins that deform the soul; and there, in each of the states, the poet is moved, now with pity, now

27

with horror, to find persons he had known on earth. But each successive hell is at the same time a recognition of what lies within himself. In his encounter with the adulterous lovers, Paolo and Francesca, he is so moved with pity that he faints; for had he not loved Beatrice to that extreme by which he knew he might have become like them, aware only of one another? T. S. Eliot has in *Little Gidding* recaptured Dante's dismay at another meeting, with his old teacher Brunetto Latini, in the 'What, are you here?' of his own encounter with the 'familiar compound ghost' of his literary masters. The empathy that so shook Dante to the heart is surely an identification of ourselves with the state of another soul; we discover ourselves in them, and them in ourselves. For the hells through which Dante moved are not places but states, all of them recognizable to every one of us.

At the bottom of the abyss, that narrows and narrows to those self-enclosed, ice-bound prisons in which the souls have lost all freedom, the poet comes to the throne of Satan. I have never undergone analysis (otherwise than through poetry and the other arts, which is after all the more ancient and normal way of self-exploration) but I understand that at an early stage of self-discovery the patient may expect an encounter with the figure Jung calls the Shadow. This figure may appear in our dreams as a sinister, repulsive *alter ego* whom we are as loath to recognise in ourselves as was Shakespeare's Prospero to accept Caliban; and yet to the monster of his isle Prospero said at last, 'This thing of darkness I acknowledge mine'. Perhaps Dante's meeting with the beast in the forest was his first glimpse of the Shadow, as a protean, theriomorphic form, like some dream monster who may inspire terror without obliging us to recognize in so alien a shape an aspect of ourselves. But, just as in a series of human dreams the same archetype may present itself in a series of guises, Dante was to meet the Shadow again, in more terrible and inescapable form. He confronts Satan, the ruler of evil who has his throne within each of us, in the most hidden and remote depth of those regions of evil we in vain deny.

The limit of the descent into Hell is the point of total inertia, the centre to which everything falls. The narrowing circles whose terraces the poet, led by Virgil, has all the while been traversing, lead to this place where no further freedom is possible. As in Poe's story of the pit and the pendulum, Hell narrows and narrows until the point is reached at which the final terror is inescapable. Here Satan is enthroned, the hidden ruler of all the hells; Jung's Shadow encountered unavoidably at the heart of the soul's labyrinth. Dante can see no way of escape; but the confrontation with the principle of evil face to face proves, on the contrary, to be the point of reversal. The journey had been, hitherto, always a descent into darker and worse places, the claustrophobia closing in until Hell's ruler is encountered and identified as the Shadow; or, as William Blake has called Satan, the Selfhood or ego which in each of us perverts our acts to selfish ends. Now that the ruler of the hells has been seen and identified, Virgil half leads, half carries the horrified Dante through a narrow passage under Satan's throne, below the hairy thighs of the half-animal, half-human figure of the Devil. What takes place is a kind of rebirth through 'a round opening'; and like the new-born Dante can now for the first time see the sky and the stars. Now there is literally—and how dramatically—a change of point of view: Satan on his towering throne is seen reversed beneath the travellers' feet; his power gone. He is no longer the ruler and the centre of the psyche. What has taken place Jung has described as re-integration of the personality when we find the Self—the 'other' mind within us—and not, as we had hitherto supposed, the ego, to be the ruler and centre of the soul.

Dante's journey surely meets the experience of many whose first step in self-knowledge has been the discovery of the hells within: under the volcano; the waste land; Blake was surely thinking of Dante when he wrote of

> The son of morn in weary night's decline,
> The lost traveller's dream under the hill.

Dante at the beginning of his spiritual adventure had no idea of even the existence of these hells; and so it is in perhaps every interior journey. Those who have read Bunyan's *Pilgrim's Progress* will remember that his journey to the Celestial City also began in the City of Destruction. But the Pilgrim had lived for many presumably contented years in that city before he recognized that familiar neighbourhood for what it was, and set out to flee from it, leaving his own family and the friends and neighbours of a lifetime. Bunyan's City of Destruction; Dante's City of Dis whose domes glow in a red sky, so like a modern city; Milton's Pandemonium, adorned with all the skills and arts of architecture and technology; or those terrible false paradises of Aldous Huxley's Brave New World where nobody is allowed to suffer or to desire anything better than perfect adaptation to existing conditions—all these are adorned with every amenity of civilized living. None of the poets has ever suggested that Hell is a place of pitchforks and boiling tar.

Dante, emerging through the opening at the bottom of Hell (the extreme limit of his own inner darkness), finds a new orientation. Whereas in the hells he has been enclosed within the caverned world of his own subjectivity, he now emerges into the greater universe and beholds the heavens and the stars above him. In Hell, native inertia had facilitated the poet's descent; but from this point he will have to climb. Did Dante here think of the line of Virgil Jung so often quotes, 'easy is the descent into Avernus, but the reascent—*hoc opus, hic labor est*'? And yet the poet undertakes the climb gladly, for he knows, now, where his journey is leading him. Once there is a goal, and that goal is seen, there can be no going back. The wise teaching of the Church is that none who has entered Purgatory can thereafter return again to Hell, the closed world with no outlet, no greater context to give meaning and orientation to life. In the hells the poet had witnessed and experienced each of the human energies misdirected in the service of the satanic ego; in the purgatories, whose states he must now traverse on his ascending spiral path, each of these energies will be set right, and the poet freed, one by one, from each of those faults we all share. In the heavens beyond, opening in widening circles, each of the seven energies or functions of the soul which in the hells had found and distorted expression as the 'seven deadly sins' will be seen in their aspect of seven cardinal virtues; for they are the same energies now operating in obedience to the divine order.

Dante's reorientation involves a new way of seeing even the hells; for now he understands that what had seemed an endless descent had all the time in reality been the first stage of the upward climb towards Paradise: while he had thought he was descending he was in truth already spiralling upwards towards the point of transformation of consciousness. Had he not emerged through that dimensionless point of reversal, to see the stars overhead and the light of dawn rising over the sea, he would never have made this discovery; for the hells are states of, precisely, absence of this light of hope, and ignorance of the whole of which even they form a part. While we are in Hell it seems that there is no way out; we are there, as it seems, eternally. Only as we emerge do we see evil in its true proportion. Once we have set foot on the Mountain of Purgatory we are free from those inner prisons—the self-enclosed worlds of the ego cut off from God—and are already aware of belonging to a greater whole.

At the summit of the mountain is the Earthly Paradise: the state of unfallen man. Thus far Virgil has led him—wisdom, or reason, or whatever may be symbolised by that figure of the 'wise old man'. But in order to enter the heavens, the worlds of the blessed spirits who behold God, wisdom does not suffice; and it is here that Beatrice comes to meet him; and it is she, the embodiment of love—of heavenly love, the love of the soul—who must lead him into those higher worlds or states that knowledge alone cannot enter. Jung's figure of the *anima*, the soul-figure, is said to be ambiguous, at once desirable and cruel, angel and temptress, beyond good and evil. We may find the shadow of Beatrice in Francesca blown by the winds of passion; but Beatrice is the soul-image purified and transfigured by the transforming experience through which the poet has passed. But when the poet invites us to gaze with him into the great cosmic mandala of the mystic rose of the heavens of which Eliot wrote

> When the tongues of flame are in-folded
> Into the crowned knot of fire
> And the fire and the rose are one

he leads us beyond the range of experience to which most of us have attained; yet he enables us to glimpse the goal we are even now travelling towards. In this poet's supreme vision of the numberless multitudes of the heavenly spirits, even Beatrice herself becomes but one among the numberless blessed souls who draw their life from God.

Dante's *Commedia* may serve to remind us that, whereas our present knowledge of the inner worlds is uncertain and fitful, there are old maps of that country. But at the end of a civilization whose concern has been almost exclusively the exploration of nature and physical space, we have all but forgotten what country it is the old maps are describing. Materialists imagine that because the hells are not to be found among the rocks or the angels where the astronauts fly that these are unreal. But there is at this time a complete withdrawal of the old projection of the hells and the heavens into an external elsewhere; a recognition that all the old supernatural population is to be found in ourselves. Not outer, but inner space promises to be the theme of a new age; and the old maps are being brought out again.

A recent volume of poems by Thomas Blackburn reflects, in many fine and deeply self-searching poems, this change of standpoint; like this on the Scandinavian demon Grendel, another shadow-figure:

After the marsh was drained and its vast monsters
Had gasped their lives out in the well-rinsed air,
Our city corporation cleaned the fosse up
And charged us sixpence to see Grendel's lair.
We thought that with the great Panjandrum banished
An era of sweet dreams was sure to start;
But gracious no, only his cave has vanished;
Don't look now, but he's walking in your heart.

Perhaps we meet Dante again not full-circle, but on a higher turn of the spiral of development. Dante suffered from the dualism of medieval Christianity which makes redemption from the hells eternally impossible. Blake was perhaps the first Christian poet (or prophet, as he called himself, for he held poets who speak for the Imagination to be the prophets of the modern world) to challenge his dualism, and to say that though all the hells remain as eternal possibilities, and although those within them may see no way of escape, none are eternally binding on those who enter them. They are part of the one universe in which we travel. 'Distinguish between the man and his present state,' Blake said. His belief that none need remain eternally in hell is more Buddhist than Christian. Yet this same belief is surely implicit—though not explicit—in Dante's poem; for he himself made the journey to be reborn through that narrow opening, thereby showing that there is a way.

Dante's journey is of course everyone's journey; but the poet is the explorer, the opener of the way, who ventures, in a state of inspiration, into regions of consciousness which in most of us remain dark and unexplored. The honour in which poets and prophets were formerly held was in virtue of this 'inspiration' from the 'other' mind.

Dante's poem holds before us images of an inner world all share; of an eternal order, not of time or place which is the measure of our humanity, the pattern, the scale (using the word in its musical sense) to which we are attuned. In those works of art which are true to the archetype we discover our own laws, our own inner order. We speak of 'beauty' because 'the beautiful' is what is true to the archetype and true to the cosmic order that upholds the world. What we call beauty brings us back to the archetype, harmonizes us with ourselves and indeed with others since it is by virtue of this inner order that we are alike. Without such works human society must suffer the kind of moral and spiritual sickness so prevalent at the present time. The necessary food of the spirit is missing; and instead of healing us and

32

restoring us to our humanity much modern art and music is (whether deliberately or in ignorance) Satanic, destructive in an almost physical sense; dislocating the psyche, as sound-waves will bring down a building. The housing in which people live, the music to which the populace listens, the visual images presented to us by a commercial society are calculated to destroy rather than to harmonize the soul. There are of course exceptions in every art, but all too few, and these against the spirit of the established values of the time.

Plato taught that all knowledge comes from memory—recollection; but not memory of our own experience of a few years of mortal life. Plato's memory is a cosmic memory, not memory as the behaviourists would define it, something gathered from the experience of the senses, but instead a memory of the universal mind from which we are, from the confined nature of perception, shut off. Have we not all the sense of some knowledge lost, or just out of reach? By common consent, within any traditional society, the poet is held to be 'inspired' by the Muse, the Holy Spirit, the Instructors—that is to say from the 'other' mind. To those who believe with the behaviourists that all knowledge comes through the senses, what meaning have Wordsworth's lines,

> Our birth is but a sleep and a forgetting,
> The Soul that rises with us, our life's star,
>   Hath had elsewhere its setting,
>   And cometh from afar
> Not in entire forgetfulness . . .?

For the behaviourists (as for the eighteenth-century philosopher Locke), the new-born come trailing no clouds of glory, bring with them no memories. But for the Platonic tradition, which makes not matter but mind its starting-point, Wordsworth's lines are not figuratively but literally true; they are after all but a paraphrase of the teaching of Plotinus. And for those who hold, in whatever terms, this belief, poetry and the other arts are the chief and indeed the normal means by which we relate ourselves to the timeless. Blake wrote of poetry, painting and music as man's three ways of 'conversing with Paradise'; which is only another way of saying the same thing.

The Platonic philosophers held that we, in our natural state, are 'asleep'. Our relationship with the timeless is expressed in a number of myths of sleep and waking, remembering and forgetting. A similar view is taken by Jungian psychology, but with an important difference. Whereas the Greeks held that the 'other' mind is wakeful and conscious, is the omniscient mind of the immortal gods, and the mortal condition a 'sleep' and a 'forgetting', the terms of modern psychology are at best ambiguous. The very term 'unconscious', though descriptive of our empirical situation in our relation to the transpersonal mind, is misleading because it suggests that conscious knowledge is in some respects more perfect; that the knowledge of the unconscious is in some sort of rudimentary state, merely potential. This is not the teaching of the ancients, nor is it of the Indian philosophers, nor of the Christian theologians who taught the omniscience of God and the relative ignorance of man.

Plato attributes our forgetfulness to the limitations of a physical body. The myth in the Tenth Book of the *Republic* to which Wordsworth's lines finally refer tells how the souls about to enter generation 'descend', like shooting stars, and then must cross a desert between the two worlds or states. They come to a river—the river Lethe, or forgetfulness. This river is interpreted by the late Platonists as ever-flowing matter; of which water is the universal symbol. The souls are thirsty for matter's sleepy draught: some drink so deeply that their oblivion of their former state is almost complete. Others drink less deeply, and arrive on earth 'not in entire forgetfulness'. All the Greek myths relating to knowledge and inspiration assume that we may in certain circumstances recover our lost knowledge of the universal mind. There are, according to Plato, three kinds of souls who are rememberers: the philosophers, who have knowledge; the lovers, who through their devotion to beauty come to knowledge of 'the beautiful itself'; and the 'musical souls', who are the artists. It is the function and the task of these to create in this world 'copies' of the eternal originals, or archetypes 'laid up in heaven', in stone or metal or music or dance or words, according to their skills. These copies will awaken in those who behold them—even if only momentarily—recollection of the eternal order of which all are part, and attunement to that order.

The poet's 'muse' is more than a literary convention: it is the experience of every creative person that inspiration comes from beyond our own knowledge. According to Plato there are nine Muses, each giving guidance in some one particular art. The poet is said to have the gift, when inspired (though not at other times), of flying to the Garden of the Muses, where he gathers, as bees gather honey, the sweetness of his song.

I think every poet knows what is meant by the muse or daimon who seems to give us knowledge we do not normally possess. Plato wrote of the Daimon of Socrates. The God of Israel 'spake by the prophets'. Shakespeare's Ariel is the very essence of the spirit who flies free but who will serve the poet-magician who knows how to control his inspirer. Milton invoked the 'Heavenly Muse' and so did Blake, with a difference: Blake was a modern man and knew that the muse is within; paraphrasing Milton, he summons the 'Muses who inspire the Poet's song' in a manner at once homely and sublime:

> . . . Come into my hand,
> By your mild power descending down the Nerves of my right arm
> From out the Portals of my brain, where by your ministry
> The Eternal Great Humanity Divine planted his Paradise. (K481)

Yeats had his 'instructors', Robert Graves his White Goddess. Often the figure of the muse is projected, as Dante projected his Beatrice or Bloch his 'beautiful lady', onto some human figure. Many still hold the old belief, inherited by Christendom from the Greeks, of the holy guardian angel who accompanies each of us throughout life. To speak for myself I cannot remember a time when I was not aware of the companioning presence of my own daimon. I never thought of this inner companion as an angel for this daimon spoke always of freedom and delight and beauty, never of such restrictive matters as religion dealt in. But if the daimon is not moral, neither is it immoral; carnal desires, or indeed any other self-interested thoughts, served only to drive away this delicate companion. Of the twin demi-gods Castor and Pollux it is said that one is incarnate, one in the other world or state; and I wonder if this myth does not describe precisely the relationship we each have with the daimon or guardian angel? Poets, in any case (Dante and Yeats were both born in the sign of Gemini), seem to be more than normally aware of this relationship with the 'other' mind. Of course there are many levels: as the aspiration, so the inspiration. Porphyry tells that the Delphic Oracle revealed that Plotinus was inspired by God himself, the universal spirit.

I attempted in a poem to express the relationship with the daimon:

> Long ago I thought you young, bright daimon,
> Whisperer in my ear
> Of springs of water, leaves and song of birds
> By all time younger
> Than I, who from the day of my conception
> Began to age into experience and pain;

35

But now life in its cycle swings out of time again
I see how old you were,
Older by eternity than I, who, my hair gray,
Eyes dim with reading books,
Can never fathom those grave deep memories
Whose messenger you are,
Day-spring to the young, and to the old, ancient of days.

The story is well known of nine daughters of Pierius who challenged the Muses, daughters of Zeus, and who were turned into magpies for their presumption. They would have fared better in the twentieth century; probably given prizes for their realism. For there is always an art of imitation which is not the product of imaginative inspiration but of the human personality, uninspired. Such verse is not without its value—it may have great wit, or political forcefulness, or it may be comic verse; but the two kinds of verse, so Blake wrote, 'ought to be known as two distinct things for the sake of eternal life'. For the sake of eternal life because it is through imaginative inspiration alone that contact is made with the eternal mind. Blake distinguished between the 'daughters of memory' (the daughters of Pierius, according to the myth) and the 'daughters of inspiration' as the mortal and the divine Muses of the poet.

Of these things we can perhaps only speak in symbolic terms; for symbol is the language of the psyche: the river of forgetfulness, the sleep of the soul, the Garden of the Muses. But is it not a truth of experience that when we are moved deeply by some piece of music or some other art, we have not, as it were, to learn from the artist, as we might commit to memory some technical process previously unknown? The symbols speak to us more clearly than words. We accompany Dante on his journey and know the place; we share the experience as if it were the work not of some other mind but of our own. And in a sense this is so; for though the personality of the artist may give colour to his work, an individual style and stamp, supreme art comes from that mind which is common to all. The poet seems to be speaking out of our own deepest knowledge. 'Ah yes,' we say. 'But how did Shakespeare, or Hopkins, or Schubert, know this?' Works of imaginative genius seem our own creation. But while such works are often less 'difficult' to understand than works of mere talent which may need footnotes to supply the references, the demands they make on us are greater than the mere gathering of information needed for the elucidation of a difficult text: such works demand *anamnesis*, the wakening of recollection; and we might prefer to forget because sleep

36

is easier and less demanding and sometimes less painful than wakeful-
ness: which is, nevertheless, that to which we must grow.

Platonic recollection is not remembering the past but remembering the timeless. 'What we remember we shall known again', is the
secret message of all beauty. These memories are also hopes; for
imagination tells both of the beginning and the end, 'mixing', as T. S.
Eliot has written, 'memory with desire'. We desire what we recol-
lect—we could not desire what we do not, in some sense, remember.
Since in the timeless world end and beginning are one, the work of
imagination evokes not mere nostalgia, but also hope; the longing to
be what we truly are. In the words of Plotinus, the soul 'makes its
memories the starting-point of a new vision of essential being'. That
is why Yeats made 'a new religion, almost an infallible Church of
poetic tradition, of a fardel of stories, and of personages, and of
emotions . . . passed on from generation to generation by poets and
painters with some help from philosophers and theologians'. Only
'some help' for the inspiration of the poets is immediate, theology
only a secondary elaboration. 'I wished for a world', he wrote, 'where I
could discover this tradition perpetually, and not in pictures and in
poems only, but in tiles round the chimney-piece and in the hangings
that kept out the draught. I had even created a dogma: "Because those
imaginary people are created out of the deepest instinct of man, to be
his measure and his norm, whatever I can imagine those mouths
speaking may be the nearest I can go to truth." '

For Yeats the 'holy city of Byzantium' was both type and symbol of
the city of the soul which the arts are for ever building, surrounding
us with images of an inner order. For him Byzantium was not only the
ancient city of Constantine but that environment of the arts in which
we live and discover ourselves; 'holy' because what art mirrors is the
eternal world. Our modern technological environment is profane
because it reflects no inner order in which the soul can recognize and
discover itself. Constantine's city was itself an architectural mandala,
built according to the plan of the heavenly Jerusalem, 'On earth as it is
in heaven'. But although the city was Christian the inspiring philosophy was still Platonic. It was Plato who first dreamed of an earthly
Republic whose laws and arts should reflect in every aspect of life a
'divine original', 'laid up in heaven'. In *A Vision* Yeats wrote of that
city;

I think that in early Byzantium, maybe never before or since in recorded
history, religious, aesthetic and practical life were one . . . the painter,

37

the mosaic worker, the worker in gold and silver, the illuminator of sacred books, were almost impersonal, almost perhaps without consciousness of individual design, absorbed in their subject-matter and that the vision of a whole people. They could copy out of old Gospel books those pictures that seemed as sacred as the text, and yet weave all into a vast design, the work of many that seemed the work of one, that made building, picture, pattern, metal-work of rail and lamp, seem but a single image; and this vision, this proclamation of their invisible master, had the Greek nobility . . .

The 'invisible master' is the Logos, the archetype, the inner order which is in truth the author of all 'inspired' art.

In his poem *Sailing to Byzantium* Yeats summarizes his own philosophy of inspiration. He begins by evoking life in all its beauty; but from nature he turns away because all in nature is flux and impermanence—in the words of another poet, 'birth, copulation, and death'. The poet must rather seek 'monuments of unageing intellect', Plato's timeless world of the archetypes. The body ages—'an aged man is but a paltry thing'—but the soul is unageing: it does not belong to 'nature'. Yet the soul can only discover its own native region from those works which are themselves expressions of the inner order:

> Nor is there singing-school but studying
> Monuments of its own magnificence;
> And therefore I have sailed the seas and come
> To the holy city of Byzantium.

He calls the icons from their walls to be his teachers; and we must here remember that the icon—a Greek conception—is not conceived or intended as a copy of nature, but as an expression of the spiritual essence of the archetypal being it depicts. Therefore the icon itself is in a sense 'sacred' and can teach, or impart knowledge of some state of being:

> O sages standing in God's holy fire
> As in the gold mosaic of a wall,
> Come from the holy fire, pern in a gyre,
> And be the singing-masters of my soul.
> Consume my heart away; sick with desire
> And fastened to a dying animal
> It knows not what it is; and gather me
> Into the artifice of eternity.

The last stanza of the poem describes, literally, the glory, the hammered gold and mosaic, of Constantine's city; the golden tree with artificial singing birds sent by the Caliph to the Emperor, which might be literally able to 'keep a drowsy emperor awake'. But that golden artifice of song is, on another level of meaning, a symbol of the poet's art that can keep the drowsy soul from sinking into forgetfulness. Yeats meant us, perhaps, to be reminded of Hans Andersen's story of the dying Emperor and the nightingale who restored him to life and drove away his terrors by her song. And does the golden bough carry also an allusion—for it is by means of such allusion that poets work—not only to Virgil's golden bough by whose magical power Aeneas was able to descend into Hades, but also to one of Yeats's 'sacred Books', Frazer's *The Golden Bough*, that great treasury of myth and symbol? The bird is also the type of Plato's 'musical soul' who sings on earth the music of eternity. Therefore the poet, 'once out of nature', aspires to be the voice of the soul and to speak from a knowledge not to be learned on earth of the timeless order of the things of the Kingdom of Heaven, which is, as all know, within; treasures which are, as the Gospel says, 'both new and old',

> . . . such a form as Grecian goldsmiths make
> From hammered gold and gold enamelling
> To keep a drowsy Emperor awake;
> Or set upon a golden bough to sing
> To lords and ladies of Byzantium
> Of what is past, or passing, or to come.

4

Poetic Symbols as a Vehicle of Tradition

T HE theme of the Eranos Conference in this year, whose number, 1968, relates us to the beginning of the Christian era, defines, for any poet, something more than a problem; a predicament. That date affirms our place within a tradition; but are we in truth still within the scope of Christendom? And if we are, for how much longer? When may not some new Year One sever our links with that Christian-European civilization within which some of us still remain, while others already do not? Are we the last of the old, or the first of the new cycle? And can the old civilization which so precariously survives still perhaps produce, like the school of Plotinus and the late Platonists, a last fine flowering of the mature wisdom of our two thousand years, so that the seed of ancient knowledge shall not be lost? Such are the questions that present themselves. During the first hour I will speak of the crisis of change, as this has been reflected in the work of English poets; in the second hour, of the nature—so far as this can be divined in the symbols of poetry—of the new cycle.

There is a sense in which the relating of past to future is always the work of any present; and a single generation may at any time risk the whole continuity of civilization and learning. Ages of accumulation are entrusted to each generation by the past, desiring to make over its treasures to the use of the future. But we all have at this time the sense of a situation unprecedented, of the end of a cycle of that Great Year of the ancients which has again become a powerful symbol at the present time. Within that symbol the poetic thought of W. B. Yeats (whose poetic thought I regard as the greatest since Shelley and Blake, his own earliest masters) is contained; it is the theme of his remarkable prose work, *A Vision*, an obscure book to many who read it first in 1928, but in 1968 a work of immediate relevance. In his most often quoted poem *The Second Coming* the poet announces his theme of the turning-point of civilization in Plato's image of the revolutions of the world in an ever-widening spiral:

> Turning and turning in the widening gyre
> The falcon cannot hear the falconer

—the limit is almost reached and the Christian era about to give place to the era of Antichrist:

> . . . but now I know
> That twenty centuries of stony sleep
> Were vexed to nightmare by a rocking cradle,
> And what rough beast, its hour come round at last,
> Slouches towards Bethlehem to be born?

This sense of impending change is something more than the mutability which is one of the enduring themes of poetry. Spenser, at the end of the sixteenth century, had a deep sense of mutability, the theme of his finest cantos. But Spenser contains whatever shadow of impending change was upon him in the old cyclic pattern of nature as it has always been celebrated in the pastoral world outside history.

> . . . all things stedfastnes doe hate
> And changed be: yet being rightly wayd
> They are not changed from their first estate:
> But by their change their being doe dilate:
> And turning to themselves at length againe,
> Doe worke their owne perfection so by fate.

Spenser's mutability is remote from Yeats's mutation. The Great Year belongs not to nature as we experience its seasonal cycles or the succession of generations, but to history, whose scale is too great for us to look for any return or discern a whole. In Shakespeare the end of some irrecoverable glory is suggested in his mysterious poem *The Phoenix and the Turtle*, by whose symbolic death, 'Leaving no posteritie',

> Truth may seeme, but cannot be,
> Beauty bragge, but 'tis not she,
> Truth and Beautie buried be.

If the Phoenix, the longest-lived bird, be the informing spirit of a civilization, Shakespeare himself is announcing the end of an era, and introducing that theme of mourning which characterized English poets of the early seventeenth century, who projected into private

41

bereavement, the fading of flowers or the death of a favourite faun, a sense of irrecoverable loss.

Yeats situates the beginning of the break-up of European unity of culture a few years before Shakespeare's birth; but the theme of world revolution did not take possession of the imagination of the poets until the second half of the eighteenth century. Inspired perhaps not so much by historic events as by the archetype which created those events, Blake, in *The Marriage of Heaven and Hell*, announced: 'A new heaven is begun'; and adds the words: 'The Eternal Hell revives'. It was Swedenborg who had announced that New Age 'in the heavens', or inner worlds, giving as its date the year 1757, the year of Blake's birth. In his writings Swedenborg had revived the ancient theme of the historic cycles, symbolized by him as a succession of 'churches', each taking its origin in some new spiritual vision which in course of time is evolved, becoming at last exhausted. The Swedenborgian New Church was to be the ultimate Christian revelation, of 'God as man', a Christian humanism; and it is from Swedenborg that Blake took the term which he made his own, the 'Divine Humanity'. Both Swedenborg and Blake constructed symbols covering the whole of human history from Adam and the Patriarchs to the end of the cycle; and, contrary to the usual Christian view of time as linear, Blake related the Swedenborgian twenty-seven Churches to the cyclic symbol of the Great Year of the Ancients. Blake concludes his account of these Churches with the line:

And where Luther ends Adam begins again in Eternal Circle.

Blake in his 'prophetic' mythological poems created a symbol of the Messiah of the Swedenborgian New Age in 'the new-born terror' Orc, the babe with fiery limbs and flaming hair destined to destroy the old order; Blake's Second Coming, like that of Yeats, is to bring a reversal of all the values of Christendom: not peace but a sword; not Eros but Ares. In his strange symbolic poem on the theme of the historic cycles, *The Mental Traveller*, Blake describes the alternation of these two contrary principles. The beginning of the Christian era is symbolized by the babe 'born in joy/That was begotten in dire woe'—and at the end of the cycle, Antichrist:

> But when they find the frowning Babe,
> Terror strikes thro' the region wide:
> They cry, 'The Babe! the Babe is born!'
> And flee away on every side.

42

> For who dare touch the frowning form
> His arm is wither'd to its root;
> Lions, Boars, Wolves, all howling flee,
> And every Tree does shed its fruit.

—an allusion to the Apocalypse of St John, in which at the end of time 'the star of heaven fell unto the earth, even as a fig tree casteth her untimely figs when she is shaken of a mightly wind'. Blake's terrible child, Orc, red and hairy like Esau, is to break loose from the manacles which bind him; as in France the forces of revolution were to break the chains of Rousseau's famous epigram of man 'everywhere in chains'. In Swedenborg's symbolic system the two brothers, Jacob and Esau, symbolise the opposite principles of the spiritual and the corporeal, who must rule in turn; and Swedenborg's prophecy of the domination of Esau is one of the roots of Blake's myth of 'the new-born terror', red Orc with his hairy shoulders who is in turn the forerunner of Yeats's 'rough beast'. Yeats, writing in *A Vision* of Blake's *Mental Traveller*, thinks of

> the Wheel as an expression of the birth of symbolical children bound together by a single fate. When we so think of it we recreate the lives of Christ and St. John as they are symbolised in the Christian year, Christ begotten in spring and brought forth in midwinter, begotten in joy and brought forth in sorrow, and St. John begotten in autumn and brought forth in midsummer, begotten in sorrow and brought forth in joy. Coventry Patmore claimed the Church's authority for calling Christ supernatural love and St. John natural love and took pleasure in noticing that Leonardo painted a Dionysus like a St. John, a St. John like a Dionysus.

So in *The Resurrection* Yeats himself situates the Resurrection—the beginning of the Christian era—in the context of the symbolic death of Dionysus; who in Blake's Red Orc, and Yeats's own 'rough beast', returns.

Blake's *A Mental Traveller* had a profound influence upon Yeats's thought, and in *A Vision* he makes many references to it. At the beginning of the Christian era, Yeats writes of 'the irrational force that would create confusion and uproar as with the cry "the Babe, the Babe is born" ', and of how, at an earlier reversal, at the time of the Roman civil wars there were many omens, and, 'greatest marvel of all, out of the calm and clear sky came the sound of a trumpet. The Etruscans declared that this trumpet meant "the mutation of the age

and a general revolution of the world".' Then as now the world felt
itself at the point of change: 'When the trumpet sounded in the sky in
Sulla's time the Etruscan sages, according to Plutarch, declared the
Etruscan cycle of 11,000 years at an end, and that "another sort of
men were coming into the world".' Plato too had a myth, comparable
to the Hebrew myth of Jacob and Esau, of 'the golden race' and the
'earth-born' men who in turn control the affairs of the world; and their
alternations underlie all Hellenic myths of history. What for one
civilization is an end, for another is a beginning; the Etruscans heard
the trumpet that heralded their doom; and Virgil, in the reign of
Augustus, was to celebrate the coming of another sort of men as a new
Golden Age: 'The cycles in their vast array begin anew; Virgin
Astraea comes, the reign of Saturn comes, and from the Heights of
Heaven a new generation of mankind descends.' So the present
world-revolution, heralded by its agents with fanatical exultation,
was for Yeats (as he noted after seeing in Paris the first performance of
Jarry's *Ubu Roi*) the reign of 'the savage god':

> Mere anarchy is loosed upon the world,
> The blood-dimmed tide is loosed . . .

Whatever Virgil's conscious intention, events were to fulfil his
prophecy in the end of Hellenism and the advent of Christianity.
Shelley, on the side of revolution and the New Age, who saw Christ as
tyrant and the earth-born Titan Prometheus as the new culture-hero,
for whom the serpent, accursed by the Hebrew and Christian myth,
was a symbol of beneficent earth and the eagle, Christian symbol of
soaring spirituality, of the tyranny of Heaven, paraphrased in the last
chorus of his drama *Hellas* Virgil's prophecy:

> The world's great age begins anew,
> The golden years return,
> And earth doth like a snake renew
> Her winter weeds outworn:
> Heaven smiles, and faiths and empires gleam
> Like wrecks of a dissolving dream.

A Platonist, Shelley, a generation younger than Blake, desired the
return of a new Hellenistic civilization;

> A brighter Hellas rears its mountains
> From waves serener far

44

—and his vision was of a new Golden Age:

> A loftier Argo cleaves the main,
> Fraught with a later prize;
> Another Orpheus sings again,
> And loves, and weeps, and dies.

Yeats in his play *The Resurrection*, whose theme is the beginning of the Christian era, reflecting on Virgil, on Blake and on Shelley, answers Shelley with a reversal of his symbol:

> Another Troy must rise and set,
> Another lineage feed the crow,
> Another Argo's painted prow
> Drive to a flashier bauble yet—

Yeats's play places the Christian Ressurection within the context of the myth of Dionysus, who, by reason of his annual sacrifice and resurrection, symbolizes, within the Hellenic tradition, all cyclic revolutions of death and rebirth, including those of history. Blake's *Mental Traveller*—a poem of central importance to Yeats's thought—was likewise based in part upon the cyclic myth of Dionysus, which he knew from Thomas Taylor's *Dissertation on the Mysteries of Eleusis and Dionysus*, a work known also to Yeats, who, no less eclectic than was Blake, had studied all available myths and symbols relating to this theme. These three poets of the Great Year express in their attitudes to the symbol three possible ways of response; Shelley would have wished to stop the wheel which must carry away the Utopia of which he dreamed:

> O cease! must hate and death return?
> Cease! must men kill and die?
> Cease! drain not to its dregs the urn
> Of bitter prophecy.

Yeats, who saw

> Conduct and work grow coarse, and coarse the soul

found comfort in the certainty that time will in its revolutions bring back

The workman, noble and saint, and all things run
On that unfashionable gyre again.

Blake, whose rapid stanzas take his Mental Traveller through the complete cycle without a pause, in that mood of dispassionate exhilaration which informs the whole poem, comes round full circle to the affirmation that the cycle runs for ever, every end a new beginning:

And all is done as I have told.

Plato, whose *Politicus* may be, for the purposes of this paper, regarded as the source of European thought on the Great Year, did not by any means regard the alternate ages of the golden race and the earth-born race as of equal value. In the Golden Age the supreme god Saturn, whose age is the state of Paradise and the rule of the spirit, conducts the world; but at the time of reversal the god relinquishes his government, leaving the world to its own devices, or, according to another myth, to the government of Jupiter (Shelley's tyrant, and, under another name, Blake's demiurge, whom he calls 'a very cruel being', Yeats's 'savage god'). The 'earth-born' race is now supreme, and an age of materialism supervenes. 'But you yourself', Plato concludes, 'have seen what the condition of the present life is, which is said to be under Jupiter. But are you able, and likewise willing, to judge of these which is the most happy?'—one of those Socratic questions which allows of only one answer.

Virgil, Blake, Shelley, and in our own time Yeats, all attempted—as also did Swedenborg—to relate the symbol of the Great Year to history. This cannot of course be done, in an exact sense, for the very reason that symbol is not history. What we can say is that the symbol itself has its periods of relevance and tends to recur when the sense of the mutation of an age takes possession of the imagination. And in such a period we have lived since in the eighteenth century the first shocks of revolution made European civilization totter.

Yet Plato, in the *Politicus*, regarded these alternations as inevitable; in the nature of things the rise and fall of civilizations, which come to an end not through failure to be or to become what they should be, but rather through their own fulfilment. When all the seeds sown at the beginning have come to fruition and every soul received its necessary number of rebirths, 'then the governor of the universe, laying aside as it were the handle of this rudder', departs; and, when this happens, 'all the gods who govern locally, knowing what has now

46

happened, again deprive the parts of the world of their providential care'. So at the present time small things as well as great bear witness to the departure of the informing spirit which created European Christendom; and indeed all traditional civilizations throughout the world. No regret at the disintegration of the ancient cultures of China and Japan, Tibet, India, or our own seems able to arrest the process. Swedenborg follows Plato in regarding the cyclic rise and decline, whether of organic or spiritual life, or of the 'churches' of successive phases of history, as in the nature of things; for everything originates in an informing spiritual impulse, which embodies itself, and declines into a rigid formality, the original impulse spent. Blake's *A Mental Traveller* is a supremely Swedenborgian account of this process within history.

Yeats in the last chorus of *The Resurrection* gives expression of this doctrine of the inevitability of the cyclic process:

> Everything that man esteems
> Endures a moment or a day.
> Love's pleasure drives his love away,
> The painter's brush consumes his dreams;
> The herald's cry, the soldier's tread
> Exhausts his glory and his might—

This view—which may be called the traditional doctrine of historic cycles (and which he had learned from Empedocles, from Vico, from Swedenborg and from Blake)—is also expressed through Yeats's symbolic *persona* Michael Robartes, who represents, in his mythology, the figure Jung has called 'the Wise Old Man'; who in *A Vision* explains the symbol:

> 'Have I proved that civilizations come to an end when they have given all their light like burned-out wicks, that ours is near its end?' 'Or transformation', Aherne corrected. I said, speaking in the name of all, 'You have proved that civilizations burn out, and that ours is near its end.' 'Or transformation', Aherne corrected once more. 'If you had answered differently', said Robartes, 'I would have sent you away, for we are here to consider the terror that is to come.'

Perhaps we are here for the same purpose. If the poets be true oracles, and if we are in truth living at a moment of cataclysmic reversal and renewal of an age, any statement made about 'the two cultures' which is less than mythological must seem inadequate. At

47

such a moment of the reversal of the gyres, our relation both to tradition and to the present must have an unprecedented character.

I first began to hear the word 'tradition' as a student at Cambridge during the 1920s; the word became current at that time through the writings of T. S. Eliot. In an often-quoted essay (written in 1917) on *Tradition and the Individual Talent* Eliot likens tradition to a series of 'monuments'; the metaphor, with its suggestion of a grave-yard, is oppressive:

> The existing order is complete before the new work arrives; for the order to persist after the supervention of novelty, the *whole* existing order must be, if ever so slightly, altered; and so the relations, proportions, values of each work of art toward the whole are readjusted; and this is conformity between the old and the new. Whoever has approved this idea of order, of the form of European, of English literature will not find it preposterous that the past should be altered by the present as much as the present is directed by the past . . . In a peculiar sense he will be aware also that he must inevitably be judged by the standards of the past.

Eliot's view of tradition is, above all, historical: history is at once the body of tradition and its measure: 'Someone said: "The dead writers are remote from us because we *know* so much more than they did." Precisely, and they are that which we know.' Tradition, so understood, is a constant accumulation, a piling-up of wealth; and we are left with the sense that a mind, or a civilization, like a house, may accumulate too much furniture. Blake understood what Eliot failed to understand, or could not bring himself to admit, the failure of the spiritual impulse which accompanies this amassing process: the spiritual impulse born as the Babe, in Blake's *The Mental Traveller*, grows old:

> An aged Shadow, soon he fades,
> Wand'ring round an Earthly Cot,
> Full filled all with gems & gold
> Which he by industry had got.

In a later book, *Notes Towards a Definition of Culture*, Eliot named three conditions without which a high degree of civilization is impossible.
The first of these is organic (not merely planned but growing) structure, such as will foster the hereditary transmission of culture within a culture: and this requires the persistence of social classes. The second is that a

culture should be analysable geographically into local cultures; this raises the problem of regionalism. The third is the balance of unity and diversity in religion—that is, universality of doctrine with particularity of cult and devotion.

It goes without saying that these three conditions have, since 1948 when those words were written, been so fast disappearing from the world as to make Eliot's terms of discussion seem rather a mockery than a solution of our present situation, the more bitter as they are more true. Eliot, speaking for a declining civilization, seeing, like the Etruscans, that 'another sort of men' were coming into the world, could offer only counsels of despair:

> We can assert with some confidence that our own period is one of decline; that the standards of culture are lower than they were fifty years ago; and that evidences of this decline are visible in every department of human activity. I see no reason why the decay of culture should not proceed much further, and why we may not even anticipate a period, of some duration, of which it is possible to say that it will have *no* culture.

Even in 1948 those were ominous words; now they come to us like a drowned sailor's last message in a bottle washed up on a desolate shore.

When as an undergraduate at Cambridge I first encountered Eliot's ideas on a tradition Catholic in religion, Royalist in politics and classical in literature, my impression was, paradoxically, of an alien mode of thought. If tradition were, as Eliot presents it, the course of history whose past is continually changed by its future, was he not disregarding the real course of traditional development in English poetry, which has been romantic, protestant, and democratic? This development may be for better or for worse, but if history be the measure, can so long, rich, and consistent a development be called a departure from tradition? Milton, if any poet, created an epic that altered the past. I had been reared on the Romantic poets and I believed in their doctrine of inspiration, with Milton's poetry, so disliked by Eliot, as its greatest poetic expression; as Dante's had been of Catholic Christendom. In *Paradise Regained* Milton's Jesus sets aside, as Satan's last and most subtle temptation, 'culture', in Eliot's sense, rejecting 'the schools of ancient sages' and 'the olive-grove of Academe', in the name of inspiration:

49

> Think not but that I know these things, or think
> I know them not; not therefore am I short
> Of knowing what I aught: he who receives
> Light from above, from the fountain of light
> No other doctrine needs, though granted true;

I was therefore, as a student, of Herbert Read's party; whose anarchy was an affirmation of inspiration as against tradition, and seemed a more fruitful way than to follow Eliot's dignified funeral-procession of the past (to borrow a simile from Henri Corbin).

The relationship between T S. Eliot and Herbert Read was that of complementary opposites; the two poets were friends, and seemed, when I was a student, like the two pillars of an arch which upheld the then literary world: I speak of the last years before the Second World War when both Eliot and Herbert Read were defining their standpoints as critics. Read, in his essay *The Poetic Experience*, seems to be addressing Eliot when he writes 'there is not one literary tradition but many traditions; there is certainly a romantic tradition as well as a classical tradition, and, if anything, the romantic tradition has the longer history'. Read based his own thought upon this romantic tradition, above all as expressed by Coleridge in his famous definition of the primary imagination as the 'living Power and prime Agent of all human Perception, and as a repetition in the finite mind of the eternal act of creation in the infinite I AM'. He liked to quote Coleridge's distinction 'between form as proceeding, and shape as superinduced;—the latter is either the death or the imprisonment of the thing;—the former is its self-witnessing and self-effected sphere of agency'. Thus, while Eliot made his plea for tradition rest upon historic transmission, Read appealed to the permanent nature of the human imagination, and found his support in the then novel psychology of Freud and of Jung. He was in fact the first literary critic to my knowledge who suggested that it was rather to Jung than to Freud that we should look for confirmation of the Romantic view of poetic inspiration. He quotes Jung's remark that 'active phantasy is the principle attribute of the artistic mentality' with the comment that he (Jung) 'nowhere seems to have pressed home the conclusions that are surely latent in the theory, namely, that the poetic function is nothing else but this active fantasy in its more than individual aspect'.

It was in relation to Jung that Herbert Read defined his position:

> I have been gradually drawn towards a psychological type of literary criticism because I have realized that psychology, more particularly the

method of psycho-analysis, can offer explanations of many problems connected with the personality of the poet, the technique of poetry, and the appreciation of the poem . . . my tendency, step by step with my increasing knowledge of modern psychology, has been to give literary criticism a psychological direction.

So, while Eliot saw culture as grounded upon a tradition without any necessary individual inspiration, Read saw as its ground inspiration without tradition; an attitude expressed in the title of an exhibition of paintings (culminating with the Surrealists) held just before the Second Word War, entitled 'three thousand years of modern art'; indeed the phrase 'the modern movement' is one which in itself expresses Read's view of all true art as essentially 'modern', always making a new beginning, without a past. Such a doctrine could not fail to commend itself to the young and to the uneducated; in this sense it is a manifesto made on behalf of the new cycle, no less inevitably associated with revolution (or anarchy, in Read's own case) than is Eliot's and David Jones's view of a tradition ripening through centuries inseparable from European Christendom and a hierarchic society.

It seemed to a young poet at that time not only the easier but the more living way. Unlike Freud, Herbert Read tacitly assumed the incorruptible purity of the soul and therefore of the fountain of inspiration. Yet his writings, in the context of a positivist and atheist climate of opinion, together with the Freudian view of the unconscious as the sum of individual and social repressions, have often been forced into the service of a generation of painters and writers whose productions are mere scribbling and automatism, grounded in nothing that Coleridge would have recognized as 'a repetition in the finite mind of the eternal act of creation'; much of it (with Freud's sanction) obscene, perverted and nihilistic, and nearly all noticeably lacking in those technical skills which only long labour and study can achieve in any art. Read expressed later his dismay at the way things were going in the Modern Movement which he had himself helped to create.

In his essay *The Poetic Experience*, he quotes as a perfect statement of what he himself wished poetry to be D. H. Lawrence, who saw in 'free verse'

the insurgent naked throb of the instant moment . . . free verse has its own *nature*, it is neither star nor pearl, but instantaneous like plasm. It

51

has no goal in either (time or) eternity. It has no finish. It has no stability, satisfying to those who like the immutable. None of this. It is the instant; the quick; the very jetting source of all will-be and has-been. The utterance is like a spasm, naked contact with all influences at once. It does not want to get anywhere. It just takes place.

Read commented on Lawrence that 'poetry of this instantaneous kind must necessarily be written in free verse. At the same time it tends to be strongly rhythmical, though this thythm is also unconscious and instinctive: the pitch and interval of natural utterance. The rhythm is found just as the words are found; by the laws of attraction which seem to operate in the unconscious mind, a law which selects equivalents in visual image, verbal expression, temporal extension.' Thus a culture which for Eliot seemed the *sine qua non* of the *ars poetica* was for Herbert Read a mere encumbrance from which the creative essence of the psyche must be freed.

When I began my study of William Blake it was under the influence of Herbert Read's psychological theory. Had not Blake claimed for his poems that 'the Authors are in Eternity' and of his Prophetic Book, *Milton* (his type of 'the inspired man'), 'I have written this Poem from immediate Dictation, sometimes twenty or thirty lines at a time, without Premeditation and even against my Will; the Time it has taken in writing was thus render'd Non Existent, and an immense Poem Exists which seems to be the Labour of a long Life, all produc'd without Labour or Study.' If there is a single poem that typifies the genius of English Romantic poetry it is Coleridge's *Kubla Khan*, 'dictated' to the poet in an opium dream. 'I regard the truth as a divine ventriloquist', Coleridge has written; and all this might seem to support Herbert Read's theory of 'instantaneous' poetry. In that perspective it is easy for ignorance to see Milton's, Coleridge's and Blake's great learning as unrelated to their inspiration; instead of being—as I was soon to discover—the indispensable language of that inspiration. Instead of the book I had projected I was to write a study of the sources of Blake's myths and symbols; and any reader familiar with the symbolic vocabulary of neo-Platonism will recognize in *Kubla Khan* a poem written in strict accordance with the iconography of that tradition, in which Coleridge was saturated.

What Read approvingly calls 'poetry of this instantaneous kind', which is neither star nor pearl (together with the taste for free verse which accompanied the theory of instantaneity), was itself the product of an assumption about the nature of the 'jetting source' which the

52

experience of thousands of years of art and poetry does not bear out. Both the practice and the theory reflect rather a brief moment in the history of psychology when it was imagined that the unconscious was as empty of forms as Locke's *tabula rasa*, the mind of a new-born child. Read conceived the psyche as a fountain of emotion but not of forms—not of those myths and symbols, archetypal figures and configurations, which have at all times been the creations of what he calls 'active fantasy' and which are at once its language and its records. The poetry of Blake and of Coleridge is not at all like 'plasm', but on the contrary a poetry of archetypal beings and symbolic events and configurations of bewildering richness and disconcerting precision. What is true of the formal content of the imagination is true also of its rhythmic forms; free-verse is by no means its typical expression—rather the contrary, a failure on the part of the poet to reach that fountain. The Irish mystic and poet AE (George Russell) writes, in *The Living Torch*, that 'the verse form is only natural when the soul speaks', because: 'The heart in love, in imagination, in meditation, mounts at times to an ecstasy where its being has become musical. Carlyle quotes a German mystic who said: "If we think deeply we think musically" ', and elsewhere he writes of free verse that 'the angel who presides over hearing shakes its head and murmurs: "No, it does not remind me of the music of the spheres." ' AE objects to free verse not because it is inspired by the deepest imagination, but precisely because it is not. Plato's fountain of the Muses, in his *Ion*, was precisely a fountain of those poetic forms which Herbert Read would discard because they seemed to him (not being plasm-like) artificial; but the whole body of the traditional art and poetry which he dismissed, with its formal, indeed mathematical, structure, the Basilica of Santa Sophia and Dante's *Commedia*, and not a few fragments of 'instantaneous' free-verse, are precisely what has, in the course of civilization, issued from that fountain, bearing upon it the stamp of ideal forms, complex and organized and, as Blake says, 'minutely articulated'.

As a writer on the essential nature of poetry, and of tradition, no one at the time of which I am writing took Yeats seriously; for his view of the nature of tradition, of inspiration, and of the *ars poetica* as a traditional art, was totally alien not only to Eliot and Read, but to the whole Anglo-American literary world of that time. I found the clue to Yeats's thought on tradition when I began to study Blake; for the first book written on Blake's symbolic system was by Edwin J. Ellis and William Butler Yeats (then in his twenties) during the 1880s. In Ellis and Yeats's commentaries on Blake's prophetic books I discovered a continual allusiveness to a tradition (taken for granted by the authors) whose existence I had not discerned in Blake because I had not known of it: a language of myth and symbol exact and coherent within its own terms. Blake's most original utterances, I now found, embodied, in a language he shared with all other 'inspired' poets, a structure and mode of thought and expression both objective and exact, and implicit in every smallest detail of his work. It was, it seemed, the Romantic poets who are most truly classical, traditional and strict in the use of the symbolic terms and forms proper to the *ars poetica*.

I began to discover that tradition and inspiration, far from being opposites, are in truth inseparable; for tradition is the record, the language, the learning of inspiration. The content of tradition, so understood, is not historical but metaphysical; nor does it relate to time, but to the timeless order. Its monuments are not a record of history, but, as Yeats has called them, 'monuments of unageing intellect', contemporaneous, belonging to history only in the style of their execution. Such works are at once records of the soul's self knowledge and its only doctrine. What tradition transmits has nothing to do with the past, being what St Augustine calls 'wisdom, that was not made, but is now what it always was and ever shall be'. In the *Bhagavad Geeta* it is called (in the words of the translation of Yeats's friend Shri Purohit Swami) 'the imperishable philosophy', 'the supreme secret', known to 'the Divine Kings', 'then, after a long time, at last it was forgotten'; it is to restore this knowledge that the divine being becomes incarnate 'whenever spirituality decays and materialism is rampant'. According to Ananda Coomaraswamy, in his essay *Is Art a Superstition*, 'symbols are the universal language of art, an international language with merely dialectic variations current once in all milieus and always intrinsically intelligible'. 'The adequacy of the symbols being intrinsic, and not a matter of convention, the symbols correctly employed transmit from generation to generation a knowledge of cosmic analogies.' The language of tradition becomes lucid not through the study of history but through familiarity with the order to which it relates; conversely, as Coomaraswamy says, 'the greater the ignorance of modern times, the deeper grows the darkness of the Middle Ages'.

A culture, in the historical sense, may embody tradition or it may not: it is possible for a whole society (and we may question our own) to depart entirely from tradition. Eliot contrasts Dante, traditional poet of European Christendom, with Blake, whom he considered outside

54

tradition because he was outside the framework of the received ideas of his time. But Coomaraswamy names Blake with Dante as the two supreme traditional poets of Europe because both are alike grounded in 'the imperishable philosophy' and its symbolic themes and language. If Dante lived and worked within a society which as a whole shared and understood that language, Blake is the outstanding example of a traditional poet in a society which as a whole had departed from tradition, and to whom therefore his symbolic language (intrinsically intelligible though it may be) appeared as dark as Coomaraswamy's Middle Ages. The affinity between the two poets is evident from the majestic power of Blake's illustrations to Dante.

The painter Cecil Collins has described tradition as 'the continuum of a universal knowledge of the purpose and meaning of life and of rebirth, transmitted from generation to generation. Certain, immortal, eternally fresh'. His definition, like that of St Augustine, stresses the ever-present nature of this knowledge; tradition, like Spenser's Great Dame Nature, is 'ever young yet full of eld'. Or one might define tradition as the body of knowledge with its accompanying language of symbol, proper to what the Platonic philosophers have called the memoria, or memory of nature.

The symbolic language—Blake calls it 'the Body of Divine Analogy'—is intelligible as a whole or not understood at all. If we possess the kind of knowledge necessary for the understanding of one period of such art we have (with due allowance for dialectic variations) the key to all.

> The Nature of Visionary Fancy, or Imagination, is very little Known, and the Eternal nature and permanence of its ever Existent Images is consider'd as less permanent than the things of Vegetation and Generative Nature; yet the Oak dies as well as the Lettuce, but Its Eternal Image and Individuality never dies, but renews by its seed; just as the Imaginative Image returns by the seed of Contemplative Thought.

So Blake wrote of the abiding archetypal symbols. Jung would have agreed about the permanence of the 'ever existent images'. Yet there is a danger, into which modern psychology itself often falls, of misreading the symbols for want of the doctrine. In this sense symbols cannot be separated from the whole transmitted body of knowledge to which they belong. Hellenic myths (of Oedipus or Psyche) or Hebraic myths (of Job or the myth of the Messiah perhaps) cannot be given a 'new' interpretation, out of context. But the necessary knowledge is even so rather metaphysical than historical; a metaphysician of some other tradition (a 'dialectic variation' of the universal language) will come nearer to the truth than an historian, however scrupulous, without the doctrine.

Academicism and avant-gardism are alike alien to tradition, for both are concerned with the how, and not the what, of art. To the traditional poet and artist, on the contrary, the what is far more important than the how; it should, indeed, be, as Coomaraswamy has said, 'the what that determines the how, as form determines shape'. Within tradition poetry and the other arts have a clear function: to awaken in the reader or auditor the primordial images, and by this means to reintegrate the time-and-place-bound ego with the eternal Self. By this standard much that today passes for literature and art (and not only within the popular subculture which has usurped these names) can only be seen as the blind painting for the blind. Such work is no more 'modern' than it is 'traditional' art: it is not art at all, for it fulfils none of the traditional functions of a work of art.

Yeats (more learned in tradition, so understood, than Eliot) defined 'supreme art' as 'a traditional statement of certain heroic and religious truths, passed on from age to age, modified by individual genius, but never abandoned'. For Yeats, as for all traditional poets and philosophers, the arts cannot be separated from religion, since both spring from the same root. Yeats invokes that source more ancient than any cult which has sprung from it and for a time celebrated its mystery: 'A great work of art, the *Ode to a Nightingale* not less than the *Ode to Duty*, is as rooted in the early ages as the Mass which goes back to savage folk-lore. In what temple garden did the nightingale first sing?'

Yeats here is speaking the language of tradition for those who are able to hear with the imagination. The song of the nightingale is poetic inspiration which comes from beyond history and is untouched by time; and that was Keats's meaning in his ode; to which Yeats is here alluding:

> Thou wast not born for death, immortal Bird!
> No hungry generations tread thee down;
> The voice I hear this passing night was heard
> In ancient days by emperor and clown:
> Perhaps the self-same song that found a path
> Through the sad heart of Ruth, when, sick for home
> She stood in tears amid the alien corn.

With Yeats's allusion to Keats's poem—one of the supreme expressions of English romantic poetry—we may contrast Eliot's: 'The ode of Keats contains a number of feelings which have nothing particular to do with the nightingale, but which the nightingale, partly perhaps because of its attractive name, and partly because of its reputation, served to bring together.' Eliot, whose view of tradition is historical, and who was (or so Yeats described him) 'without apparent imagination', has failed to comprehend the truly traditional character of Keats's symbol. It is not the 'reputation' or the history of the nightingale, or its name, which makes the symbol valid; one might as well speak of the reputation of the sun and moon. But the intelligibility depends upon the reader's faculty of recognition; Eliot failed to 'read' Keats's symbol not through want of academic learning on either side, nor ignorance of natural history, but purely and simply because he was not open to the language of cosmic analogy implicit in the symbol. Keats's poem has the character of all truly traditional works of art: it relates the present to the timeless. The transition from the bird-song to exiled Ruth would have, for Eliot, 'nothing particular to do with the nightingale' because the transition is not logical: it is made below the formal surface of the poem and arises out of the experience of the symbol; the bird-song from the timeless world reminds the listener that the soul's situation in the time-state is that of exile; and of the soul's exile a female figure is symbolically acceptable, not from a logical or formal, but from an imaginative transition; not so much to the conscious as to the unconscious mind. Ruth, widowed and in exile, is the traditional and ever-present figure of Psyche herself; who in the mythological story of Cupid and Psyche also recognized her divine lover as a *voice*, fittest symbol of the communication of the invisible world.

Birds and their voices have been held oracular from the beginning of time; the hero of folklore who can understand the speech of birds has the key to supernatural wisdom; and in poetry the bird-voice has the same meaning: it speaks from 'the age-long memoried self'; whether it be Shakespeare's

> . . . Bird of loudest lay
> On the Sole Arabian tree

or his lark who sings at 'Heaven's gate'; or Shelley's lark that pours its—song from 'Heaven, or near it'; Milton's who sings

> From his watch-towre in the skies

57

or Blake's whose

> . . . little throat labours with inspiration; every feather
> On throat & breast & wings vibrates with the effluence Divine

or Yeats's bird of art, 'of hammered gold and gold enamelling'

> . . . set upon a golden bough to sing
> To lords and ladies of Byzantium
> Of what is past, or passing, or to come.

The peacock of Byzantine iconography has the same timeless intelligibility; whose harsh cry seemed to Yeats a more fitting symbol of the mysterious utterance of the superhuman than the sweetness of lark or nightingale. Even if the bird-voice be of evil omen it is nonetheless the inspired utterance of the superhuman speaking from, and to, the imagination; Shakespeare's

> . . . shriking harbinger
> Foul precurrer of the fiend

or Poe's

> Quoth the raven, Nevermore.

Such symbols are so to say words in the language of traditional poetry; which is itself the language of the *memoria*.

There is a sense in which the traditional language of symbols can never be learned but only 'revealed'. Yet symbolic discourse has its tradition and its learning, its continuity, its continuous allusiveness, not throughout some single culture only but universally. If, as seems likely, our own civilization should break down, the intrinsically intelligible language of tradition might form the only living link with whatever future there may be; tradition may be disinterred no older than when it was buried; it is the perpetual lamp within the tomb of a buried civilization. Lark, nightingale and peacock will be, for the imagination, what they have always been when Eliot's row of monuments, the records of history, tell us no more of those who constructed them than do the broken inscriptions and crumbling walls of the tombs on the Via Appia.

The captains, merchant bankers, eminent men of letters,
The generous patrons of art, the statesmen and the rulers,
Distinguished civil servants, chairmen of many committees,
Industrial lords and petty contractors, all go into the dark.

It would be less than just to Eliot to suppose that tradition was for him only a receding vista of monuments of forgotten greatness; he held culture to be 'essentially the incarnation of the religion of a people'. 'No culture has appeared or developed except together with a religion: according to the point of view of the observer, the culture will appear to be the product of the religion, or the religion the product of the culture.' Believing as he did that Christianity is the last and perfect expression of the 'wisdom that was not made' he saw in Christendom not only the highest actual, but also the highest possible culture.

David Jones, in his seminal essay *Art and Sacrament*, affirms the religious nature of art even more strongly than does Eliot: '. . . the activity called art is, at bottom, and inescapably, a "religious" activity, for it deals with realities, and the real is sacred and religious.' If, as David Jones argues 'the real is sacred' it follows that art must be sacramental, since everything in nature is a sign or (to use the alchemical term) 'signature' of that which informs it: Blake's 'Divine Analogy', Swedenborg's 'correspondence'. Therefore, he writes:

> . . . because the Church is committed to 'Sacraments' with a capital S she cannot escape a committal to sacrament with a small s, unless the sacramentalism of the Church is to be regarded as a peculiar and isolated phenomenon. We know that such a view is not to be entertained and that the sacramentalism of the Church is a thing normal to man and that a sacramental quality is evident in the past works of man over the whole period of his existence so far known to us.

Thus David Jones makes the ground of culture not, like Eliot, history, but the unchanging nature of the relationship in which we as human beings stand to our world.

Within tradition—or as David Jones would say within the real—no distinction can exist between sacred and profane. 'Let us tell them the painful truth'—so wrote Coomaraswamy ('they' are the art-critics)—'that most of these works of art are about God'; and elsewhere: 'In a traditional society there is little or nothing that can properly be called secular.' Yeats understood this when he wrote: 'I wished for a world where I could discover this tradition perpetually, and not in pictures and in poems only, but in tiles round the chimney-piece and in the hangings that kept out the draught.' Conversely it might be said that even when profane artists decorate churches with Madonna or Crucifix, they are not expressing tradition but destroying it; for the work of art expresses the mind that informs it, regardless of function; and a modern church may be no more expressive of the spiritual world than a petrol-station. 'People speak of sacraments with a capital "S" ', Jones writes, 'without seeming to notice that sign and sacrament with a small "s" are everywhere eroded and in some contexts non-existent. Such dichotomies are not healthy'; and again, 'the period in which we live now is alien to sign, sacrament and sacramental acts, and not one of us can totally escape that alienation'. Is not bad religious art itself the proof of failure of vision? AE wrote: 'No Church today can convince me that it is inspired until the words arising from it even in anger break in a storm of beauty on the ear.' Hardly a description of the 'New Mass'.

What troubled Eliot (and there is so much justice in his criticism of Blake), what troubled David Jones, and what must trouble any poet of this time who does not share the current profane view of the real, is communication; for, as he states in the Preface to *The Anathemata*, 'the forms and materials which the poet uses, his images and the meanings he would give to those images, his perceptions, what is evoked, invoked or incanted, is in some way or other, to some degree or other, essentially bound up with the particular historic complex to which he, together with each other member of that complex, belongs'. David Jones, within the limits of the situation, succeeded better than any other English writer in achieving a traditional art still within the Christian 'unity of culture' which had the quality of (to use his own word) 'nowness'. This is doubtless because he takes for his ground not the historic aspect of Christendom but the permanent aspect of the sacramental; and because he sees history as itself a symbolic and sacramental event; 'sacred history', the expression in time of the timeless. The Muse, as he says, 'is indifferent to what the poet may wish he could feel, she cares only for what he in fact feels'. It is perhaps for this reason that the poetry of Eliot communicates rather his deep regret for the passing of Christendom than any sense of its continuance in an age that cries not 'The Babe is born!' but 'God is dead'.

It is said that the old symbols and myths (common to poetry and religion) have worn thin with use; but symbols of the sacred become meaningless only when they no longer serve to relate us to the primordial images; which necessarily happens when the superhuman is (as in our 'humanist' society) denied. So seen, the 'demythologizing' process at work within Christendom is not so much a work of religious reform as the operation within the Church itself of a mentality alien alike to poetry and to religion: for 'the arts abhor any loppings off of meanings or emptyings out, any lessening of the totality of connotation, any loss of recession and thickness through'. David Jones, in that same Preface, gives an example: 'water is called the "matter" of the Sacrament of Baptism. Is "two of hydrogen and one of oxygen" that "matter"?' He goes on to ask 'whether there is a radical incompatibility between the world of "myths" and the world of "formulae" '. Seen so, a 'demythologized' religion must appear a contradiction in terms. H2O describes so small and (qualitatively speaking) insignificant an aspect of 'water' that we may wonder how it has come about that so many persons at this time would see no inadequacy in the definition. Such a work as Bachelard's *L'Eau et les Rêves*—a qualitative redefinition of the matter 'water'—seems relevant in this context.

At such a time, Jones asks:

> What *is* valid as material for our effective signs? Normally we should not have far to seek: the flowers for the muse's garland would be gathered from the ancestral burial-mound—always and inevitably fecund ground, yielding perennial and familiar blossoms . . . It becomes more difficult when the bulldozers have all but obliterated the mounds . . . and where was this site, where were these foci there is *terra informis*.

But the bulldozer is itself a symbol of the phase of destruction and obliteration in which we are living, a phase no less 'normal' than civilization in its prime; we are not outside the scope of the ancient symbol of the Great Year but all too terribly within it. Coleridge wrote in his notebook, 'There be Spirits that are created for Vengeance—in the time of Destruction they pour out their force and appease the Wrath of him that made them.'

'We must, in this "time of destruction" ', Jones reminds us, 'also remember that no metamorphosis since pre-historic times is in any way comparable to the metamorphosis that we are now undergoing.' Coomaraswamy took the measure of the situation when he wrote: 'We are considering a catholic or universal doctrine, with which the humanistic philosophies of art can neither be compared nor reconciled, but only contrasted.' For there has never before in human history been a culture based upon denial of the sacred. He writes of 'the withering touch of our civilization' on primitive peoples; but we ourselves are the principal sufferers, our consciousness, as Jung wrote, 'torn from its root and no longer able to appeal to the authority of the primordial images'.

The question seems to be not whether we can or cannot separate art from religion, but to what form of religion we can, in the modern situation, relate art and poetry? Only one of the poets of the generation of Eliot, Read and Jones has come near an answer: I mean, of course, Yeats. Yeats was, though not a Christian, no less aware than Eliot and Jones of the failure of communication in the absence of a shared culture grounded in a shared religion. 'Had not Europe shared one mind and heart, until both mind and heart began to break in fragments a little before Shakespeare's birth?' Eliot and David Jones looked back to pre-Renaissance Europe, Yeats to Byzantium, as periods of what, in *The Trembling of the Veil*, he calls 'unity of culture': 'I delighted in every age where poet and artist confined themselves gladly to some inherited subject-matter known to the whole people, for I thought that in man and race alike is something called "Unity of Being".' At one time Yeats had hoped perhaps to discover or to restore, in Ireland, such a unity of culture, not based solely upon Christianity but also upon the shared mythology and history of the race from pre-Christian times: 'Have not all races had their first unity from a mythology which marries them to rock and hill?' Yeats, at a time of the breakdown of Christendom, searched for an older tradition which might survive the change: 'I ceased to read modern books that were not books of imagination, and if some philosophic idea interested me, I tried to trace it back to its earliest use, believing that there must be a tradition of belief older than any European Church, and founded upon the experience of the world before the modern bias.' At the same time he began to study the visions and thoughts of the country people of Ireland; not only for traces of a pre-Christian tradition, but also because perhaps the country people might have remained nearer to the primordial images. But even though he achieved in Ireland a partial success (and Ireland had retained a more living and imaginative sense of the Catholic faith than perhaps any other European country) he wrote at last that 'the dream of my early manhood that a modern nation can return to Unity of Culture, is false; though it may be we can achieve it for some small circle of men and women, and there leave it till the moon bring round its century'. The attempt to discover how best, at the end of a cycle, to embody and communicate tradition occupied Yeats's thought for many years. This orientation, in the absence of shared cult and culture, might still be possible through poetry and the arts.

For the poets stand near the primordial images; and of William Blake's New Age, announced in those prophetic books written a hundred years before, which he was the first to edit and publish, Yeats was the first disciple. In 1897, in his essay *William Blake and the Imagination*, he wrote of Blake that 'in his time educated people believed that they amused themselves with books of imagination, but that they "made their souls" by listening to sermons and by doing or by not doing certain things. When they had to explain why serious people like themselves honoured the great poets greatly they were hard put to it for lack of good reasons. In our time we are agreed that we "make our souls" out of some one of the great poets . . . while we amuse ourselves, or, at best, make a poorer sort of soul, by listening to sermons or by doing or by not doing certain things.' Elsewhere, in *Autobiographies*, Yeats expands this concept of a religion of art. He believed that 'whatever the great poets had affirmed in their finest moments was the nearest we could come to an authoritative religion, and that their mythology, their spirits of water and wind, were but literal truth'. 'I had even created a dogma: "Because those imaginary people are created out of the deepest instinct of man, to be his measure and his norm, whatever I can imagine those mouths speaking may be the nearest I can go to truth." When I listened they seemed always to speak of one thing only: They, their loves, every incident of their lives, were steeped in the supernatural.' They possessed, in contrast with the fixed and externalized symbols of cult, numinosity.

This might seem, to those whose nostalgia is for societies which possess unity of cult and culture, a second best. To Blake it did not seem so, as we may see from a letter upon the subject which he wrote in October 1801 to his friend and fellow Swedenborgian, the sculptor Flaxman. The Swedenborgian New Age he saw as the reign of the Imagination: 'The Kingdoms of this World are now become the Kingdoms of God & his Christ & we shall reign with him for ever & ever. The Reign of Literature & the Arts Commences. Blessed are those who are found studious of Literature & Humane & polite accomplishments. Such have their lamps burning & such shall shine as the stars.'

Poetic inspiration, for Blake, was the reality of which cult is merely an expression. 'The Religions of all Nations are derived from each Nation's different reception of the Poetic Genius, which is every-where call'd the Spirit of Prophecy.'

It must be said that if Blake made of religion a mode of poetry, he also made poetry a sacred art; it was, according to Blake, not the poets but 'priesthood' who had misunderstood the gods, 'choosing forms of worship from poetic tales . . . Thus men forgot that All deities reside in the human breast'. It is not the poetic tales which are irreligious; and with their return from the cult to 'the human breast' the gods do not lose their reality but find it. It is in poetry and the arts that the primordial images are most themselves, and speak most immediately to the imagination of modern mankind.

The transference of the sacred from cult to poetry has surely been implicit in the English poetic tradition ever since the Renaissance; and if this be so my instinctive unease with Eliot's attempt to affirm a tradition to fit a theory, while failing to see that tradition in a living sense was present in just those English Romantic poets who seemed to him most to be without it, was well grounded. English poetry, basically neo-Platonic, polytheistic and mythological, remained a channel for tradition when other means failed. If, as Yeats has somewhere written, England possesses the poorest philosophic literature in the world, it possesses in compensation the most philosophical—or rather the most metaphysical—poetry of any modern nation. When Milton theologizes he writes, as Blake observed, 'in fetters'; his theology few now would take seriously, while his poetic myth of lost Paradise is unageing. Blake had no hesitation in saying that 'Milton's Paradise Lost is as true as Genesis or Exodus'; historical 'evidence' is nothing, for the works of Moses, like those of Milton, are 'Poetry, and that poetry inspired'.

The poets and painters of the Renaissance did not, surely, turn to the Pagan gods and their myths because these seemed more true, or even more beautiful than the Christian, but because, being freed from cult, the old gods had, paradoxically, become more valid as symbols of the primordial images; the archetypal figures of Apollo and Venus and the rest once more plastic in the imaginations of Botticelli, Spenser and Shakespeare; freed from cult, they moved once more towards their source.

As a child I could not read Milton's *On the Morning of Christ's Nativity* without an inner protest that the birth of Christ should have been the occasion of the banishing of the whole Greak pantheon; did Milton himself share that sense of desolation?

And mooned *Ashtaroth*,
Heav'ns Queen and Mother both,
   Now sits not girt with Tapers holy shine,

64

The Lybyc *Hammon* shrinks his horn,
In vain the *Tyrian* Maids their wounded *Thammuz* mourn.

Milton, the supreme poet of inspiration, should have left demythologizing to the iconoclasts of a puritanism which had lost all vital connection with the primordial images. No poet has a right to rejoice when the gods are banished.

The Renaissance return to the Hellenic gods (Milton's perhaps insincere attempt to place them in a theological hell notwithstanding) was a stage in the renewal of access to those archetypes and primordial images whose final release took place in the Romantic poetry of the end of the eighteenth century; in Blake's astonishing pantheon, in Coleridge's dream myths, in the neo-Hellenism of Keats and Shelley. As if to celebrate their return to 'the human breast' Blake renamed the primordial images; four principal gods and their consorts or 'vehicles'; the soul-figure or anima, Jerusalem, with her shadow Vala, 'the goddess Nature'; 'Satan the selfhood', the human ego, Jesus the Imagination; and a multitude of 'sons' and 'daughters' of the principal gods, each with their attributes, mythical enactments and transformations. Blake was no less learned in ancient mythologies than Milton, Coleridge, Shelley or Yeats; scholarship can uncover the sources of most of his myths and figures in neo-Platonic, Gnostic, Hermetic and Alchemical myths and theology; but his reason for renaming the gods was, I think, just to give back to them their strangeness, their namelessness, their numinosity; the sacred character which as cult images they had lost long ago, and as conventional literary images had again lost. Therefore he re-created the Kore as the Little Girl Lost of *Songs of Innocence and Experience*, and for Apollo with his lyre and arrows gave us Los with his alchemical furnaces and his printing-press. It is the function of tradition to perpetuate the primordial images, not the names by which they may have at various times been known. Cult mistrusts eclecticism, but poets delight in it, for the poetic symbols are enriched by all they have gathered from the beginning of the world. They borrow their beauty from all who have used them before; we may not know their descent but 'our nerves quiver with a recognition they were shaped to by a thousand emotions'—to quote Yeats yet again.

The history of imaginative poetry is of such continuous renewal, of renaissance; whether, like Milton's Satan, or Shelley's Prometheus, or Yeats's Cuchulainn, some old god or hero is given new life; or, as with Shakespeare's heroic or Blake's mythological personages, re-created

65

by the poets. 'Perhaps even these images, once created and associated with river and mountain, might move of themselves, and with some powerful, even turbulent life'—so Yeats expressed his desire that the Irish poets might achieve what Blake had done, who gave form to the Four Zoas, or Shelley who re-animated the myth of Prometheus.

The doctrine of poetic inspiration is itself traditional; Greek theology is derived (whether symbolically or historically) from the poet-hero Orpheus; and Plato in the *Ion* states the received doctrine:

> . . . the Muse, inspiring, moves men herself through her divine impulse. From these men, thus inspired, others, catching the sacred power, form a chain of divine enthusiasts. For the best Epic poets, and all such as excel in composing any kind of verses to be recited, frame not those admirable poems from the rules of art; but possessed by the Muse, they write from divine inspiration.

The poet is called by Plato 'sacred', for he is unable to write unless divinely inspired:

> . . . till the Muse entering into him, he is transported out of himself, and has no longer the command of his intellect . . . the god, depriving them of the use of their intellect, employs them as his ministers, his oracle singers, his divine prophets; that when we hear them we may know, it is not these men who deliver things so excellent; these, to whom intellect is not present; but the god himself speaking, and delivering his mind to us.

Herbert Read in his essay *The Nature of Criticism* calls this passage (which he quotes in support of his own view of inspiration) 'the final elaboration of the primitive metaphor'; for to him the 'breath' of God seemed to him no more than a figure of speech. But Blake said 'Plato was in Earnest; Milton was in Earnest' when they spoke of the Muse; for the Muse of poetry is not a metaphor for enhanced feeling, but 'they believed that God did visit them Really and Truly'. 'Inspiration', Coomaraswamy writes, 'can never mean anything but the working of some spiritual force within you.' Perhaps at this time we are once more prepared to understand the traditional belief that the poet is after all instrumental, though of who or what the divine ventriloquist may be we may no longer—or not yet—be prepared to say. But the traditional view once more seems more credible than any humanist attempt to replace it.

AE speaks both for the Orphic tradition and for the religion of art when he writes:

> I think, indeed, that almost the only oracles which have been delivered to humanity for centuries have come through the poets, though too often they have not kept faith with the invisible . . . but at times they still receive the oracles, as did the sibyls of old, because in the practise of their art they preserve the ancient tradition of inspiration and they wait for it with airy uplifted mind.

Blake, who had read the *Ion* in his contemporary (and at one time friend) Thomas Taylor's translation (quoted above), objected to Plato's over-insistence on the poet's deprivation of the use of his intellect: in his *Vision of the Last Judgement* he wrote: 'Plato has made Socrates say that Poets & Prophets do not know or Understand what they write or Utter; this is a most Pernicious Falsehood. If they do not, pray is an inferior kind to be call'd Knowing? Plato confutes himself.' Blake is right in poin·ing to what is surely one great difference between poetic inspiration and madness. Yeats too stresses the wholeness of being in men of genius—'the two halves of their nature are so completely joined that they seem to labour for their objects, and yet to desire whatever happen, being at the same time predestinate and free, creation's very self'. He calls genius a crisis which joins 'the age-long memoried self' for certain moments to the trivial daily mind which he calls 'trivial' in comparison with the 'age-long memoried self'. Yeats had less respect than had Plato for the human intellect. Blake's daily mind was by no means trivial; nor Milton's, nor Yeats's; yet when these speak of the 'other' mind of inspiration all do so with a reverence as towards the sacred; 'the authors are in eternity', Blake said of his poems: 'And tho' I call them Mine, I know that they are not Mine', being of the same opinion with Milton when he says 'That the Muse visits his Slumbers & awakes & governs his Song when Morn purples the East.'

Milton composed in the early morning, inspired, by his own confession, by his dreams; he sings (so he writes) with 'mortal voice', but with the assistance of his 'heavenlie Muse';

> . . . yet not alone, while thou
> Visit's my slumbers Nightly, or when Morn
> Purples the East: still govern thou my Song.

The invocation of the Muse is by no means empty or formal; and so

Milton follows the Platonic tradition in the opening passage of his great poem:

> Sing, Heav'nly Muse, that on the Secret top
> Of *Oreb*, or of *Sinai*, didst inspire
> That Shepherd, who first taught the chosen Seed
> In the Beginning, how the Heav'ns and Earth
> Rose out of *Chaos*: or if *Sion's* Hill
> Delight thee more, and *Siloa's* Brook that flow'd
> Fast by the Oracle of God . . .

Milton's Muse is more real than the web of Cromwellian theology in which he vainly attempted to ensnare her, forcing her from Olympus to Sinai and disowning her heathen relations:

> But drive farr off the barbarous dissonance
> Of *Bacchus* and his Revellers, the Race
> Of that wild Rout that tore the *Thracian* Bard
> In *Rhodope* . . .

—so he disclaims Orpheus and the Orphic tradition—

> For thou art Heav'nlie, shee an empty dreame . . .

But poetry knows nothing of such theological distinctions; nor does inspiration from the sleeping mind take kindly to monotheism: Milton acknowledges the Orphic tradition even in his disclaimer.

Yet Blake follows Milton in his rejection of the Greek and his affirmation of the Hebrew as the purest expression of 'inspiration', not on theological or sectarian grounds but because the Greek Muses were, so he says, 'daughters of memory' whereas the Bible is the work of the 'daughters of Inspiration', the distinction between the Socratic 'human' knowledge and the prophetic tradition of the Holy Spirit. Blake is certainly unjust, not only to the Orphic tradition, but also to Plato, whose *anamnesis*—recollection—is an awakening of innate knowledge and akin to inspiration. But the Hebrew prophetic tradition may certainly be seen, as Blake saw it, as the purest expression of the doctrine of inspiration, and Blake's 'Jesus the Imagination' as the true Messiah of the Prophets: 'we of Israel taught that the Poetic Genius (as you now call it) was the first principle and all the others merely derivative; which was the cause of our . . . prophecying that all Gods would at last be proved to originate in ours & to be the tributaries of the Poetic Genius.

Yeats follows Blake in his declaration of faith (in his late *General Introduction for my Work*); only his Christ is a little farther from theology, not static and unchanging but multiform and in perpetual mutation:

> My Christ, a legitimate deduction from the Creed of St Patrick as I think, is that Unity of Being Dante compared to a perfectly proportioned human body, Blake's 'Imagination', what the Upanishads have named 'Self': nor is this unity distant and therefore intellectually understandable, but immanent, differing from man to man and age to age, taking upon itself pain and ugliness, 'eye of newt and toe of frog'.

This multiplicity is certainly to be discovered in Blake's 'world of Imagination', where 'All Things are comprehended in their Eternal Forms in the divine body of the Saviour, the True Vine of Eternity, The Human Imagination . . . around him were seen the Images of Existences'. Perhaps Plato's 'garden of the Muses' implies the multiplicity of that world, which not even Milton's Puritan austerity was able altogether to exclude; for all poets are by nature polytheists. Shelley, no less religious than Milton, was no less anxious to reject Christianity than Milton the Greeks, and for the same reason—in order more strongly to affirm the reality, diversity and richness of the celestial hierarchies. Shelley in *Prometheus Unbound* drew much from the Hellenic descriptions of the daimons, especially those of Proclus, and Apuleius *On the God of Socrates*:

> . . . those subtle and fair spirits,
> Whose homes are the dim caves of human thought,
> And who inhabit, as birds wing the wind,
> Its world-surrounding aether; they behold
> Beyond that twilight realm, as in a glass,
> The future . . .

Coleridge, a Christian by profession, created from a dreamworld Albatross and Daimon, phantom ship and Abyssinian Maid, figures whose ambiguous atmosphere is numinous indeed, but certainly not Christian. Not even Blake's pantheon produces upon us an effect so strongly magical, so immediately supernatural, as do Coleridge's myths, which seem to spring more immediately from the 'age-long memoried self' than do any others in English poetry.

In whatever form, under whatever name, all imaginative poets have, like Yeats, hailed 'the superhuman', whether as heavenly Muse, or as 'woman wailing for her demon lover'; the intention in all cases is the same—to evoke the wisdom of the *memoria*.

At no time before the present would it have been possible for a poet—Edwin Muir—to have written that 'it is clear that no autobiography can begin with a man's birth, that we extend far beyond any boundary line which we can set for ourselves in the past or the future.' Yeats arrived at a similar concept, through his early studies of the techniques of magic, whose underlying principles he defines in his essay *Magic*:

(1) That the borders of our mind are ever shifting, and that many minds can flow into one another, as it were, and create or reveal a single mind, a single energy.
(2) That the borders of our memories are as shifting, and that our memories are a part of one great memory, and the memory of Nature herself.
(3) That this great mind and great memory can be evoked by symbols.

For Yeats magic was less a kind of poetry than poetry a kind of magic. The symbols of poetry and the other arts have the power to evoke those universal forms which they embody. They speak from the *memoria* of the poet to the same *memoria* in the reader; they are the language in which 'the great memory' communicates itself throughout human civilization. Edwin Muir, who never practised any form of magical evocation, experienced visionary insights into this mind, which he has described in his autobiography *The Story and the Fable*. In a series of waking dreams he seemed the spectator of what seemed a vision of the creation itself; and in those visions saw archaic seas and monsters, eyeless sea-creatures and unknown forms and—what astonished him more—angels, whose conformity to the established notion of an angel 'instead of making them unreal, made them more convincing, giving them the actuality of a rare species of which one has often read, about which there has been some controversy, and which one now sees with one's own eyes. On the other hand, the dragon and the sphinx seemed to be completely self-created; so far as I know there was no subject-matter in my mind from which I could have fashioned them. And the whole atmosphere of the dream was strange and astonishing: its exhilarating speed, its objective glory, above all its complete lack of all that is usually meant by human.' This collective life, upon which individual lives come and go like waves

70

and ripples upon a great sea of being, Edwin Muir calls the Fable: 'In themselves our conscious lives may not be particularly interesting. But what we are not and can never be, our fable, seems to me inconceivably interesting. I should like to write that fable, but I cannot even live it; and all I could do if I related the outward course of my life would be to show how I had deviated from it.'

This multiple and multiform Self has been described by no modern poet better than by AE in *Song and its Fountains*:

> I have vivid sense of a being seeking incarnation here, beginning with those faint first intuitions of beauty, and those early dreamings which were its forerunners. It was no angelic thing, pure and new from a foundry of souls, which sought embodiment, but a being stained with the dust and conflict of a long travel through time, carrying with it unsated desires, base and august, and, as I divined of it, myriads of memories and a secret wisdom. It was not simple but infinitely complex . . . It had worshipped in many houses of prayer and kept the reverence it had paid, and had been in many a gay and many a ruined heart. Out of ancient happiness it could build intoxicating images of life, and out of ancient sorrows it could evoke a desolating wisdom. . . . I suspect of that inner being that it is not one but many; and I think we might find out if our meditation was profound that the spokes of our egoity ran out to some celestial zodiac. And, as in dream, the ego is dramatically sundered into this and that and thou and I, so in the totality of our nature are all beings men have imagined, aeons, archangels, dominions and powers, the hosts of darkness and the hosts of light, and we may bring this multitudinous being to a unity and be the inheritors of its myriad wisdom.

Blake was describing the same source of more than individual knowledge when he wrote to John Flaxman: 'In my Brain are studies & Chambers fill'd with books & pictures of old, which I wrote and painted in ages of Eternity before my mortal life, & those works are the delight & Study of Archangels.' Coleridge too spoke of '. . . the power of imagination proceeding upon the *all in each* of human nature' by *meditation* rather than by observation. This inner being, which continually seeks embodiment in all art of the imagination, finds its equivalent in symbol and image; as in a mirror it finds its images in nature; and what David Jones has called the sacramental nature of art consists in this continual seeking and finding of an equivalence in nature for meaning. Coleridge came perhaps nearer than any other poet who has considered these things to an understanding of this mental process in which meaning seeks in the apparently external world its language of sign. He wrote in his notebook:

71

In looking at objects of Nature while I am thinking, as at yonder moon dim-glimmering through the dewy window-pane, I seem rather to be seeking, as it were *asking* for, a symbolical language for something within me that already and for ever exists, than observing anything new. Even when that latter is the case, yet still I have always an obscure feeling as if that new phenomena were the dim awaking of a forgotten or hidden truth of my inner nature. It is still interesting as a word—a symbol. It is Λ δ γ ο ς, the Creator, and the Evolver!

In Shakespeare he saw a supreme expression of this mind:

Shakespere shaped his characters out of the nature within; but we cannot so safely say, out of his own nature as an individual person. No! this latter is itself but a *natura naturata*,—an effect, a product, not a power. It was Shakespeare's prerogative to have the universal, which is potentially in each particular, opened out to him, the *homo generalis*, not as an abstraction from observation of a variety of men, but as the substance capable of endless modifications, of which his own personal existence was but one, and to use this one as the eye that beheld the other, and as the tongue that could convey the discovery.

So near did Coleridge come to Blake's intuition of the human individual as 'but a form and organ of life'. Or again:

It is throughout as if a superior spirit more intuitive, more intimately conscious even than the characters themselves not only of every outward look and act, but of the flux and reflux of the mind in all its subtlest thoughts and feelings, were placing the whole before our view; himself meanwhile unparticipating in the passions, and actuated only by that pleasureable excitement, which had resulted from the energetic fervour of his own spirit in so vividly exhibiting, what it had so accurately and profoundly contemplated.

In the light of such accounts, the Miltonic invocation of the Muse takes on new meaning:

> . . . Heav'nlie borne,
> Before the Hills appear'd, or Fountain flow'd,
> Thou with Eternal Wisdom didst converse . . .

To converse with 'eternal wisdom' is and always has been in the nature of the poetic genius.

The life-giving exhilaration, the inexhaustible rich abundance of the forms that rise from the 'age-long memoried self', their numinosity, fulness of meaning and intelligibility is in contrast with the sense of exhaustion of forms, the emptyings-out, the break-up of a civilization, the obliteration of records, Eliot's fragments shored against ruin, which we find when we look at tradition from the point of view of cult and culture. If anything the abundance and glory of the imaginative world, the sense of the sacred, the sense, even, of an order, a pleroma, becomes greater as we approach the present. Blake is more 'full of gods' than Milton, Yeats than Shelley; Edwin Muir and AE both exclaim that no poem they have written can possibly do justice to that world perceived in vision. Is it possible that the break-up of those very forms which Eliot identified with tradition is itself a manifestation of the same imagination which created those forms and which those forms for a certain time communicated and expressed? Indian theology recognizes the triple aspect of the divine being, as creator, preserver and destroyer; and Shelley, who hails that 'wild spirit' under the symbol of the wind, as 'Destroyer and preserver' had perceived a religious truth and his words are prophetic when he invokes the destroyer:

> Thou from whose unseen presence the leaves dead
> Are driven, like ghosts from an enchanter fleeing.

But the destroyer also safeguards the future:

> . . . O, thou,
> Who chariotest to their dark wintry bed
>
> The winged seeds, where they lie cold and low
> Each like a corpse within its grave, until
> Thine azure sister of the spring shall blow
>
> Her clarion o'er the dreaming earth . . .

Seen in terms of the Great Year and its cycle the phase of destruction of forms has its place. Blake, least sentimental of men, wrote that 'the Oak dies as well as the Lettuce, but Its Eternal Image & Individuality never dies, but renews by its seed; just so the Imaginative Image returns by the seed of Contemplative Thought; . . .' Yeats too had this thought when he wrote, in *The Tragic Generation*, 'Is it true that our air is disturbed, as Mallarmé said, by "the trembling of the veil of the Temple", or that "our whole age is seeking to bring forth a sacred

73

book"? Some of us thought that book near towards the end of the last century, but the tide sank again.' No single sacred book, perhaps, but a transformation of consciousness more significant still, an opening of the Book of Life itself, the *memoria*, a new access to the primordial images, no longer to be approached through any religious cult, but, as Jungian psychology and the testimony of the poets alike bear witness, by a return to the source. At this time we have no shared cult, no collective mythology which speaks to us with the immediacy of our dreams and visions of the primordial images themselves. I do not believe it was for lack of learning that Blake discarded the named gods for the unnamed; indeed I spent many years of study in proving the opposite; the reason for such rejection is not, as Eliot thought, 'meanness of culture' so much as a profound intuition of the character of the New Age. What if the Sacred Book whose immanence was felt by Mallarmé and Yeats were the same as those 'books' Blake perceived in his 'brain', the archetypal world, with its records of 'the age-long memoried self'? With the universal realization of the interior and universal nature of the gods, cult, which is local in time and place, must fail; or at all events our attitude to its symbols undergo a change. But our age sees the cult-images as provisional and local forms. Yeats's learning in the symbolic tradition was no less than Milton's, who points to every source upon which he has drawn, in order to enrich and widen the allusiveness of every symbol. Yeats's purpose was the same, but his means different; his sources are only partially divulged; 'It is only by ancient symbols, by symbols that have numberless meanings beside the one of two the writer lays an emphasis upon, or the half-score he knows of, that any highly subjective art can escape the barrenness and shallowness of a too conscious arrangement, into the abundance and depth of nature.' Yeats's image of tradition is not localized; its allusiveness is limitless, like a 'half-faded curtain embroidered with kings and queens, their loves and battles and their days out hunting, or else with holy letters and images of so great antiquity that nobody can tell the god or goddess they would commend to an unfading memory'. Thus what from the point of view of cult may seem a loss, is from the point of view of poetry an enrichment.

'Have I proved that civilizations come to an end when they have given all their light like burned-out wicks, and that ours is near its end?' Swedenborg envisaged a succession of 'churches', and each church, its light spent, undergoes the archetypal event known as a Last Judgement. This archetype was the theme of Blake's most ambitious pictorial composition, which expressed his own vision of the consummation of an age. 'When Imagination, Art & Science, all Intellectual Gifts, all the Gifts of the Holy Ghost, are look'd upon as of no use, & only Contention remains to Man then the Last Judgment begins.' That event Blake variously describes; in its simplest terms: 'The Last Judgment is an Overwhelming of Bad Art & Science'; and if we consider that the Judge is the Imagination, and what is judged is whatever a temporal personality or a civilization has made or done, the definition is more far-reaching than it might seem. It is an awakening of consciousness: the Human Imagination 'Coming to Judgment among his Saints & throwing off the Temporal that the Eternal might be Establish'd'. A Last Judgement so understood is inevitable in the nature of things, since we contain within ourselves the Judge.

Such a coming-to-consciousness, whether on an individual or on a collective scale must produce that dramatic division contained in all accounts and depictions of that consummation; the destruction of the damned and the resurrection of the saved. All that belongs to the constructions of the human ego must be consumed; whatever is of the living imagination will rise from its grave; we are ourselves both the saved and the damned. Or, seen in terms of history, cult and culture are consumed, vision survives. Has our civilization come to such a moment? We can no longer shelter in its collapsing forms.

A great deal of contemporary literature and visual art is an expression of the process of disintegration. Loss of form characterizes such so-called art; and in poetry perhaps first became evident in that vogue of free-verse which captivated a generation of poets of whom Eliot and Pound are representatives, who evidently felt that its broken cadences expressed the spirit of their time. Such would be the traditional judgement of that 'free verse' which Lawrence and Read saw as an 'emancipation'. Eliot's relinquishments, 'a rejection of all rhythms and metaphors used by the more popular romantics', give to his *Four Quartets* their character of a Requiem. He could write formal lyric, but does so in a valedictory spirit, as when in *East Coker* he calls such a lyric

A periphrastic study in an out-worn poetical fashion.

'Ezra Pound has made flux his theme', Yeats wrote of him; impressed by Pound's immense conviction, born of the assurance that certain poets have at certain times that they are speaking for their age. Pound possessed this gift, the 'unabridged transitions, unexplained ejaculations that make his meaning unintelligible'—so Yeats noted—notwithstanding. Both Pound and Eliot identified themselves with European culture, and its break-up; their own conviction, their readers' assent to their broken forms, and Yeats's inability to accept either their poetic theory or practice seem aspects of a single fact. Yeats had not identified himself with that civilization, or that break-up; his orientation was not historical but metaphysical. Much contemporary writing since reflects less the death than the subsequent decomposition of the corpse, and can hardly be called an expression of any phase of the life or culture of western Christendom. If in this disintegration we have Shelley's 'pestilence-stricken multitudes' of dead leaves, in a few visionaries, may we hope, are the winged seeds which must for the present lie 'cold and low'.

Hitherto it has been taken for granted in our modern civilization that what all share is the external world; and if the inspiration of the poets has survived, as something more than a convention, within a materialist civilization—some residue of the old belief in the 'sacred' nature of the poet survived—the response of most readers to the primordial images poetry has held before them has been a response of the unconscious; though perhaps all the more compelling for that very reason. But, Yeats asks, 'what can one do when the age itself has come to Hodos Chameleontos'—the 'way of the chameleon', of those evershifting images of the 'age-long memoried self'? And he quotes from the Chaldean Oracles, used in the rituals of the magical Society of which he was a member: 'Stoop not down to the darkly splendid world wherein lieth continually a faithless depth and Hades wrapped in cloud, delighting in unintelligible images.' The traditional function of a shared mythology and cult is to give coherence to this flux. But if the new Sacred Book be the transpersonal mind itself, a new generation is about to find itself, without guide or compass, in the presence of a mysterious world of inexhaustible richness, but strange and terrible. The breadth and stability of the ancient cultures, sustained by myth and cult, is not for us; and yet the return to the source may be—or could conceivably be—the beginning of a renaissance of an unprecedented kind. 'The blessed spirits must be sought within the Self which is common to all,' Yeats wrote in *A Vision*; and to a fellow-member of the Society of the Golden Dawn: 'Individuality is not as important as our age has imagined.' Blake knew that the

76

'stupendous visions' of the archetypal world are collective and not personal; 'vision is seen by the Imaginative Eye of Every one according to the situation he holds . . .', he wrote; and 'the Last Judgment is one of these Stupendous Visions. I have represented it as I saw it; to different people it appears differently, as everything else does.'

Yeats was familiar with visions of this archetypal nature, a number of which he describes in *The Trembling of the Veil*; how, for example, a certain magical symbol would evoke, in those to whom it was shown, some archetype—the Garden of Eden is one such symbol which he describes at length—but with differences of detail in each evocation. So much did he take it for granted that such visions are objects of knowledge, that he treated his own insights into *anima mundi* and those of others just as a scholar in some other field would collect fragments of related material, piecing together the fragments to construct a complete whole. So having evoked a vision of the moon—'a naked woman of incredible beauty, standing upon a pedestal, and shooting an arrow at a star'—he gathered related symbols from folklore, from archaeology, from Greek mythology and from the dreams of friends, or from children, or from works of imaginative fiction by members of his circle, to complete his partial vision. 'Myths are the activities of the Daimons', he believed; and regarded what he had seen as an event in 'a world where myth is reality'. The vision or dream occurred not long before the outbreak of the First World War, and Yeats related the visionary event to what was presently to be realized in history. When many years later he used the symbols in poems, he did so in an entirely impersonal way, relating the vision to the ancient myth of Dionysus (*Two Songs from a Play I*), slain at the onset of a new age; and to the death of Parnell, seen as an Irish culture-hero (*Parnell's Funeral*).

The anonymity of traditional art is a necessary outcome of its character as the expression of a transpersonal mind. Yeats (who had no love for the socialist ideal) in *Four Years* writes: '. . . I wanted to create once more an art where the artist's handiwork would hide as under those half-anonymous chisels, or as we find it in some old Scots ballads, or in some twelfth- or thirteenth-century Arthurian romance.' 'Elaborate modern psychology sounds egotistical . . . when it speaks in the first person, but not those simple emotions which resemble the more, the more powerful they are, everybody's emotion, and I was soon to write many more poems where an always personal emotion was woven into a general pattern of myth and symbol'.

77

Seeing that a vision could divide itself in divers complementary portions, might not the thought of philosopher or poet or mathematician depend at every moment of its progress upon some complementary thought in minds perhaps at a great distance? Is there a nation-wide multiform reverie, every mind passing through a stream of suggestion, and all streams acting and reacting upon one another, no matter how distant the minds, how dumb the lips? . . . was not a nation, as distinguished from a crowd of chance comers, bound together by this interchange among streams or shadows? (*Hodos Chameleontes*).

Yeats could not endure 'an international art, picking stories and symbols where it pleased', for such eclecticism oversteps the bounds of the *memoria* and must tend rather to disintegrate than to create an organic imaginative unity. Yeats believed, with Dionysius the Areopagite, that 'he has set the borders of his nations according to his angels'; '. . . the nations were sealed at birth with a character derived from the whole, and had, like individuals, their periods of increase and decrease'. 'Nations, cultures, schools of thought may have their *Daimons*. These *Daimons* may move through the Great Year like individual men and women and are said to use men and women as their bodies, to gather and disperse those bodies at will,' he wrote in *A Vision*.

The breakdown of regional and racial group-souls, of vital collectivities of cult and culture, class and caste, is one of the most disquieting processes we witness in the modern world. What is the inner life of the displaced masses without memory or culture which occupy those modern machine-created non-places everywhere the same? On the face of it the modern crowd would seem to be a return to chaos, a product of the process of the disintegration of civilization. What is the dream of the crowd? Perhaps it is collectivity as such. Edwin Muir, as a young socialist in Scotland, as he relates in his *Autobiography*, seemed, in a mass political rally, to glimpse a 'part of the fable' which has not yet manifested itself clearly in the world, which he called a 'universal purification'.

It was as if I had stepped into a fable which was always there, invisibly waiting for anyone who wished to enter it. Before, ugliness, disease, vice and disfigurement had repelled me; but now, as if all mankind were made of some incorruptible substance, I felt no repugnance, no disgust, but a spontaneous attraction to every human being. I felt this most intensely during the first May Day demonstration I attended.

78

David Gascoyne, moving from Surrealism to an existential Christianity, the only living English poet who possesses in a significant degree the prophetic vision, made this collective participation the theme of his poem *Night Thoughts*. He evokes a vision of the modern 'megalometropolis' as horrific as any of Dante's hells, the sense of separation, loneliness and alienation; and then invokes the being whom Blake calls the Imagination, the Upanishads the Self, and Plato the One:

'O be the One, that I may never be alone in knowing that I am. Let my lost loneliness be illusory. Allow to me a part in Being, that I may thus be part of One and All.'

Yeats himself, prophet of the Great Year as Blake of the New Age, wrote in *A Vision* of a kind of exhilaration which comes when we accept the change:

. . . when the limit is approached or past, when the moment of surrender is reached, when the new gyre begins to stir, I am filled with excitement. I think of recent mathematical research; even the ignorant can compare it with that of Newton . . . with its objective world intelligible to intellect; I can recognise that the limit itself has become a new dimension, that this ever-hidden thing which makes us fold our hands has begun to press down upon multitudes.

5

Waste Land, Holy Land

Y OU have done me the honour of inviting me to give the Warton
    Lecture for 1976; and since I am a poet I must conclude that it is
as a poet that you wish me to speak; not from learned sources but from
my own experience of the literary scene as one of the generation who
emerged from childhood in the mid-twenties.

Yeats wrote, before the First World War, of 'the rise of soul against
intellect, now beginning in the world'. Subsequent history, and
literary history, may not seem to support his prophecy; there is little
soul and much intellectual arrogance in our world. Yet the voice of
the greatest of poets is always prophetic, and Yeats's vision embraced
a time-scale far beyond those superficial waves and wavelets of fashion
upon the ebb and flow of a greater tide. His younger contemporaries,
both in this country and in America, who because they reflected
current ideologies thought they understood the direction of history
better than Yeats did, ridiculed the great poet's preoccupation with
that whole range of knowledge belonging to the soul and its nature.

Auden accused Yeats of not having a sympathetic attitude toward
the most progressive thought of his time; by which he presumably
meant (I quote) 'the social struggle toward a greater equality' which
'has been accompanied by a growing intellectual acceptance of the
scientific method and the steady conquest of irrational superstition'.
But scientific method has not proved so universal a way to knowledge
as Auden's generation had thought; reformist ideologies have been
seen to fail; while the transforming power of the words of our
century's supreme 'singing-master of the soul' continues to work
towards the fulfilment of his prophecy.

It seems to me a very short time since I was myself a young and
most obscure poet caught up in that war; not as a combatant but as a
fugitive. Now I surprisingly find myself old, looking back on it all,
and wondering about the issue of that battle. And it may be that my
time has come to turn back the pages of my own book of life, and tell
you what it was like to be of the soul's party at that time when
intellect—rational, scientific intellect—held the field. I am no victor;

at best a survivor; but since the story of those years has been told so often in terms of the then (and still now) current values, it should perhaps be known that there were some who did not assent to those values and who would tell the story differently.

I have chosen the title, 'Waste Land, Holy Land', because these are the terms in which I now see the struggle that was taking place. T. S. Eliot, the other major poet of my time, has once and for ever described the Waste Land of the modern world; that profane world in which the soul can only suffer exile. For the soul is, as Edgar Allen Poe understood, native of another country:

> Lo, in yon brilliant window-niche
> How statue-like I see thee stand,
> The agate lamp within thy hand,
> Ah! Psyche, from the regions which
> Are holy land.   (*To Helen*)

It was T. S. Eliot who gave its true name to our time and place: the Waste Land. His judgement had nothing to do with politics, with W. H. Auden's social struggle; Eliot's truth was the truth of the soul, unable to endure a world in which many would, before the two world wars, have seen a picture of prosperity. He declared our world waste and his great poem is a lamentation because life in that country has withered at the roots. I first read a poem by T. S. Eliot in a magazine I picked up by chance, *The Criterion*. I was at the time (1926) so ignorant as never to have heard his name and I therefore had, as a first-year undergraduate, the pleasure of discovering him for myself; for the impact was instantaneous and tremendous. Here, I felt—and how many others felt as I did—is a voice that speaks the unspoken, the nameless disquiet in which I, as a member of my generation, found myself. That generation (and we were fortunate) had been brought up on Shakespeare and the Romantic poets and Palgrave's *Golden Treasury*; 'modern' poetry was the Georgian poets who wrote of rural life, Walter de la Mare, and Gilbert Murray's translations of the Greek drama. Going up to Cambridge in the mid-1920s as a student of natural sciences, I found the ground cut from beneath me; those old assumptions made by the Romantic poets, for whom poetry was the natural speech of the soul, withered in the light of logical positivism, dialectical materialism, and the prestigious 'science' of the Cavendish Laboratory, which recognized no soul at all. Eliot's poems explored with undeniable truth the state of being which must, without that fiction or reality which the age had disallowed, pass for the real world.

81

This was the region, this the soil, the clime my generation must inhabit; the romantic dream had failed and we found ourselves imprisoned in a profane and soulless reality no poet had as yet explored.

Here I must say that I am not venturing to attempt a 'criticism' of Eliot's poetry nor an evaluation of it; only I am recalling the impact of that poetry upon myself and others of my generation of *entre deux guerres*. Those who read his poetry now may find in it more than we did, read it more accurately or in truer perspective; but that first impact is irrecoverable. In words of Dantesque gravity Eliot's poetry gave words to an experience whose truth found its echo in our own condition. We did not read his poems in any perspective at all: rather we were in them, ourselves figures in the sad procession of Eliot's London, that 'unreal city' in whose unreality lay its terrible reality. We knew that city by participation, knew it too well to criticize or evaluate. We knew the Thames whence Spenser's nymphs had departed, the rat-infested shore and the gasworks. Of the glory of Cleopatra's barge or Gloriana's there remained only the luxury of Bond Street. When Goldsmith's 'lovely woman stoops to folly' it matters; there is Mr Primrose to seek his fallen daughter and bring her home; but now, the joyless seduction of a tired typist in her transient furnished room matters neither to herself nor to anyone else. Instead of the pride of work there is the joyless procession of wage-earners over London Bridge and the echo of Dante's 'I had not thought death had undone so many'. Indeed we may often have misunderstood the poet whose words we borrowed as a kind of magical incantation to help us to bring under control the situation of our own lives. For my generation had not yet become accustomed to a soulless world and continued to mourn an absence no longer felt—or no longer consciously felt—by the generation who succeeded us. I remember chanting to myself from *Ash Wednesday* the words

> Because I do not hope to turn again
> Because I do not hope
> Because I do not hope to turn.

Eliot's words lent a kind of valedictory dignity to the turning away from a lost Paradise we still remembered, the halting rhythms of his free verse kept pace with our own knowledge that the 'viewless wings of poesy' were now only 'vans to beat the air'.

Eliot's is the voice of the suffering soul which cannot endure a world stripped of every sanctity by those very ideologies adhered to by most of those who at that time acclaimed him: I remember the shocked surprise with which we learned that Eliot was a Christian. He described our world within the context of the Christian religion, but we saw his burning indictment merely as true to life.

Psyche is in exile, yet again and again the poet invokes her suffering or absent figure; she is the 'Lady of silences, Calm and distressed' who is the 'End of the endless/Journey to no end'; the weeping garden girl who weaves the sunlight in her hair; the 'silent sister veiled in white and blue'; she is Marina, the absent daughter whose return brings peace, and whose very name suggests the long sea-wandering years of separation. Who are all these feminine figures, or the 'Lady whose shrine stands on the promontory' but Poe's Psyche with her inextinguishable lamp whose country is the holy land, the 'garden where all loves end', our native Eden now withered into the waste land by her absence? Eliot's poetry gave utterance to the suffering of a profane society which had no place for the soul to whom alone belong the shrine, the garden and the end of every journey.

Already in *The Love Song of J. Alfred Prufrock* the poet has entered the Waste Land; the poem is prefaced by a passage from the *Inferno* and there immediately follows an invitation to another descent:

> Let us go then, you and I,
> When the evening is spread out against the sky
> Like a patient etherised upon a table;
> Let us go, through certain half-deserted streets,
> The muttering retreats
> Of restless nights in one-night cheap hotels
> And sawdust restaurants with oyster-shells:
> Streets that follow like a tedious argument
> Of insidious intent
> To lead you to an overwhelming question. . . .

We have entered the joyless realm and the landscape is familiar. Every image suggests sickness and despair; the evening sky, no longer Hopkins's 'dappled-with-damson-west' charged with 'the grandeur of God', can anaesthetize but cannot heal; it is passively 'spread out', the sickness of the patient 'etherized' as for an operation of perhaps fatal outcome transferred to the sky itself since place and state are one and indivisible. The streets are 'half-deserted' as if life has ebbed from them. Instead of home-coming we are reminded of the impermanence of the houses. St Teresa likened life to a night in a bad inn; and here

83

there are 'one-night cheap hotels' where the 'sleep' of life is restless and haunted by 'muttering' (whose? It can only be our own). We are led not to any solution, but towards an 'overwhelming question':

> Oh, do not ask, 'What is it?'
> Let us go and make our visit.

J. Alfred Prufrock's land is waste because, in search of love (for the poem is called a love song) or perhaps because, like that legendary knight, he does not know the question, or does not dare to ask it, of the Holy Grail, that sacred presence that appears in this world and yet belongs also to another. In the trivial world in which he is trapped the question cannot be asked nor the answer told. Useless to say

> . . . 'I am Lazarus, come from the dead,
> Come back to tell you all, I shall tell you all'—
> If one, settling a pillow by her head,
> Should say: 'That is not what I meant at all.
> That is not it, at all.'

Prufrock also dreams, but in those dreams he can find nothing to help him in waking life, to which he must return as to a death:

> We have lingered in the chambers of the sea
> By sea-girls wreathed in seaweed red or brown
> Till human voices wake us, and we drown.

The world of his dreams is cut off from his waking life as utterly as Lazarus's experience beyond the grave; and perhaps these realms are the same, being regions of the inner life, of the timeless, which has no longer any place in or way of access to the world where men and women meet one another only on a level of triviality, where there is only the all-consuming passage of time: 'There will be time, there will be time', Prufrock says; but for him time is not as for Blake, 'the mercy of eternity'; it brings only old age and death: 'I grow old, I grow old' is the form of Prufrock's despair.

The city, being man's creation, is a more immediate reflection of the spiritual condition of a civilization than is 'nature'; yet nature too can be a waste land, reflecting the inner desert. Edwin Muir's poem *The Cloud* describes the profanation of the arcadian image of the countryman tilling his fields by the teaching that 'God is dead' propagated by the Marxist variant of our Western materialism. The

poet and his wife were driving through country roads in Czechoslovakia to attend a Communist propaganda lecture:

> At a sudden turn we saw
> A young man harrowing, hidden in dust, he seemed
> A prisoner walking in a moving cloud
> Made by himself for his own purposes;
> And there he grew and was as if exalted
> To more than man, yet not, not glorified:
> A pillar of dust moving in dust; no more.
> The bushes by the roadside were encrusted
> With a hard sheath of dust.
> We looked and wondered; the dry cloud moved on
> With its interior image.

Coming away from the lecture which exalted the peasant and his toil
while denying in him the divine image,

> . . . we longed for light to break
> And show that his face was the face once broken in Eden,
> Beloved, world-without-end lamented face;
> And not a blindfold mask on a pillar of dust.

What Edwin Muir felt was an absence of something that should have
been there, for Eden is man's native place, or condition; and so is
Eliot's waste land haunted by an absence, precisely, of the holy of
whose sanctuaries he gave us so many symbols, especially in his later
poems. Their placing, like highlights in a dark picture, is all important: Little Gidding, the place where prayers have been said; the
Garden with its pool that fills with light; or any

> . . . intersection of the timeless moment
> Is England and nowhere. Never and always.
> (Little Gidding)

It is we who consecrate or desecrate; and cities also have been holy.
Jerusalem is the very type of the image of man's inner heaven realized
on earth; and Yeats's Holy City of Byzantium in which 'religious,
aesthetic and practical life were one . . . and this vision, this proclamation of their invisible master' the vision of a whole people. Eliot
discerned in our world an absence—of all things the hardest to
discern, still harder to identify. The death of God, the death of the

soul—name as we will the withdrawal of the inner vision from the outer world—lays waste the earth. Eliot situated the profane world in that place in the soul's order of values to which it belongs—in the hells, the kingdom cut off from life.

To the talented group of writers who followed Eliot, Psyche's country was not in question. Auden and Day-Lewis and their friends were concerned with the political and economic reform of modern industrial society and the 'social struggle towards a greater equality'. One might ask, 'Equality to what?' To Muir's 'blind mask in a pillar of dust' or the traditional Christian 'image of God'? These poets were indeed moralists, and initially of Marxist politics and the Marxist view of man, though Auden later became a Christian, preaching tolerance and charity towards fallen humanity in a fallen world. They no less than Eliot were concerned with the modern urban landscape but with the object of arousing the slumbering political conscience. Their concern was neither to illuminate the drab with reconciling beauty (as James Joyce had re-created Dublin in the light of imagination, humour, love, and acceptance); nor, like Eliot, to voice the protest of the soul in exile. Utopia, not the Kingdom of Heaven, was their goal; and their work was immediately successful with a generation of waste-landers for whom the outer world had come to seem the whole world. Auden was not concerned with an absence, nor with Prufrock's 'overwhelming question', nor with the shrines and sanctuaries of the soul; rather his object was to focus our attention upon the time-world whose signs and symptoms he so brilliantly read. The world is sick—yes—but, whereas Eliot had understood that the remedy is reconsecration, for the poets who succeeded him it was social reform. Fear, horror, guilt, shock, cancer, the grave, jump out of Auden's early poems to startle the reader into repentance like devils in a morality play, against a scene of hard-edged machines—aircraft, and 'the helmeted airman', plate-glass, 'silted harbours, derelict works', arterial roads, fast cars, 'the cigarette-end smouldering on the border'. He involves his reader by the skilful placing of the definite article, implying that we know that world as well as he does: not 'a helmeted airman' or 'a Sport Hotel' or 'an infected sinus' but 'the'—the one we know, the one in which we secretly or guiltily participate: 'Those handsome and diseased youngsters'; 'that distant afternoon . . . they gave the prizes to the ruined boys'. He drives home the imputation of guilt, the inescapable implication in the public world:

You cannot be away, then, no,
Not though you pack to leave within an hour,
Escaping humming down arterial roads.

When I first read these poems I did not feel myself to be one of the 'we' Auden sought to mobilize, the 'us' of 'our time' with its shared world of the documentary film and the news bulletin, a world everywhere permeable to the mass media and a collectivity from which no distance can any longer separate us, the dance-band at the Sport Hotel

Relayed elsewhere to farmers and their dogs
Sitting in kitchens in the stormy fens.
('Consider This and in our time')

His appeal to a supposedly, and within its own terms a really shared, contemporary scene, with its well-placed allusions to Nijinski and Diaghilev (gently cajoling our snobbery) to the van der Lubbe trial and Churchill and Hitler and the rest—why did I not feel the intended response, 'Yes this is the real world, scene of our actions and our moral choice'? For Auden was a most persuasive moralist—his tone is often positively evangelical, full of imperatives—'watch', 'consider', 'summon', 'mobilize', 'It is later than you think'.

Now I can see more clearly than anyone noticed at the time the sleight-of-hand Auden practised on his readers. He sought to cut off the soul from any retreat into those inner sanctuaries where under social conditions of every kind men and women have found refuge and another reality. It seemed to me that Auden, that man of impressive worldly wisdom, and his 'we' sought to close the escape routes and to round us up like a flock of sheep to be driven into his pen, away from that inner country that is everyone's priceless and unpurchased birthright, the imaginative ground we each inhabit. If it can be said that dreamers have too little sense of political realities, too little desire for social change, can it not also be said that political and social unrest afflicts not so much the poor and the ignorant but above all those who have, by our modern ideologies, been driven out of these inner sanctuaries, be these religious shrines or places of dreams? Eliot saw that our profane society was a hell precisely because cut off from that ground; the succeeding generation thought, like Milton's fallen angels, that the 'unreal city' could be made tolerable—could be made Utopia—by social reform.

In this sleight-of-hand Auden was not so much the creator as one expression of the mentality of his time; for current ideologies, and notably Marxism, assume that our humanity belongs totally to the outer world their power-structures can control, that we are economic and social beings only, that our whole environment is comprised within the daily scene. This assumption totally neglects that other half of life in which every individual is free to turn aside into a secret and inviolable universe entirely inaccessible to their collective imperatives.

Again let me disclaim any intention of attempting a critique of Auden's poetry; I am merely describing my own response to that school of writers. Some would consider it the first duty of the poet to be politically 'engaged'; others might reply that political change can improve the human condition only in very limited ways; while poetry and the other arts, by building for the soul invisible sanctuaries and regions of contemplation, by exploring and extending the scope of our humanity, from Dante's beatitude to his hells, from Shakespeare's Forest of Arden to Lear's heath, has created—that it is its especial virtue that it can so create, at all times and in all places—areas of inner freedom that we can, and do, inhabit, however circumscribed our outer conditions may be. The fallacy that man lives by bread alone has never been more prevalent than in this century. I did not choose to exchange my inner worlds for Auden's hard-edged reality; if a world may be called real which curtails our humanity of half its realm. Had not Eliot, for that very reason, called the same city 'unreal'?

Believing as I do that poetry is in its proper nature the language of the soul; that its proper function is to create for us images of an inner order all share, to open into every present those secret doors, those ways in; to consecrate and redeem for every generation some parcel of the surrounding waste, I cannot feel that those poets of the thirties, brilliantly and admirably as they may have performed some other necessary social role, were fulfilling the proper and vital task of the poet. Genius, Yeats said, is a crisis which joins for certain moments the sleeping and the waking mind. Only at such moments are we fully human, fully ourselves; and for what else does the poem, the work of art, exist, if not to bring about this union?

Auden was, I think, deeply suspicious of—perhaps feared—the 'other' mind whence comes inspiration. We clashed, I remember, over Blake, when, at a party in New York, at the time when I was giving a series of lectures on Blake in Washington, Auden challenged me to admit that Blake was, when all is said and done, 'dotty'. He

88

could never have responded to the purpose of our great prophet,

> . . . I rest not from my great task!
> To open the Eternal Worlds, to open the Immortal eyes
> Of Man inwards into the Worlds of Thought, into Eternity
> Ever expanding in the Bosom of God, the Human
> > > > Imagination.
> > > (K623)

Because Eliot and Auden described the same modern urban scene in the same sharply defined images of contemporary situations, the two poets were often compared when they ought rather to have been contrasted. Eliot's London is closer to Blake's, whose 'streets are ideas of Imagination', than to Auden's well photographed documentary world. Yet even Yeats failed to distinguish, in Eliot's early poems, between the image and its intent. In his much-criticized Introduction to the *Oxford Book of English Verse* he wrote that 'Eliot has produced his great effect upon his generation because he has described men and women that get out of bed or into it from mere habit; in describing this life that has lost heart his own art seems grey, cold, dry'. Yeats made the common mistake of taking Eliot's realistic images at their face value; he if any poet should have taken note of those bright shafts of illumination from another dimension—those clues that tell us that Eliot was at all times describing the actual in terms of the absent; for the hells are such precisely in terms of that from which they are absent; as no poet since Dante has understood more profoundly than did Eliot. While 'Apeneck Sweeney', type of the totally profane man for whom life is just three things, 'birth, and copulation, and death', could coldly watch the hysteria of the prostitute whose human face is no more than

> This withered root of knots of hair
> > Slitted below and gashed with eyes,
> This oval O cropped out with teeth:

Eliot reminds us of the unnoticed wisteria by the window behind his 'golden grin'; or that

> The nightingales are singing near
> The Convent of the Sacred Heart.

The nightingale is Keats's 'immortal bird', type of that music heard by all successive generations; Eliot's 'Convent of the Sacred Heart' the sanctuary of the love that Sweeney profanes.

Yeats made his anthology before 1935; before Eliot had written his *Four Quartets*. But even then he should have heeded those images whose function is to locate, to identify, to comment upon, the action: the Convent of the Sacred Heart; the weeping girl with her arms full of flowers; 'the lost lilac and the lost sea voices'; all these are things that should be and are not: illuminations of the sacred.

Auden and Day-Lewis in forcing us to confront the social evils of our time shifted the ground of conscience from the inner to the outer world; and many of us felt that we had no answer to give, at that time, to these political poets. Not so Yeats; who, though he read their work, he says, with 'some excitement', saw that 'Communism is their *Deus ex Machina*, their Santa Claus, their happy ending, but speaking as a poet I prefer tragedy to tragicomedy'. In other words, he is accusing *them* of being the escapists. 'It was easier to look at suffering if you had somebody to blame for it, some remedy in mind,' he wrote. Tragedy comes from within; politics is tragicomic in so far as disaster can at any point be averted by manipulation of outer circumstances. Yeats, an old man of long experience of politics, could say to these young poets who sought to make the good and evil of our inner experience seem less 'real' than social ills, 'No matter how great a reformer's energy a still greater is required to face, all activities expended in vain, the unreformed.' The force of these words, largely unheeded at the time, is now inescapable: the political reformer may alter circumstances; poetry and the other arts can change what we inwardly are.

Auden, as is apparent in his mistrust of Blake and his 'eternal worlds', mistrusted and feared what comes from the imagination, from beyond reason's little conquered territory. It is characteristic of him that in *The Sea and the Mirror* he should have treated Ariel as a suspect figure: Prospero would miss him, with his flights of fancy and indeed his insights—Auden allows him these—but the balance falls on the side of disillusionment, which is presented as the 'real' with which all the characters must come to terms. Never has poet so extolled the light of common day. As the ship sails away from the enchanted island, Prospero speaks:

> . . . Alonso's heaviness
> Is lost; and weak Sebastian will be patient
> In future with his slothful conscience—after all, it pays;
>   Stephano is contracted to his belly, a minor

90

But a prosperous kingdom; Stale Trinculo receives,
    Gratis, a whole fresh repertoire of stories, and
Our younger generation its independent joy.
    Their eyes are big and blue with love; its lighting
Makes even us look new; yes, today it all looks so easy.
    Will Ferdinand be as fond of a Miranda
Familiar as a stocking? Will Miranda who is
    No longer a silly lovesick little goose,
When Ferdinand and his brave world are her profession,
    Go into raptures over existing at all?
Probably I overrate the difficulties;
    Just the same, I am very glad I shall never
Be twenty and have to go through that business again,
    The hours of fuss and fury, the conceit, the expense.

So all that enhances life, all that lifts us, albeit momentarily, beyond our everyday selves, is illusory and silly; we must settle down to be ordinary, to be tolerant, and to die. The young lovers have not seen a momentary vision of the gods who move our lives: they are deluded—'our younger generation' who will know better when they are our age. Their eyes are 'big and blue' (the denigration is implicit) with love; to them sacramental (and the Church after all is on their side) which Prospero now calls 'that business' with even an implication of 'the expense of spirit in a waste of shame'. Miranda as a 'stocking'—an inhuman, indeed a shocking image—is more real than the Miranda who sees the whole world renewed in her own Paradisal vision; redemptive, as Eliot in his own comparable figure of Marina implies, of that world itself. Auden would say that Shakespeare, after all, made Prospero bury his magic wand and return to the world; but did he mean those who had visited the Island to forget it? Or is not that Island rather a symbol of the Platonic 'other' world from which the soul descends into ours, 'not in entire forgetfulness'? Was not that island to remain the rectifying vision of those who remember it? Is it not precisely the task of the poet to ensure that we do not cease to 'go into raptures over existing at all' when young love is only a memory?

In justice to Auden we must remember that he did write of all-too-human love with great compassion. His love-poem with the opening lines

Lay your sleeping head, my love,
    Human on my faithless arm

is a most moving expression of love as it must be for those who have

91

forgotten. But without the archetype, the image of the soul that Eliot never relinquished, the 'Lady of Silences', the quasi-divine 'Lady whose shrine stands on the promontory', the all-too-human must lose its dignity and that sacred core which, as Conrad said, is at the heart of every human love. Eliot knew, perhaps better than Auden himself, the waste land of human love when that sacred core has been lost: Sweeney is a figure that is too nakedly hellish for any humanist to confront.

Had Yeats made his anthology ten years later he would have found poets more after his own heart than Auden and his circle; poets in whom he might have seen the beginnings of the fulfilment of his own prophecy of the 'rise of soul against intellect'. It was with relief that readers who had, obscurely if not consciously, failed to find imaginative sustenance in Auden's kind of poetry, turned to Dylan Thomas, whose earthly paradise is made of the simple elements of a country childhood. The word 'holy'—a word that had not been found in poetry for many years—is characteristic of him; all is praise and celebration. What symptoms of political and economic sickness Auden might have seen no less in the valleys of Wales than in the Pennines it is easy to imagine: Thomas found holy land. The people of Milkwood live in their dreams, good and bad, their inner lives woven and interwoven with the outer life of their village, incorrigibly oblivious to all collectivizing propaganda.

Auden looked for the steady conquest of the irrational: Vernon Watkins, from his early *Ballad of the Mari Lwyd* and throughout his work, reminds us that the house of life stands in a great surrounding darkness that is also native to us; whose voices speak to us from a timeless world with a strange oracular tongue, reminding us of what we are. The dead are not, for him, non-existent: they are a dimension of ourselves, their communications, as for Eliot, 'tongued with fire/ Beyond the language of the living'. Our universe is not the world of politician and newscaster but of the soul's history.

It may be objected that, whereas T. S. Eliot and Auden were aware of the predicament of urban mankind, these Welsh poets knew nothing of the urban environment with its consequent ideologies which has thrown so many into a state of spiritual alienation. One poet—too little known—did notably seek to rediscover the holy land in the waste land.

David Gascoyne understood that it is man-made false values and sick states of mind which alone obscure the holy land everywhere and always present. So with the 'nondescript terrain' of *The Gravel-Pit*

Field, 'a stretch of scurfy pock-marked waste' that 'sprawls laggardly its acres till/They touch a raw brick-villa'd rim'. Seen with the eye of vision

> . . . each abandoned snail-shell strewn
> Among these blotched dock-leaves might seem
> In the pure ray shed by the loss
> Of all man-measured value, like
> Some priceless pearl-enamelled toy
> Cushioned on green silk under glass.

He beholds the apotheosis of this waste land; freed from utilitarian or sociological values we may project upon it, even such a field in its 'extreme abasement' is seen in another light as

> Between this world and the beyond
> Remote from men and yet more real
> Than any human dwelling-place:
> A tabernacle where one stands
> As though within the empty space
> Round which revolves the Sage's wheel.

Eliot, in one of his *Preludes*, tells of walking at night in London streets aware of the sleepers who will presently and tragically awake

> Impatient to assume the world.

The poet is moved by the mystery of their sleep,

> . . . moved by fancies that are curled
> Around these images, and cling:
> The notion of some infinitely gentle,
> Infinitely suffering thing.

David Gascoyne's *Night Thoughts* is London's nocturn; a phantasmagoria of illusion and loneliness, in which this poet, not focused upon the harsh realities of day, reflects:

'The boundaries of the senses are not often clearly realised. The Infra and the Ultra are fields easily forgotten. Out of hearing stays unthought-of; out of sight is out of mind. And yet, how haunted we all are.' He 'half hopes to overhear—that haunting thing'. It is through this nameless 'being' that 'We are closer to one another than we realise. Let us remember one another at night, even though we do not know each other's names.' The poet calls us together not in the harsh light of waking day, but in participation of the inner, hidden regions of the sleeping mind.

Day-Lewis in his poem *The Flight* attempted to make a specifically machine-age poem (doubtless at the time sharing Auden's enthusiasm for science) celebrating the air-ace and his craft, implicitly setting these beside Achilles and Cuchulain, those bronze-age heroes and their armour. The courage is doubtless the same in our technological age as in any other, but I think the poem fails because some artefacts are so complete an expression of the soulless mentality that conceived them as not to be susceptible of any symbolic imaginative existence otherwise than as symbols of that soullessness. This was the considered view of Eliot's friend the poet and painter David Jones, whose poem *In Parenthesis* is at once the epic of modern warfare (his theme is the trenches of the First World War) and a consecration of the most waste of all land, the battlefield. But it was not our modern technology he praised:

I said, Ah! what shall I write?
I enquired up and down.
                    (He's tricked me before
with his manifold lurking-places.)
I looked for His symbol at the door.
I have looked for a long while
                    at the textures and contours.
I have run a hand over the trivial intersections.
I have journeyed among the dead forms
causation projects from pillar to pylon.
I have tired the eyes of the mind
                    regarding the colours and lights.
I have felt for His Wounds
                    in nozzles and containers.
I have wondered for the automatic devices.
I have tested the inane patterns
                    without prejudice.
I have been on my guard
                    not to condemn the unfamiliar.
For it is easy to miss Him
                    at the turn of a civilization.

I have watched the wheels go round in case I might see the living creatures like the appearance of lamps, in case I might see the Living God projected from the Machine. I have said to the perfected steel, be my sister and for the glassy towers I thought I felt some beginnings of His creature, but *A, a, a, Domine Deus*, my hands found the glazed work unrefined and the terrible crystal a stage-paste . . . *Eia, Domine Deus*

(The Sleeping Lord, 1974)

If Jones has written an absolutely modern epic of war it is not because he saw modern warfare as unprecedented but because he discerned in the English Tommy in his khaki uniform the timeless figure of the soldier, in modern warfare, the same war that was waged at Troy, or at Badon Hill, or sung in the epic of the Welsh battle of Catraeth or in the *Chanson de Roland*. If in *In Parenthesis* tin helmet and barbed wire are of a like significance with the Cross and the Crown of Thorns, it is because those who wore them and died upon them share our humanity. Machines may be unprecedented but to the men of the battlefield the 'strange shapes of death' are what they always were. If it has seemed to some that modern warfare is worse than the sacking of Jerusalem by Titus and Vespasian, or the massacre of Drogheda by Cromwell, or the French retreat from Moscow, it is because of the numbers involved; to the individual soldier the situation is neither better nor worse. Death on the battlefield is one of the situations mankind has confronted from time immemorial; and in that situation other ages have been able to find imaginative meaning, however dark. Death, after all, is one of the unchangeable elements of our human existence. Our human range is finite; progress can bring no joy greater than men and women have at all times experienced; nor can there be any situation of unprecedented evil, cruelties and abominations worse than other ages have known. Under whatever political regime—in Utopia itself—our humanity is attuned to a scale of joy and grief which is ever the same. Suffering is immeasurable, as joy also is, in quantitative terms; weapons may be unprecedented but death is not.

In a profane world death is as meaningless as life; and in this respect alone perhaps is modern warfare unprecedented: our wars and our peace alike are waste land. In his great poem David Jones has shown that in our own age, as in other ages, the hells are harrowed. Indeed if the worst conceivable situations which our humanity may have to confront lie beyond the scope of poetry, then poetry itself is a mere diversion.

David Jones's battlefield is certainly not a presentation of that 'passive suffering' Yeats said was no theme for poetry. The situation is redeemed by the presence—the imaginative as well as the physical presence—of men in all their poignant physical vulnerability, but also in the dignity of their confrontation. Auden's 'helmeted airman' is not human but a spare part of a machine: we are not shown his face. Jones's soldiers of the London Welsh Infantry in tin helmet and khaki puttees tell us who they are, bringing with them their own memories and those of their race. Because of their presence the battlefield itself becomes holy ground.

> This Dai adjusts his slipping shoulder-straps, wraps close his misfit outsize greatcoat—he articulates his English with an alien care.
> My fathers were with the Black Prinse of Wales
> at the passion of
> the blind Bohemian king.
> They served in these fields,
> it is in the histories that you can read it, Corporal—boys Gower, they were—it is writ down—yes.
> Wot about Methuselum, Taffy?
> I was with Abel when his brother found him,
> under the green tree.
> I built a shit-house for Artaxerxes.
> I was the spear in Balin's hand
> that made waste King Pellam's land.
> I took the smooth stones of the brook,
> I was with Saul
> playing before him.

In Dai's Boast (which runs to some five or six pages) he tells us who he is; he stands on the everlasting battlefield of the earth in his full human stature and even in the dignity of his human free will, albeit the free will to accept but not to change the event. Wherever man is present the sacramental consecration is possible; even on the battlefield. Perhaps especially on that field, where so much is demanded of men, who often surpass themselves; 'the "Bugger! Bugger!" of a man detailed had often about it the "Fiat! Fiat!" of the Saints'.

Finally, Edwin Muir, the poet who of all those I have known, most clearly realized that we live in two worlds and that our waking life is rooted in the soul's timeless country. I remember with what gratitude I first listened to him saying so simply all those things I had scarcely allowed myself even to think. But Edwin, for all his quiet gentleness, had a mind that no tide or wind of fashion could deflect from the certainties of his insight. Very early in our acquaintance he asked me if I ever wrote poems from dreams, and I said No. He told me that I should because dream is so important a part of our reality, an aspect of our world and of ourselves. We live in the waking day for little more than half of our time and perhaps even less of our being. There is a life of the night also:

> I have been taught by dreams and fantasies,
> Learned from the friendly and the darker phantoms

—so he wrote in one of his last poems. Again and again he speaks of the knowledge of the night:

> The night, the night alone is old
> And showed me only what I knew,
> Knew, yet never had been told;
> A speech that from the darkness grew
> Too deep for daily tongues to say,
> Archaic dialogue of a few
> Upon the sixth or the seventh day.
> And shapes too simple for a place
> In the day's shrill complexity
> Came and were more natural, more
> Expected than my father's face
> Smiling across the open door.
> *(Day and Night)*

And yet of all his contemporaries it was Muir who was most directly involved in the political tragedies of Europe before and after the Second World War. He saw at first hand the rise of Nazism in Germany; the disasters that befell Czechoslovakia (he was Director of the British Institute in Prague) first from the German occupation, then following the Communist *coup d'état*. But he understood the outer event in terms of the inner, and saw that the worst violations were those upon the soul. None of his many explicitly descriptive poems better expresses the everlasting paradox of aggressor and victim than *The Combat*, written from a dream. The conflict was one he witnessed in the world of his time, but in the dream the emotion is naked; external events are after all but an expression of the eternal conflict within ourselves, and is not even history the enactment of our dreams? Over and over again the aggressor, the 'crested animal in his pride' and the victim, 'a soft round beast as brown as clay', repeat the battle in which the dream-victim is always defeated and yet never destroyed.

97

Edwin Muir had at one time taken his dreams to a Jungian analyst, but had soon realized—the analyst also—that these visions properly belonged to the domain of the poet; never to be explained, only to be made known. In a poem entitled *The Poet* he writes of that living and hidden source:

> What I shall never know
> I must make known,
> Where traveller never went
> Is my domain.

Even Jung's great reverence for the holy land of the psyche fell short of the poet's experience; Plato's 'garden of the Muses' has ever been the poet's source of inspired knowledge; it is the psychologists who are the newcomers.

I have spoken of these poets I have known, who were my friends, in an attempt to discover, and in their enduring words to communicate my own belief that poetry is the proper language of the soul; a speech that never ceases to tell those who are in the time-world of a timeless region that lies beyond the reach of intellectual judgements and evaluations. When the frontier of our consciousness is closed we inhabit a waste land to which neither wealth nor culture can impart life, which no social reform can restore. Thus understood poetry is no mere adornment of the everyday scene but a necessary knowledge of our immortal selves. Because this is so I believe that Yeats's prophecy of the 'rise of soul against intellect' must, sooner or later, fulfil itself, since it is a return to the norm, grounded not only in tradition but in the real nature of things. Truth, Yeats wrote—and he meant the truth of the soul, not of the intellect—'can never be discovered, but may be revealed'; as Muir also understood when he wrote, of Psyche's holy land,

> Look once. But do not hope to find a sentence
> To tell what you have seen. Stop at the colon:
> And set a silence after to speak the word
> That you will always seek and never find,
> Perhaps, if found, the good and beautiful end.
> You will not reach that place.   (*Images*, I)

6

Hopkins: Nature and Human Nature

FEW poets carried to fame, as Hopkins was, on a tide of fashion, speak, as he does, no less immediately to the present generation than to my own in the 1920s. Political and religious ideologies come and go, as do literary fashions; but Hopkins meets us in the one world all share—Catholic and Communist, Imagist and Existentialist, sacramentalist and positivist—the world of the senses, the natural world. Out of our common treasury of sensible nature Hopkins brings 'things both new and old'; the song of the lark, woods carpeted with bluebells in spring, leaf and shadow and cloud moving in the wind; the scents, sounds and feel of things. In 'God's Grandeur' he speaks of our cities where

> Generations have trod, have trod, have trod;
>   And all is seared with trade; bleared, smeared with toil;
>   And wears man's smudge and shares man's smell: the soil
> Is bare now, nor can foot feel, being shod.
>
> And for all this, nature is never spent;
>   There lives the dearest freshness deep down things.

It is this immaculate freshness of the earthly Paradise his poetry gives back to us. Never has the word 'nature' been so richly complex in fulness of meaning as for the Victorians. To the Victorian scientist nature was still something he could, like the painter and the poet, observe with his senses. Yet, from Galileo to Newton, vistas of space had opened; with Darwin, vistas of time. Wordsworth's *Prelude* became the sacred book of a new 'natural religion', whose universe seemed infinitely grander in its mystery than the cosmology of the Churches. History, not nature, had long been the context of Christian theology; and scholars could still in the eighteenth century argue that the earth was created in 4004 BC. Hopkins had learned from Ruskin that scientific structural minuteness of observation which makes his 'inscapes' live for us with such truth and realism. The Lake Poets he thought 'faithful but not rich observers of nature'. But through them, and no less through the paintings of Constable, Turner and their successors—for Hopkins might have been a painter, like some other members of his family, had he not been a poet—he was heir to the richest inheritance any nature poet ever received from his immediate predecessors.

But Hopkins did more than enrich, extend, particularise, the Wordsworthian 'nature' of the Victorians. If Wordsworth re-situated human kind in nature, as prodigals welcomed back to our native country, it remained for Hopkins to re-situate nature in the context of man, and both man and nature within the Christian context which sees man, if not as the be-all, at all events as the end-all of creation. We cannot go 'back' to nature, in the Wordsworthian sense of the pre-human kingdoms. Now that Wordsworth's Lake District has shrunk to a small area of threatened 'environment', Hopkins's 'Binsey Poplars', with its recognition of the scope of human destructiveness, seems prophetic. For better or worse, it is the human kingdom that now reigns on earth, threatening to cut the very roots of the Tree of Life:

> Ten or twelve, only ten or twelve
> Strokes of havoc únselve
>   The sweet especial scene,
> Rural scene, a rural scene, .
> Sweet especial rural scene.

But in a far more fundamental sense Hopkins's view of nature begins where Wordsworth's ends. The poem in which he broke that silence self-imposed when he entered the Society of Jesus, 'The Wreck of the Deutschland', celebrates—if that is the word—the encounter of the human soul with nature in her terrible aspect. What hell had been to the older religion, deluge and earthquake and volcano and, above all, shipwreck were to the new 'natural religion', the dark side of the mystery. Hopkins, more realistic than Wordsworth, understood that there could be no piety, natural or supernatural, which leaves out of account 'the raging of the stormy sea and the destructive sword' that Blake called 'portions of eternity too great for the eye of man'. The universe of science seemed to make nothing of the Christian view of man as the object of God's special concern. What to Wordsworth or Turner or Thomas Hardy might seem natural accident within an indifferent universe, the priest must proclaim as the act of God: he understood that the God who is, is terrible:

> And here the faithful waver, the faithless fable and miss.

'The Wreck of the Deutschland' is at once a superb expression of the counter-reformation ideal of sacrifice, and of nineteenth-century reason wrestling with the nature of an inhuman universe. Hopkins's 'martyr-master' stands with Hardy's blind President of the Immortals, or Lear's gods, who 'kill us for their sport':

> I did say yes
> O at lightning and lashed rod;
> Thou heardst me truer than tongue confess
> Thy terror, O Christ, O God.

In such a cry of vanquishment and submission, what an expression of faith! We must turn to the Psalms or to the Book of Job for a comparable heroic realism. So understood, this world, such as it is to human sense and human experience, is the place of existential encounter with God in his immediate personal dealings with man. At every time, in every place and situation, we stand within that confrontation.

> Thou hast bound bones and veins in me, fastened me flesh,
> And after it almost unmade, what with dread,
> Thy doing: and dost thou touch me afresh?
> Over again I feel thy finger and find thee.

No poet was ever more concrete. Perhaps his unmitigated realism was reinforced by Loyola's Spiritual Exercises, in which the physical details of the Passion are built up in vivid mental images. Hopkins re-situated symbol in physical fact. In a sermon he once preached on that potent symbol associated with his Order, the Sacred Heart, he characteristically insisted on carnal fact: 'There would', he concedes, 'no doubt be something revolting in seeing the heart alone, all naked and bleeding, torn from the breast' but, he goes on, 'Christ's heart is lodged within his sacred frame and there alone is worshipped.' Not a word about not taking the symbol literally. It is this physicality, this incarnational character, that Yeats understood to be the element in Christianity which scandalised the Greeks. In Yeats's play *The Resur-*

101

rection a Greek touches the side of the risen Christ; he recoils with the cry, 'The heart of a phantom is beating'; for, to the Platonic Greeks, the Resurrection of the Body is an outrage. The followers of Yeats's Dionysus sing 'As though God's death were but a play'; but for Hopkins the test of all reality is by flesh and blood.

Yet in Hopkins's realism the symbolic dimension is present. The strength of a symbol is its truth on all levels, including the physical; Coleridge spoke of 'the translucence of the Eternal through and in the Temporal'. 'The Wreck of the Deutschland' is no less symbolic than 'The Ancient Mariner'; nor was Hopkins less familiar than Coleridge with that whole range of neo-Platonic symbolism which likens mortal life to the storm-tossed voyage of Odysseus. The symbol survives in the Anglican rite of baptism in the prayer that the child 'may so pass the waves of this troublesome world, that he may come into the land of everlasting life'. But in Hopkins's poem the symbol is fully incarnated in the physical event. No sea-crossing of dream is so real or so soul-searching as shipwreck on the high seas.

There was no sympathy between the Jesuit and the young Yeats when their mutual friend Katharine Tynan tried to bring them together in Dublin. Hopkins in a letter to Coventry Patmore objected to a poem by Yeats:

> Now this *Mosada* I cannot think highly of . . . It was a strained and unworkable allegory about a young man and a sphinx on a rock in the sea (how did they get there? what did they eat? and so on: people think such criticisms very prosaic; but commonsense is never out of place anywhere, neither on Parnassus nor on Tabor nor on the Mount where our Lord preached . . .

Hopkins, Pater's most brilliant pupil, could have been among the Decadents had he so chosen; he was unimpressed by that decadent chimera the Sphinx.

Of course he was too narrow; and in this respect a man of his time. The twentieth century accords to dreams a reality to which the Victorians were blind. Yeats's 'rough beast' has proved none the less real because it came 'out of *Spiritus Mundi*'. But to each poet his excellence. For Hopkins no dragon of the psyche could strike the terror of 'endragonèd seas'; and he found his nightmare where

> Only the beakleaved boughs dragonish[1] damask the tool-
> smooth bleak light; black.

Even when in an introspective poem he wrote

> O the mind, mind has mountains; cliffs of fall
> Frightful, sheer, no-man-fathomed

it is likely that he had real cliffs in his mind's eye. In July 1884 he wrote to Bridges, 'Yesterday I went to see the cliffs of Moher on the coast of Clare, which to describe would be long and difficult. In returning across the Bay we were in some considerable danger of our lives'.

Perhaps it is his insistence on physical fact, his bringing of all experience to the test of the incarnational here and now of this world made Hopkins seem so much one of themselves to the positivists of Cambridge in the 1920s. Yet in nothing is he more Catholic than in the sacramentalism of his physicality, which brings the encounter with 'the living God' to the proof of the senses.

But when we think of 'nature' in Hopkins's poetry we think not of 'the beat of 'endragonèd seas'', nor 'cliffs of fall', but of 'rose-moles all in stipple upon trout that swim', of the sensuous sensual delight of 'spring's universal bliss'. May, 'When weeds, in wheels, shoot long and lovely and lush', was Hopkins's month, as it was Shakespeare's in that same Thames valley both poets loved.

Bluebells were his especial flower, described in his journal as they returned each spring in a wood near Stonyhurst. Here is his entry of May 1871:

In the little wood/opposite the light/they stood in blackish spreads or sheddings like the spots on a snake. The heads are then like thongs and solemn in grain and grape-colour. But in the clough/through the light/ they came in falls of sky-colour washing the brows and slacks of the ground with vein-blue, thickening at the double, vertical themselves and the young grass and brake fern combed vertical, but the brake struck the upright of all this with light winged transomes.

Then he gives the bluebells as they speak to other senses:

The bluebells in your hand baffle you with their inscape, made to every sense: if you draw your fingers through them they are lodged and struggle/with a shock of wet heads; the long stalks rub and click and flatten to a fan on one another like your fingers themselves would when you passed the palms hard across one another, making a brittle rub and

103

jostle like the noise of a hurdle strained by leaning against; then there is the faint honey smell and in the mouth the sweet gum when you bite them. But this is easy, it is the eye they baffle. They give one a fancy of panpipes and of some wind instrument with stops—a trombone perhaps. The overhung necks—for growing they are little more than a staff with a simple crook but in water, where they stiffen, they take stronger turns, in the head like sheephooks or, when more waved throughout, like the waves riding through a whip that is being smacked—what with these overhung necks and what with the crisped ruffled bells dropping mostly on one side and the gloss these have at their footstalks they have an air of the knights at chess.

There is much more, as if he could find no end to the simple yet limitless reality before his eyes.

At Oxford Hopkins had made a special study of the pre-Socratic philosophers, and especially of Parmenides the Eleatic; who, according to Aristotle, believed in none but a sensible reality: 'It is and that it is impossible for it not to be, is the way of belief, for truth is its companion.' In his student notes Hopkins said of Parmenides 'His feeling for instress, for the flush and foredrawn, and for inscape/is most striking and from this one can understand Plato's reverence for him as the great father of Realism.' In his description of bluebells Hopkins is affirming, with inexhaustible minuteness, with inexhaustible delight, 'It is'. In his notes on Parmenides he comments, '. . . indeed I have often felt when I have been in this mood and felt the depth of an instress or how fast the inscape holds a thing that nothing is so pregnant and straightforward to the truth as simple *yes* and *is*.' 'I do not think I have ever seen anything more beautiful than the bluebell I have been looking at. I know the beauty of our Lord by it': for only of the bluebell here and now can we say 'it is'. It could as well have been an ash-twig or an ear of green corn, or a bird's feather: whatever is here and now before his eyes is the most beautiful because it alone is fully real. Being is the attribute not of what was—Proust's *temps perdu*—or of what will be, the heaven of the otherworldly; but only of what is present to human sense. This is nature poetry in its essential purity—the poetry of the outer world, the macrocosm, seen in the mirror of the sense, but (so far as is humanly possible) unclouded by subjectivity.

Coleridge had felt the same overwhelming imaginative impact of the Parmenidean existentialism: 'Hast thou', Coleridge wrote in *The Friend*, 'ever raised thy mind to the consideration of existence, in and by itself, as the mere act of existing? Hast thou ever said to thyself thoughtfully "It is" . . . If thou hast indeed attained to this, thou wilt have felt the presence of a mystery, which must have fixed thy spirit in awe and wonder'. It was, I think, Herbert Read who first called Hopkins an existentialist; and here again positivist and sacramentalist meet on common ground. Hopkins looked not for the immortality of the soul but for the resurrection of the body. In 'The Leaden Echo and the Golden Echo' he wrote,

> See; not a hair is, not an eyelash, not the least lash lost; every hair
> Is, hair of the head, numbered.

All these are kept, the poem says, 'yonder'; but Hopkins is not really a poet of the other world, Plotinus's 'yonder' of which this world is the lovely image or shadow. 'The comfort of the resurrection' lies in the promise that the 'it is', here so fleeting, will there be made eternal; not another world, but this world experienced after another manner.

How many of the poems affirm the here and now present to the poet's senses, as in 'Hurrahing in Harvest' (the italics are mine):

> Summer ends *now; now*, barbarous in beauty, the stooks rise
> Around. . . .

or in 'The Windhover':

> I caught *this morning* morning's minion, king-
>   dom of daylight's dauphin, dapple-dawn-drawn Falcon . . .

and in 'The Starlit Night':

> Look at the stars! look, look up at the skies!
>   O look at all the fire-folk sitting in the air!
>   The bright boroughs, the circle-citadels there!
> Down in dim woods the diamond delves! the elves'-eyes!
> The grey lawns cold where gold, where quickgold lies!

It is with no inward eye that Hopkins beholds bird and stars and harvest fields, but in the ever-new immediacy of sensation. Memory, though it may transmute and distil, though it may immerse in the magical atmosphere of dream, can never recapture the inexhaustible 'isness' of sensible reality. It is in the absolute, the ever-new existence of things from which Hopkins took, and to which he gives, that peculiar, intense and vivid delight that we find in no other poet.

Hopkins's most characteristic images are really long complex nominatives—not so much phrases as words, naming the 'It is': 'drop-of-blood-and-foam-dapple/Bloom'; 'Wiry and white-fiery and whirlwind-swivellèd snow'; 'wimpled-water-dimpled, not-by-morning-matchèd face'. Adam in Paradise did not describe but 'named' the creatures; for the nominative is the nearest that man can come to nature. Of these lost names Hopkins recaptures for us a few fragments—for they are limitless as being itself—in his poetry; 'The Windhover' is a complex Parmenidean affirmation:

> . . . dapple-dawn-drawn Falcon, in his riding
> Of the rolling level underneath him steady air, and striding
> High there, how he rung upon the rein of a wimpling wing
> In his ecstasy!

What is, according to Parmenides, is 'a finite, spherical, corporeal plenum and there is nothing beyond it'. All exists for ever within the whole, each thing in its place, instressed by 'the bonds of strong Necessity', the laws of nature. The Parmenidean plenum comes very near the modern picture of the universe in which space and time are relative, are dimensions. Nothing therefore can be considered in itself, as if in isolation. There is only one whole—the all; and truly modern is Hopkins's sense of what we now call ecology—the structure of the whole of a landscape, or cloudscape, or river valley. Like Ruskin, like Turner himself, he studied closely not only the 'inscape' of some single leaf or single tree, but whole natural formations of wind and cloud, rock and water. Cloudscape is instressed by wind, as in 'Nature is a Heraclitean Fire':

> Cloud-puffball, torn tufts, tossed pillows[1] flaunt forth, then chevy on an air-
> built thoroughfare: heaven-roysters, in gay-gangs[1] they throng; they glitter in marches.

Or the Binsey Poplars with the play of wind and sun and shadow:

> My aspens dear, whose airy cages quelled,
> Quelled or quenched in leaves the leaping sun,
> All felled, felled, are all felled;
> Of a fresh and following folded rank
> Not spared, not one
> That dandled a sandalled

Shadow that swam or sank
On meadow and river and wind-wandering weed-winding bank.

The 'inscape' is not of the trees alone but of the whole 'sweet, especial, rural scene'. The characteristic continuous motion of the long-stalked aspen-leaves, first seen in play against the morning sky as they 'quelled or quenched the leaping sun', then in the no less lovely play of the shadows, 'sandalled' because they seem to tread the ground, while others 'swam or sank' in the water, imparts to a rivery landscape the trees' delicate motion. The image is not the sum of its parts but a living indivisible whole.

In his latest poems Hopkins's great unified images have the coherence of musical phrases. The opening lines of the sonnet 'Spelt from Sibyl's Leaves' is like a single word that utters the approach of darkness:

Earnest, earthless, equal, attuneable,[1] vaulty, voluminous,
. . . stupendous
Evening strains to be time's vást,[1] womb-of-all, home-of-all,
hearse-of-all night.

Hopkins at Oxford had noted that 'the two [Parmenidean] principles are fire and earth or, as he puts it, "ethery flame of fire, comforting the heart (he is thinking of it perhaps as a vital principle), marvellously subtle, throughout one with itself, *not* one with the other" and "unmeaning (α' $\delta\alpha\eta$) night, thick and wedgèd body" '. Nature's 'million-fuellèd bonfire' is Heraclitean; but those characteristic images of fire breaking from reluctant earth are surely Parmenidean: 'It will flame out, like shining from shook foil'; 'As kingfishers catch fire, dragonflies draw flame'. In 'The Windhover' fire breaks from the clods of earth as

. . . shéer plód makes plough down sillion
Shine, and blue-bleak embers, ah my dear,
Fall, gall themselves, and gash gold-vermilion.

The 'fresh-firecoal chestnut-falls' of nature have their human echo in the splendid image of Felix Randal at 'the random grim forge' striking fire from the 'thick and wedgèd body' of the iron; the man is matched in the 'great grey drayhorse' with his 'bright and battering sandal' whose iron also strikes fire from stone.

As there is no separation of parts in an ecological whole, so the oneness of being is received through every sense at once—sight, touch, taste; and above all through the poet's fine musician's ear. In 'The Sea and the Skylark' the song of the bird is evoked in a single seamless phrase:

> Left hand, off land, I hear the lark ascend,
> His rash-fresh re-winded new-skeinèd score
> In crisps of curl off wild winch whirl, and pour
> And pelt music, till none's to spill nor spend.

In a wonderful letter to Bridges he explains what his friend had found obscure:

> "Rash-fresh more" (it is dreadful to explain these things in cold blood) means a headlong and exciting new snatch of singing, resumption by the lark of his song, which by turns he gives over and takes up again all day long, and this goes on, the sonnet says, through all time, without ever losing its first freshness, being a thing both new and old . . . the skein and coil are the lark's song, which from his height gives the impression (not to me only) of something falling to the earth and not vertically quite but tricklingly or wavingly, something as a skein of silk ribbed by having been tightly wound on a narrow card or a notched holder or as fishing-tackle or twine unwinding from a reel or winch. . . .

The letter goes on to describe how 'the lark in wild glee races the reel round, paying or dealing out and down the turns of the skein or coil right to the earth floor, the ground, where it lies in a heap, as it were, or rather is all wound off on to another winch, reel, bobbin, or spool in Fancy's eye by the moment the bird touches earth and so is ready for a fresh unwinding at the next flight'. Again, the whole passage is one long nominative phrase. For Hopkins the lark is its song as the windhover is its flight; form—inscape—is the signature of the 'instress' of energy, 'live and lancing like the blowpipe flame', to use the poet's own image of the creative act of God. No bird of Hopkins's could be put in those natural history museums dear to Victorians; for the bone and feather is only the signature of the soaring singing life whose impress it bears:

> Each mortal thing does one thing and the same:
> Deals out that being indoors each one dwells;
> Selves—goes itself; *myself* it speaks and spells,
> Crying *Whát I dó is me: for that I came.*

There is a curious convergence between Hopkins and Blake, both of whom opposed to the materialist view of nature the more ancient — and also more modern — view of each creature as an unique and distinct impulse of life; 'their habitations/And their pursuits as different as their forms and as their joys'—as Blake says.

It was the Rev. M. C. D'Arcy S. J. who once said to me—and I have since wondered if he had Hopkins in mind at the time—that 'all poets are pantheists'; for if Hopkins could not permit himself to think as a pantheist he could not prevent himself from feeling as one.

> The world is charged with the grandeur of God.
> It will flame out, like shining from shook foil;
> It gathers to a greatness, like the ooze of oil
> Crushed. . . .

That other nature mystic of the Society of Jesus, Teilhard de Chardin, perceived that transubstantiation, the central mystery of the Catholic faith, must in its nature transform the whole world. He describes in *Hymn of the Universe* a vision which came to him in meditation before a monstrance: 'I had then the impression as I gazed at the host that its surface was gradually spreading out like a spot of oil but of course much more swiftly and luminously'. This flow of whiteness extended until it seemed to be 'illuminating the universe from within, and everything were fashioned of the same kind of translucent flesh. . . . So, through the mysterious expansion of the host the whole world had become incandescent, had itself become like a single giant host.' Had become, in other words, the mystical body; the Parmenidean 'It is' becomes, in the vision of the cosmic Christ, the Biblical 'I am'.

Again there is a strange convergence of Hopkins, Teilhard, and Blake. Blake's masters—Paracelsus, Jakob Boehme, Swedenborg—were all within, or strongly influenced by, the tradition of alchemy, with its consistent refusal—down to Goethe and his most recent follower, Rudolf Steiner—of a mechanistic view of nature. There is a *deus absconditus* scattered, distributed, like the dismembered body of Osiris, throughout the physical world. Like Osiris this hidden god must at last be reassembled and resurrected. In a long magnificent passage inspired by these esoteric teachings Blake wrote that

> . . . Man looks out in tree & herb & fish & bird & beast
> Collecting up the scatterd portions of his immortal body
> Into the Elemental forms of everything that grows   (K355)

109

and concludes:

> . . . wherever a grass grows
> Or a leaf buds, The Eternal Man is seen, is heard, is felt,
> And all his sorrows, till he reassumes his ancient bliss. (K356)

Blake's Eternal Man is, like Teilhard's Christ, the Emergent Person of the universe; and Hopkins in 'Hurrahing in Harvest' had divined the same cosmic being:

> I walk, I lift up, I lift up heart, eyes,
> Down all that glory in the heavens to glean our Saviour.

As plainly as Blake or as Teilhard, Hopkins saw the world as His body:

> And the azurous hung hills are his world-wielding shoulder
> Majestic—as a stallion stalwart, very-violet-sweet!—
> These things, these things were here and but the beholder
> Wanting. . . .

Hopkins even in his earliest writings often observes a tendency in natural forms towards the human countenance. In a journal he writes of clouds: 'fine shapeless skins of fretted make, full of eyebrows or like linings of curled leaves'; 'rotten-woven cloud which shapes in leaf over leaf of wavy or eyebrow texture'; 'Rarer and wilder packs have sometimes film [of vapour] in the sheet, which may be caught as it turns on the edge of the cloud like an outlying eyebrow'. Hopkins as he gazes at these shape-shifting clouds, or at the stars 'fire-féaturing heaven', seems to be awaiting some ultimate metamorphosis he felt to be imminent. Blake had written: 'Think of a white cloud as being holy, you cannot love it; but think of a holy man within the cloud, love springs up in your thoughts, for to think of holiness distinct from man is impossible to the affections.' So it certainly was for Hopkins, as here in 'The Wreck of the Deutschland':

> I kiss my hand
> To the stars, lovely-asunder
> Starlight, wafting him out of it; and
> Glow, glory in thunder;
> Kiss my hand to the dappled-with-damson west:

110

Since, tho' he is under the world's splendour and wonder,
    His mystery must be instressed, stressed;
For I greet him the days I meet him, and bless when I understand.

The 'instressing' of the divine mystery again reminds us of Blake, and the Hermetic travail of nature as it struggles to give birth to the Eternal Man. It is in human consciousness—in Blake's 'divine humanity'—that nature's mere being becomes a person; man is the 'beholder wanting'. Blake had said that 'Nature without Man is barren'; he was criticising Wordsworth's 'natural religion'. Hopkins too, at once more modern and more faithful to tradition, restores to man the centrality of which nineteenth-century science seemed for a time to have deprived us:

    And what is Earth's eye, tongue, or heart else, where
    Else, but in dear and dogged man?

Dear and dogged man: for the priest, as for the communist, there is only man; one Adam, one Christ. Far from Hopkins was 'the cult of the individual'. He loved the natural man with a priestly and compassionate love. If Wordsworth too often approached common humanity in the spirit of the man with a questionnaire, Hopkins never did so. Felix Randal the farrier is his son in religion; so is the young bugler to whom he gave his first communion:

    . . . I in a sort deserve to
    And do serve God to serve to
    Just such slips of soldiery Christ's royal ration.

In the young boy server of the handsome heart, the brothers at the Stonyhurst school play, he saw in human nature a beauty that moved him to exclaim, in 'Brothers':

    Ah Nature, framed in fault,
    There's comfort then, there's salt;
    Nature, bad, base, and blind,
    Dearly thou canst be kind;
    There dearly thén, deárly,
    I'll cry thou canst be kind.

Faithful to his realism, his Christian incarnationalism, he cared for the body no less than the soul: 'What I most dislike in towns and in

111

London in particular', he wrote in a letter, is 'the illshapen degraded physical (putting aside moral) type of so many of the people.' For him a man is never more human, more fully expressive of our 'nature', than in physical action. As the bird is its flight and its song, so a man is what he does: 'Acts in God's eye what in God's eye he is'. Felix Randal's deathbed thoughts are dismissed in a manner prosaic and perfunctory:

> Impatient, he cursed at first, but mended
> Being anointed and all;

But the farrier is made immortal in the physical glory of his act:

> When thou at the random grim forge, powerful amidst peers,
> Didst fettle for the great grey drayhorse his bright and battering sandal!

With the eye of a sculptor he sees the beauty of Harry Ploughman's 'sinew service':

> Hard as hurdle arms, with a broth of goldish flue
> Breathed round; the rack of ribs; the scooped flank; lank
> Rope-over thigh; knee-nave; and barrelled shank—
> Head and foot, shoulder and shank—
> By a grey eye's heed steered well, one crew, fall to;
> Stand at stress. Each limb's barrowy brawn, his thew
> That onewhere curded, onewhere sucked or sank—
> Soared ór sánk—,
> Though as a beechbole firm, finds his, as at a roll-call, rank
> And features, in flesh, what deed he each must do—
> His sinew-service where do.

The worst outrage against the common man—Tom the Navvy—is unemployment; for so he is unable to enact what he is, is no more himself than 'a dare-gale skylark scanted in a dull cage':

> . . . by Despair, bred Hangdog dull; by Rage,
> Manwolf, worse; and their packs infest the age.

By the same token there is no heroism of the mind to equal the simple heroism of the soldier who pledges his body to his country's service. We would be wrong to dismiss Hopkins's praise of soldiers and sailors as Victorian militarism: to do so would be to miss the gospel simplicity of the test—a man cannot give more than his life:

> '. . . So God-made flesh does too:
> Were I come o'er again' cries Christ 'it should be this'.

The young soldier is the type of Christ's sacrifice:

> Yes. Whý do we áll, seeing of a soldier, bless him? bless
> Our redcoats, our tars? Both these being, the greater part,
> But frail clay, nay but foul clay. Here it is: the heart,
> Since, proud, it calls the calling manly, gives a guess
> That, hopes that, makesbelieve, the men must be no less;
> It fancies, feigns, deems, dears the artist after his art;
> And fain will find as sterling all as all is smart,
> And scarlet wear the spirit of wár thére express.

We think of Hardy, of the Trumpet Major and his sailor brother, or Sergeant Troy who dazzled Bathsheba Everdene with sword-play, in which Hopkins would have seen something more than trivial, for 'the spirit of wár thére express'.

He did in fact greatly admire Hardy, unrivalled novelist of natural humanity, of simple people whose expression is all in their action: Giles Winterbourne, planter of trees; Gabriel Oak, shearing sheep. He loved William Barnes, too: 'It is his naturalness that strikes me most,' he wrote to Coventry Patmore, 'he is like an embodiment or incarnation or manmuse of the country, of Dorset, or rustic life and humanity. He comes, like Homer and all poets of native epic, provided with epithets, images, and so on which seem to have been tested and digested for a long age in their native air and circumstances and to have a *keeping* which nothing else could give.'

Perhaps because of his almost nostalgic affection for human simplicity from which he was himself, by birth, education and vocation so far removed, Hopkins sometimes adopted dialect words whose richness and aptness in their own context appealed to him: sometimes splendidly, as 'didst *fettle* for the great grey drayhorse his bright and battering sandal!' But what in Barnes (or in the speech of lay-brothers and simple parishioners) he admired as 'in keeping' is, in his own educated English diction, sometimes embarrassingly out of keeping; Felix Randal, 'anointed *and all*'; the cockney 'seeing *of* a soldier'; 'his treat' for the bugler-boy's first communion, and the use of native

113

Scotch words in poems written in Scotland by this very English Englishman.

'Duns Scotus's Oxford' praises the philosopher not for his originality but as 'of realty the rarest-veinèd unraveller'—Parmenides' reality, the same for all. In his sonnet on Henry Purcell 'the poet wishes well to the divine genius of Purcell and praises him that, whereas other musicians have given utterance to the moods of man's mind, he has, beyond that, uttered in notes the very make and species of man as created both in him and in all men generally'. One might say that nineteenth-century Romantic poetry also gives utterance to 'the moods of man's mind'; and in his generation Hopkins stands almost alone as representing the classical view of man. If Romanticism is a flowering of the highly civilized ideal of the fullest possible realization of the uniqueness of every individual human being—Browning's *Men and Women*—Catholicism (and within its narrower limits Marxism) never loses sight of the classical bedrock of common humanity: man and woman. By a seeming paradox—so Hopkins understood—the greatest genius comes nearest to the universal human nature; having fewer blemishes, perhaps, to obscure the 'image of God' in which Everyman is created.

In the same way he considered the judgement of an educated man to be marked not by that 'originality' so overvalued in the academic world, but by a nearer and truer approximation to the human norm. He reproved his friend Robert Bridges, in a letter, for his singularity: 'So far as I see, where we differ in judgment, my judgments are less singular than yours; I agree more than you do with the mob and with the *communis criticorum*. Presumably I shd. agree with these still more if I read more and so differ still more from you than now'—so he teases his distinguished friend, who for so long withheld Hopkins's poems from publication on account of what seemed to him their singularity and incomprehensibility.

Coventry Patmore too comes in for a rebuke for being too far removed from the old Adam: '. . . there is an old Adam of barbarism, boyishness, wildness, rawness, rankness, the disreputable, the unrefined in the refined and educated. It is that that I meant by tykishness (a tyke is a stray sly unowned dog) and said you have none of; and I did also think that you were without all sympathy for it and must survey it when you met with it wholly from without. . . . I thought it was well to have ever so little of it,' he concludes, 'and therefore it was perhaps a happy thing that you were entrapped into the vice of immoderate smoking, for to know one yields to a vice must help to

114

BRENHINOÐ Ý NÝ SOÐ

WHAT SAYS HIS MABINOGI:
SON OF MAIR WIFE OF
JOBBING CARPENTER
IN VIA NASCITVR
LAPPED IN HAY PARVVLE
BVT WHT DOES HIS BOAST SAY:
ALPHA ES ET O THAT WCH
THE WHOLE ORBIS CANNOT HOLD
ÆÞELINȝ TO THE HEVN KINȝ
SHEPHERD OF GREEKLAND
HARROWER OF ANNUN
FREER OF THE WATERS
CHIEF PHYSICIAN AND
DVX ET PONTIFEX
GVLEDIG NEFOEÐ and
WALÐA OF EVERY LAND

MODIS
NADOLIG
MVLTIS QVE
BENDIGAID
MVLTIFARIVM

A·DALANT·ANRHEG

I *Inscription*, David Jones (private collection).

II *The Chapel Perilous*, 1932, 19″ × 14″, pencil, ink and watercolour
(Collection of Helen Sutherland).

III *The Annunciation in a Welsh Hill Setting*, David Jones 1963-4, 30″ × 22″, pencil and watercolour (Collection National Museum of Wales).

IV *Procession of Fools*, 1940, $14\frac{1}{2}'' \times 19\frac{1}{4}''$, pen and indian ink (Collection The Dartington Hall Trust).

V *The Oracle*, Cecil Collins 1940, $15\frac{3}{4}'' \times 21''$, pen and indian ink (private collection).

VI *The Artist's Wife*, Cecil Collins 1948, 16½" × 17", oil (private

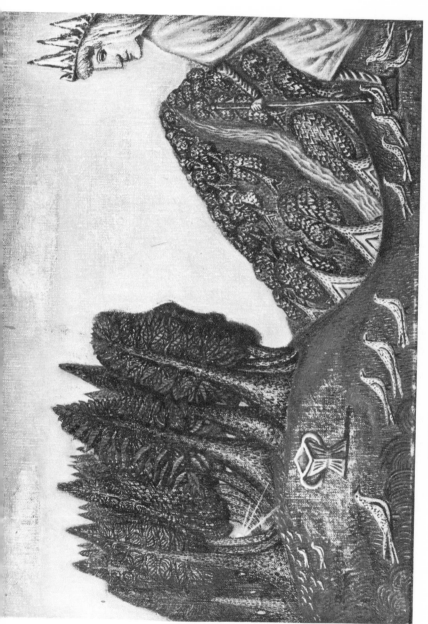

VII *The Return*, Cecil Collins 1943, oil (private collection).

VIII *Angels Dancing with the Sun and the Moon,* Cecil Collins 1950, oil (private collection).

humanise and make tolerant.' Hopkins admired Stevenson's *Dr Jekyll and Mr Hyde* and felt, most refined, most sensitive, most cultured of gentlemen and most scrupulous of priests, that he understood it from within.

Why then was Hopkins so merciless on his own 'poor Jackself'? 'My vocation puts before me a standard so high that a higher can be found nowhere else,' he had written to his Anglican friend, Canon Dixon. To blame the Society of Jesus for his self-imposed vow to write no poetry unless expressly ordered to do so in the service of his vocation would be absurd; the Society has fostered (for the greater glory of God) every kind of talent. At most the Society provided a context which permitted, which perhaps approved of, Hopkins's surely mistaken belief that the immolation of his talent was a gift more pleasing to God than its exercise. There is in the history of the Church (we may see it by walking round any gallery of Christian art) a strain of perverse morbidity, an excessive dwelling upon the tortures of martyrdom, as if these tragic consequences of evil were good in themselves. How well Hopkins knew that 'energy is eternal delight', not only in flower and bird, but in Felix Randal, in Harry Ploughman; yet forbade it to himself:

> . . . only what word
> Wisest my heart breeds dark heaven's baffling ban
> Bars or hell's spell thwarts. . . .
>
> ('To seem the stranger lies my lot, my life')

In Hopkins's invocation of 'lightning and lashed rod' there is both heroism and—I cannot but feel—some unresolved and finally self-destructive morbidity; which in no way lessens the greatness of the poetry in which he has recorded his encounter with the 'martyr-master' of his dark faith, as in 'Carrion Comfort':

> But ah, but O thou terrible, why wouldst thou rude on me
> Thy wring-world right foot rock? lay a lionlimb against me?
>   scan
> With darksome devouring eyes my bruisèd bones? and fan,
> O in turns of tempest, me heaped there; me frantic to avoid
>   thee and flee?

The image suggests Blake's illustration to the Book of Job in which Satan the Selfhood, master of disguises, masquerades, with cloven hoof, as the Most High. The conceit in 'The Wreck of the Deutschland' which compares God's infliction of suffering to the crunching of a ripe and luscious but bitter fruit suggests Moloch rather than Christ:

> How a lush-kept plush-capped sloe
> Will, mouthed to flesh-burst,
> Gush!—flush the man, the being with it, sour or sweet,
> Brim, in a flash, full!

The 'gush'—'flush' bursting image is repellent as the exquisitely painted bleeding wound of some martyrdom or crucifixion.

Yet in our own extremity, with what fullness, with what dignity of endurance he companions us. As many of the Psalms, or the Book of Job, those ancient poems to which countless generations have turned in their darkest sorrow, Hopkins has in his 'terrible' sonnets found words of utterance for whoever, 'pitched past pitch of grief', finds himself in the utmost solitudes of desolation. The quality, the degree of sensitivity, recalls a passage in Proust whose insomnia made the night seem endless:

> I wake and feel the fell of dark, not day.
> What hours, O what black hoürs we have spent
> This night! what sights you, heart, saw; ways you went!
> And more must, in yet longer light's delay.
> With witness I speak this. But where I say
> Hours I mean years, mean life. . . .

Nothing is simple: and we may see in Hopkins's seemingly needless self-immolation the heroism of the life-venturing mountaineer or air-pilot who for its own sake succumbs to 'the fascination of what's difficult'. Are not those spirits who explore the utmost limits, the extremes of joy and grief, all the states of the human soul, the growing-point of our humanity? 'The whole creation groaneth and travaileth in pain until now,' St Paul wrote; 'His mystery must be instressed, stressed'; and the instress of creation falls on 'dear and dogged man'. In man nature struggles to give birth to the hidden god, the Person of the universe. This for Hopkins is the epiphany (as for Blake before him and Teilhard de Chardin since) towards which, in ecstasy as in grief, we strive. 'The just man'—and for Hopkins the just man is redcoat and tar, the seaman of the Deutschland, 'handy and brave' 'pitched to his death at a blow', is the farrier and the ploughman, the simple people of 'a house where all were good/To me, God knows, deserving no such thing', the lay-brother who 'watched the door'—the just man

116

Acts in God's eye what in God's eye he is—
Chríst for Christ plays in ten thousand places,
Lovely in limbs, and lovely in eyes not his
To the Father through the features of men's faces.

7

David Jones and the Actually Loved and Known

ALTHOUGH I knew David Jones over a number of years, and have loved his work for as long (first his paintings, later his writings) when it comes to writing about him I wonder if I am equal to the task. Few would now dispute that he is a very great maker both in words and in those other 'signs'—as he would have said—pictorial images. But he is also a very difficult writer because of the great wealth and range of his allusiveness—his technique both as a painter and writer depends to a very great extent upon allusion—which for many, even of those who take pleasure in his work, is a largely unshared background. Few of his readers—certainly not myself—possess his wide knowledge of history, of etymology, of the Christian Liturgy, of many crafts and many ways of making and doing, not to mention those Welsh sources which for most are the worst stumbling-block of all. In his paintings too, to all appearances so delicately fragile a texture of natural forms—flower petals, animals, trees, water and light—not only is the visual complexity far greater than appears at first glance, but, again, the fullness of allusion and implication is so very much greater than we have come to expect that we may miss it altogether and wrongly see him as an impressionist. A painting of Turneresque evanescence is entitled *Manawyddan's Glass Door*: have we fully seen and experienced that painting until we have given due weight to the mythology behind the allusion to the magical house of one of the gods of the Welsh 'otherworld', only to be entered as the house turns, and within which time and place is not as it is for us? David certainly could not have painted it without that sense of a luminous 'parenthesis' in another world than ours implicitly contrasted with the darker period 'in parenthesis' of which he has written in his book about his experience in the trenches of the First World War. He painted *Manawyddan's Glass Door*, a seascape full of the radiance of Faery, soon after his return from that War. Both in the painting, at first glance an impression of light-effects over the sea near Brighton, and in the war-epic, at first reading a realistic description of life in the trenches, he is concerned with states of being, with the creation of a work in which inner and outer reality are so interfused that they are not to be separated. In a passage describing 'the folk tradition of the insular Celts' (in his essay 'The Myth of Arthur'), he is also describing his own qualities as a painter. This tradition

> . . . seems to present to the mind a half-aquatic world—it is one of its most fascinating characteristics—it introduces a feeling of transparency and interpenetration of one element with another, of transposition and metamorphosis. The hedges of mist vanish or come again under the application of magic . . . just as the actual mists over peat-bog and tarn and *traeth* disclose or lose before our eyes drifting stumps and tussocks. It is unstable, the isles float, where was a *caer* or a *llys* now is a glassy expanse.

I first met David at the house of our mutual friend Helen Sutherland. I had of course seen some of his paintings before this closer familiarity; for he was always appreciated by his fellow artists in both arts, although even now scarcely known to 'the general public', for whom he is too subtle, too delicately gentle a spirit for those who see in gentleness weakness and in violence strength. In Helen Sutherland's house, Cockley Moor, near Ullswater, there were many of his works, some painted in Helen's former house, Rock Hall in Northumberland, and some at Cockley Moor; some indeed during periods when both David and I were staying in the house, where Helen loved to have her painters and writers come to work. David was less happy painting at Cockley Moor than he had been at Rock; not because the fell-side and the birch-trees from the windows were less beautiful, but because history had not moved over that landscape. The Romans had not come nearer than the ridge of High Street, on the horizon; no holy well or burial site or ancient battle had consecrated the landscape. In physical appearance the Lake District scenery is not unlike the Welsh hills he had painted in earlier years when he was a member of Eric Gill's community at Capel-y-ffin; but, lacking the consecration of sites by mankind's story, it lacked, for David, a necessary dimension. Wordsworth could enjoy 'nature' untouched by man; but for David, as for Blake, 'nature without man is barren'. At Rock Hall he painted the little church and named it *Chapel Perilous*; *Roland's Tree* (see *plate II*) is a tall pine like any other, and certainly not the tree under which the hero of the *Chanson de Roland* actually died; but it was rooted in

119

soil enriched by the blood of the armies of Charlemagne and by their stories. He loved painting animals; but it mattered to him that these too had significance not only in the natural world but in human history. His first preserved drawing, made as a child, of a dancing bear on its rope, may already have meant the more to him because the name of King Arthur derives from *Arktos*—the bear. The Welsh ponies he often painted might have descended from the cavalry horses of Arthur's Romano-British cavalry; the freeing of their horses by knights who survived the last battle of Arthur, and who, many of them, ended their days in religious houses, is an episode he lovingly describes in an essay on 'The Legend of Arthur'. David's little horses have all chivalry behind them. The consecration of chivalry as conceived in Arthurian romance, and especially by the holy latter-days of the knights, in consequence of which their horses were freed, consecrates the horses too, many generations after. This is not explicitly communicated in the painting; they are in no way laden with visible symbols of the past that for David they may recall; they are obviously not 'symbolic' horses, but real Welsh ponies; and yet it is there as a quality which any sensitive person can feel, unable perhaps to give a name to that sense of romance and mystery which belongs to David's horses. In the same way the petals of the daffodils David so exquisitely painted in a radiant glass chalice are altogether real, down to that subtle spiral twist of the outer perianth petals that the Welsh daffodils have. But, as David himself has written, in the wonderful Preface to *The Anathemata*:

If one is making a painting of daffodils what is *not* instantly involved? Will it make any difference whether or no we have heard of Persephone or Flora or Blodeuedd?

I am of the opinion that it will make a difference, but would immediately make this reservation: Just as Christians assert that baptism by water 'makes a difference', but that many by desire and without water achieve the benefits of that 'difference', so, without having heard of Flora Dea, there are many who would paint daffodils as though they had invoked her by name.

I do not know what associations David had in mind as he painted an elegant Victorian teapot, or a pair of scissors—his mother's I believe they were—but the point is that, beyond that thrice-distilled quality of delicate line and luminosity of colour, the associations were always there as an intrinsic part of the experience of painting a perfectly real flower or tree or teapot. They were for him 'signs'—symbols—of many recessions; and for him every such 'sign' was in its degree sacramental. 'Ars knows only a sacred activity', he wrote in an essay entitled 'Art and Sacrament', since 'the notion of "sign" cannot be separated from this activity of art'. His symbols have nothing to do with the unconscious; David was a Thomist and an Aristotelian; he was not concerned with a mythological inner landscape (as for example that of Cecil Collins): the real is for him always incarnate. But incarnation is itself a sacramental meeting of heaven and earth. Nothing in 'the unconscious' could ever have for David a mystery comparable in dignity with the actually seen and known.

The phrase 'actually loved and known' occurs in the Preface to *The Anathemata*, and leads us to the heart of the secret of that 'difference' we find in David Jones's work, to which it is so hard to put a name. The artist, he constantly insists, is a 'sign-maker'; that is to say, he presents us with images, pictorial or verbal, that stir in us those associations, those overtones of meaning, that enrich and deepen the experience of the senses by speaking also to other levels of our being. And David wrestled in bitterness of heart with the difficulty in our time, of discovering valid signs—signs that would speak to a generation forgetful of tradition and taught to look no further than the senses—still able to stir in us the rich complex of association that he wishes to communicate.

> The whole complex of these difficulties is primarily felt by the sign-maker, the artist, because for him it is an immediate, day by day, factual problem. He has, somehow or other, to lift up valid signs; that is his specific task.
>
> In practice one of his main problems, one of the matters upon which his judgment is exercised . . . concerns the validity and availability of his images. It is precisely this validity and availability that constitutes his greatest problem in the present culture-situation.

And he gives a specific example:

> If the poet writes 'wood' what are the chances that the Wood of the Cross will be evoked? Should the answer be 'None', then it would seem that an impoverishment of some sort would have to be admitted. It would mean that that particular word could no longer be used with confidence to implement, to call up or to set in motion a whole world of content belonging in a special sense to the mythus of a particular culture and of concepts and realities belonging to mankind as such. This would be true irrespective of our beliefs and disbeliefs. It would remain true even if we

were of the opinion that it was high time the word 'wood' should be dissociated with the mythus and concepts indicated. The arts abhor any loppings off of meanings or emptyings out, any lessening of the totality of connotation, any loss of recession and thickness through.

I think it was in his book *The Innocent Eye* that Herbert Read developed his idea of the artist's vision being 'innocent', immediate, like that of a child who sees something for the first time, with a kind of wonder and immediacy never to be recaptured.

But as Blake would say 'the opposite is also true'. Proust, in his remarkable critical writing, *Contre Saint-Beuve*, characteristically develops his theme that we never do see anything in this 'pure' sense; always, even in childhood, a perception is a palimpsest of memories. The thing seen awakens memories clear or dim or a mere stirring of feeling to which we cannot give a name; as a hawthorn hedge in flower (to take an example from Proust's own writings) sets astir a whole complex of memories and associations, of first love, of hawthorn in the church of Combray on a feast-day of the Blessed Virgin, and so on. There is no such thing as a simple experience; knowledge is in its very nature complex, evocative, associative. As we live so does our experience gather richness from associations remembered and forgotten. It is this living texture that comprises our knowledge; one might almost say our being.

Furthermore a culture is no mere matter of book-learning. One of the misfortunes of our time is that the acquisition of information has come to replace that total experience of an inherited tradition that David calls 'the mythus'; something rooted in all the ways of feeling and living and doing and being that belong to a particular culture; a culture that begins at home. We know anything and everything, but that total experience of what is our own we have all but lost. One thing is no more ours than another; we may even be 'authorities' on some 'subject', but at the same time not belong in any living way to that body of information we possess only with our minds. It makes no difference to the quiz-man or the examiner whether we learned what we know at our mother's knee or 'heard it on the telly'; but to David such things were all-important, because it is not what we know but the quality of our knowing that is all-important. The knowledge of the 'fact-man' is dead information; a computer could retain it as well as the human brain. Knowledge has become indistinguishable from hearsay, which is not living knowledge but something extraneous, irrelevant, not rooted in our own identity or that of our family or religion or anything related to our life. It belongs to an external environment unrelated to what we are. Such extraneous knowledge does not make us aware of who we are but rather destroys in us all discernment of what is truly ours; those traditions, as he says in the same Preface,

> . . . in which one has oneself participated or heard with one's own ears from one's own parents or near relatives or immediate forebears. These things received in childhood are of course fragments or concomitants only of the whole above-mentioned complex. I am thinking only of the means whereby those concomitants and fragments reached me. I am speaking of channels only, but of immediate channels and such as condition all that passes through them, and which condition also one's subsequent attitude to all the rest. These I judge to be of the most primary importance. It is through them that 'all the rest' is already half sensed long before it is known.

For David Jones knowledge is inseparable from love; we can only 'know' in a living and real sense what we love. The poet must 'work within the limits of his love. There must be no muggings-up, no "ought to know" or "try to feel", for only what is actually loved and known can be seen *sub specie aeternitatis*.' The images the poet uses must be 'significant and warm'; true for the heart as well as for the mind.

For David the 'actually loved and known' must therefore be in the first place experienced. In this sense we can only love and know whatever comes to hand: those things we know as children, the soldiers David as a little boy got out of bed to watch as they rode past his parents' house, his mother putting him back to bed afterwards; the tools of his grandfather's craft of boat-building; the Welsh songs his father sang. The first test of what is ours is that it is 'given'. Although this is arbitrary, yet in a world whose texture is woven without a break from past to future our own place in that unbroken web is far from arbitrary: it is our situation within a totality common to all. 'Nowness' is for David all-important; it is where we stand in our relation to the whole of the past and the whole of the future, it is where past and future meet, are actualised and incarnated. 'I have made a heap of all I could find'—so he begins his Preface: 'Part of my task has been to allow myself to be directed by motifs gathered together from such sources as have by accident been available to me and to make a work out of those mixed data.'

123

Most readers of David Jones find great difficulty in coming to terms with his particular sources. Few know the Welsh language, or even the Welsh mythology; though most of us feel that the Arthurian legends are in some sense our own. Again, the Latin liturgy of the Catholic Church is unfamiliar to most English readers, even those who may be Christian. David's third field of experience is the trench warfare of the First World War; again an experience known at first hand to few of his readers now though still probably—at least superficially—more within Everyman's imaginative reach than the other two. And yet he does not insist upon our sharing his particular knowledge or terms of reference: rather he seeks to remind us that we each have our own. This may indeed be the real difficulty; for there are many readers who would rather be given by an author a whole heap of information, however remote, than be quietly reminded, on every page, that Everyman has his own unique place in a total mythus; be sent, as it were, in search of his own ways of access into experiences which only so can the author share with us.

Once, in New Orleans, I was the guest of the City Librarian; grace was said in a language unknown to me—Hebrew. I was unaccountably moved by this confrontation with so ancient a tradition. 'Those who do not know who they were cannot know who they are,' my host said. And not long afterwards an American classical scholar described a barbarian to me as one who has no past. It is participation in what David Jones calls some 'cultural mythus' that makes us civilized; barbarism can invade from within any society which allows its traditions to be forgotten. David himself had no illusions about the dangers of our own situation. He saw it as the end, if not of all civilization, at all events of *a* civilization, the two thousand years of European Christendom, which itself rests upon two thousand years of Greek, Egyptian and Hebrew civilization. This terminal situation is in a sense the occasion (though not the theme) of all his work.

David, though he often, and with powerful exactitude, gave expression to his fears for the future, nevertheless thought it important to build upon such fragments of the living tradition as he himself had inherited. It is by default that the cultural mythus is lost; it must be renewed in a living present. This renewal of an inherited mythus he has surely accomplished. There is about all his work that element of 'nowness'—as he calls it—which he saw as an essential mark of all significant art.

The generation which has succeeded that of David Jones and the two contemporary writers he most admired (Eliot and Joyce) seems to have largely lost the historic sense. For David history was not something merely learned but the space within which he lived. For him the past was all contemporaneous; and this not because he or anyone else knew more than a few fragments of the past but because time is an unbroken unity within which we are situated. He never saw any present object—horses or daffodils no less than such human *signa* as Roman inscriptions or the Catholic Liturgy—without being aware of its dimension in history; a dimension not of natural science but of human experience. Perhaps a watershed now lies between these three great writers who could still use history as their sounding-board and a generation that seems more at home with ever-contemporaneous nature than with the records of man, to whom alone history belongs. I think of St John Perse, for whom history was itself a branch of natural history. Have we then already entered the new dark age foretold by Eliot and certainly also feared by David Jones?

David's knowledge was rooted in life; in his own life. This for him was the sole guarantee of its livingness. Because his Welsh-born father used to sing and speak to his London-born son in the Welsh tongue, not only the songs and words he so learned to love and to identify as his own inheritance came, for David, within the ambiance of things capable of being actually loved and known; but, with these, all the 'matter of Wales', its history, its literature, its mythology; for these are but an extension of what his father spoke or sang. So, when he himself became a foot-soldier in the British army, the old Roman oath, *idem in me*—'the same (holds good) for me' —held good for David and for all his companions in the trenches of 1916. The army he saw as a way of life, a human condition, the same at all times and places. He had no less a sense of identity with the Roman forces in the city of Jerusalem about the time of the crucifixion; with the Welsh cavalry defeated by the Saxons at the battle of Catraeth; with all armies whose condition he shared in his time and place, than with the Royal Welch Fusiliers, Company B, to whom his *In Parenthesis* is dedicated. 'Insofar as he has access to it, by however attenuated a strand of inheritance, the entire past is at the poet's disposal.'

For him the Catholic Church was above all the living experience of all Christians throughout the two thousand years of its history. 'Apostolic succession' was for him no empty phrase; it defines the difference between a living tradition and book-learning. Christianity has come down to us not through its books and monuments but through men and women and by 'the laying on of hands'—human hands of parents and priests of the Church. Only in Israel is a tradition bound more closely to life itself, being bestowed by birth into a certain human context. David never forgot that the words the people until so recently repeated in every Mass, *domine non sum dignus ut intres sub tectum meum*, had first been spoken, in the Latin language, by a real Roman centurion. Needless to say he was in despair over the liturgical 'reforms' and the vernacular Mass which were, in his view, a break with history, with the living and immediate daily presence of the whole past of the Church. David was a deeply and widely read man, but with a difference. Whereas scholarship is concerned with erudition for its own sake, David's reading was an exploration of his own living world, his roots and the roots of his own people. His knowledge was a part of himself, all contemporaneous because all an extension of his own life.

David writes as if his range of knowledge were just what for him had happened to come to hand; and in a sense this is so. Had his father's family not come from Wales, he would hardly have incorporated into his work all those Welsh names and place-names which give so much trouble to his Anglo-Saxon readers, who might fairly protest that the author should think of his public. He did also 'happen to' serve in the British army; and the Christian religion also 'happened' to be his inheritance, though not in its Catholic form. But as David would have seen it, however far some Protestant sect may have deviated, it still remains a branch, or at least a twig, upon the single tree of Christendom, of which the Roman Church is the bole. For David, who traced all back to beginnings, it was not a mere personal or aesthetic preference that led him to the Catholic faith, but the indivisibility of history; to have called himself a Christian in a less than total sense, to have dissociated himself from the total past of the Church, would not have seemed possible to him. Nor was he (though deeply studious of the Catholic Liturgy and of Thomist theology) sectarian; I have more than once heard him speak with familiar affection of those Welsh Methodist hymns which are likewise part of the cultural mythus of Wales.

But David Jones is not a personal writer: he is a national writer, a bard in the strict sense of the word. He invites us to participate not in a private world but in a shared and objective world, to which each of us is attached by the same texture of living strands as is the poet himself. The discovery of these fine, devious, yet living threads of attachment in ourselves likewise is powerfully effected by his writings. His poetic intention (as he makes plain in his essay on Arthur) is to make us aware of the whole historic context in which we participate:

To conserve, to develop, to bring together, to make significant for the present what the past holds, without dilution or any deleting, but rather by understanding and transubstantiating the material, this is the function of genuine myth, neither pedantic nor popularizing, not indifferent to scholarship, not antiquarian, but saying always: 'of these thou hast given me have I lost none.'

David was deeply concerned with communication, with a common language of 'effective signs'. In the Preface to *The Anathemata* (p. 25) he wrestles with the problem:

> . . . as I see it, we are today so situated that it is pertinent to ask: What for us *is* patient of being 'actually loved and known', where for us is 'this place', where do we seek for what is 'ours', what *is* available, what *is* valid as material for our effective signs?
>
> Normally we should not have far to seek: the flowers for the muse's garland would be gathered from the ancestral burial-mound—always and inevitably fecund ground, yielding perennial and familiar blossoms, watered and, maybe, potted, perhaps 'improved' by ourselves. It becomes more difficult when the bulldozers have all but obliterated the mounds, when all that is left of the potting-sheds are the disused hypocausts, and when where was this site and were these foci there is *terra informis*.
>
> To what degree, for instance, is it possible for the 'name' to evoke the 'local habitation' long since gone? I do not raise these questions in order to answer them, for I do not know what the answers may be, but I raise them in order to indicate some of the dilemmas which have been present with me all the time.

These are not the words of a writer who is really and literally making a 'heap' of fortuitous private memories; and in fact his three personal themes are also and at the same time ways into our common heritage. This is so with the Welsh material; for in Wales alone is preserved the 'matter of Britain' which is the common inheritance of the whole island. If the English nation still responds to any mythology it is the myth of Arthur, the 'once and future king', 'the Sleeping Lord' who will come again in the hour of need; and the allied mythology of the Holy Grail, that symbol hovering in a mysterious half-light between Celtic prehistory and Christian medieval chivalry. David did not live to see a young generation in search of the holy places of this island—the Glastonbury Tor, the Chalice Well, Iona and the megalithic temples. He would have been glad to know that he was not mistaken in his belief that the need for roots, the need for holy places,

127

is ineradicable. His faith that Arthur may return because 'what's under works up'; and his more radical faith in man as a 'sign-making animal' who cannot exist without some participation in a mythus, is certainly justified in this renewal of the search for the sacred, here and now and in this world. Arthur and the Grail, the heritage of those 'ancient Britons' who survive as the Welsh nation, are effective signs that still give to England as a whole whatever national mythology we may still possess. From the Welsh legends come also Shakespeare's kings, Lear and Cymbeline, and 'blessed Bran' whose head is buried 'under the White Mount in London' for the protection of the land. The epic battle of Catraeth celebrated in *Y Gododdin* was fought at Catterick by Welsh cavalry riding from Edinburgh to meet the Saxon invaders of the isle. David constantly insists that Wales is the custodian of the oldest living tradition in this island, our common heritage.

> . . . all things connected with this tangle [the Arthurian legends] should be of interest to people of this island, because it is an affair of our own soil and blood and tradition, our own inscape, as Hopkins might say—it is the *matière de Bretagne*.

In the Preface he writes of

> . . . the basic things: the early mixed racial deposits, the myth (mythus) that is specifically of this Island, the Christian Liturgy, and the Canon of Scripture, and the Classical deposits. I list these four thus for mere convenience. Clearly they comprise in our tradition a great complex of influences and interactions which have conditioned us all. To say that one draws upon such deposits does not imply erudition; it suggests only that these form the *materia* we all draw upon, whether we know it or not, to this degree or that, in however roundabout a way, whether we are lettered or illiterate, Christian or post-Christian, or anti-Christian.

These things are not so much ours as we theirs, since we are what the whole past has made us.

It is not necessary therefore that the reader should share the poet's background of exact knowledge: what does matter is that the poet is writing from such a background. The reader is aware, even when ignorant of their relevance, of certain names and allusions that we take on trust in the knowledge that these are firm foundation in a real and therefore in a shared world. They may or may not awaken our curiosity to follow up the clues the writing offers; in either case they establish a historical retrospect; and because they are pieces of reality they do somewhere link up with whatever similar, though different, pieces we may ourselves possess. The poet does not thrust his own facts upon us, but rather uses these to remind us of our own, often untreasured but nonetheless precious, fragments of the same totality.

'The points of difficulty are points of precision,' Peter Levi wrote in an essay on the poetry of David Jones; we can always trust that precision to lead us to what is significant; to some treasure preserved by his favourite muse, Clio, the muse of history.

Dr N. K. Sandars, an authority on the prehistoric art of Europe, has written some of the most illuminating of the growing number of critical essays on David Jones. For David, man is *homo faber*, man the maker. David follows Aristotle in his definition, 'Art is a virtue of the practical intelligence.' In an age when verbalization is overrated at the expense of other forms of expression the archaeologists are in some ways the best equipped to evaluate David Jones's craftsman's ability to read the human story told by all that man has made and done with his hands. What Dr Sandars finds in him is unfailing truth to the known; 'the well-made objects, the right actions' for him converge and concentrate, showing us the world as a 'logical palimpsest where ages and persons juggle their differences and are found to be one age and one person, man, the maker. "We were then *homo faber, homo sapiens* before Lascaux and we shall be *homo faber, homo sapiens* after the last atomic bomb has fallen." ' Destruction and destructiveness notwithstanding he sees the mark of man everywhere to be the hand of the maker. Dr Sandars instances one of David's 'signs'; an image in *The Anathemata* in which he describes a needle-case made in the prehistoric past before the last ice-age:

> An aureole here
> for Europa's tundra-*beata*
> who of duck's bone had made her needle-case.
> And where the carboniferous floor
> yields from among the elk-bones and the breccia
> this separated one
> the date of whose cause is known alone to *him*.

Dr Sandars comments: 'The needle-case *was* made of duck's bone, and it is necessary that we should know it, for the flights of duck from the glacier-dammed lakes were the stuff of life, the needle meant clothes, safety from frost-bite in the near arctic cold, the ability to hunt and to survive.' But to David this knowledge about wearers of the skins of 'thick-felled cave fauna' was not mere archaeological data: these people were our own people, *'beata'*, people for whom Christ died—

> that follow the Lamb
> from the Quaternary dawn.
> Numbered among his flock
> that no man may number
> but whose works follow them.

To quote Dr Sandars again, 'David Jones takes this great heap of the past and tells it not as history, but as something we have experienced in our own flesh; it is closer to direct memory than anything else. Collected memories, recollected experience of things that once happened, either to ourselves, or our parents, half-forgotten stories of a mother or a grandmother. It is his, and through him *our family* story that David Jones is writing down.'

In both his completed works, and also in his wonderful fragment *The Sleeping Lord*, the experience narrated is a collective experience. *In Parenthesis* is the more accessible, for the soldiers who together go into battle are individual persons with names and faces and turns of speech; of whom the central figure, John Ball (to all intents and purposes David himself), is one in that companionship of the army described by the phrase *idem in me*. David himself considered it a less important work than *The Anathemata*, and most of his critics agree, though not perhaps most of his readers. The hero, we feel, should have a human face. The collective central Person (who is a succession of anonymous persons) of *The Anathemata* does not awaken our love in the same passionate way as do the men of B-company of the Royal Welch Fusiliers. Perhaps because I am old enough to remember that war and its slang and its songs and those postcards from 'the front' embroidered with lace and the allied flags and can remember my father's school-boys who used to come to tea-parties on their brief 'leave', wearing that sour-smelling khaki uniform of 'the trenches', I cannot read *In Parenthesis* without a pain in the heart. *The Anathemata* one is bound to admire as a superb texture of words and images but it is not, to me, a moving book. To David I think it was supremely moving; its images for him were 'warm'; and perhaps to a truly devout Catholic they are also 'warm'; for he writes:

> In a sense the fragments that compose this book are about, or around and about, matters of all sorts which, by a kind of quasi-free association, are

apt to stir in my mind at any time and as often as not 'in the time of Mass'. The mental associations, liaisons, meanderings to and fro, 'ambivalences', asides, sprawl of the pattern, if pattern there is—these thought-trains (or, some might reasonably say, trains of distraction and inadvertence) have been as often as not initially set in motion, shunted or buffered into near sidings or off to far destinations, by some action or word, something seen or heard, during the liturgy. The speed of light, they say, is very rapid—but it is nothing to the agility of thought and its ability to twist and double on its tracks, penetrate recesses and generally nose about. You can go around the world and back again, in and out the meanders, down the history-paths, survey *religio* and *superstitio*, call back many yesterdays, but yesterday week ago, or long, long ago, note Miss Weston's last year's Lutetian trimmings and the Roman laticlave on the deacon's Dalmatian tunic, and a lot besides, during those few seconds taken by the prebyster to move from the Epistle to the Gospel side, or while he leans to kiss the board or stone (where are the tokens of the departed) or when he turns to incite the living *plebs* to assist him.

Yet it would be wrong to think that *The Anathemata* is a different *kind* of work from *In Parenthesis*. We may read the latter as a more than usually detailed documentation of an episode in the First World War; but that was not how the author intended us to understand his book. In a sense the theme is the same as that of *The Anathemata*, human life seen in the light of eternity:

> I did not intend this as a 'War Book'—it happens to be concerned with war. I should prefer it to be about a good kind of peace—but as Mandeville says, 'Of Paradys ne can I not speken propurly I was not there; it is fer beyonde and that for thinketh me. And also I was not worthi.' We find ourselves privates in foot regiments. We search how we may see formal goodness in a life singularly inimical, hateful, to us.

In these words from the Preface to *In Parenthesis*, there is not a trace of bitterness; still less of irony, or self-pity. Many times it has been pointed out that for David life in the trenches was not, as Yeats objected was true of many war poets, a matter of 'passive suffering'. Yeats rightly said (indignantly as he has been blamed for this) that passive suffering is no theme for poetry. For David Jones the situation of men in even the worst conditions of war was certainly not one of mere passivity; most of B-company are killed in action but they are not therefore cannon-fodder; they are still enduring the human condition with courage and fear, with companionship and patience, and their death is not meaningless. The 'good kind of peace' he saw afar off is not wholly absent from them, or from the total impression of the book.

The timeless moment of an eternal Now which is the theme of *The Anathemata* is already implicit in *In Parenthesis*. To this I will return. The first time David ever saw the Mass celebrated was at 'the front'. A priest was saying Mass in the wooden barn of some deserted French farm. David was not a Catholic at that time, but watched through a crack in the woodwork, noticing the hands of the priest as he gave the consecrated bread to the waiting men who were about to go into battle, probably to die; the kind of visual detail of 'making and doing' that as an artist and craftsman he was likely to remember. I have always associated with that vivid memory the *Ancient Mariner* engraving that shows the priest awaiting the people who 'go together to the church' in Coleridge's poem; those bread-blessing hands were, for David, both 'significant and warm'. It was the Mass and its timeless significance for humanity in all times and places, even on the eve of battle, that for him 'made sense of everything', offering to all who are born and who die 'a good kind of peace'. It is this which makes of David's characteristically humble disclaimer in the preface to *In Parenthesis* neither a complaint nor an accusation but a declaration of his Christian faith; none the less heartfelt because of the great distance he places between himself and his companions and 'Paradys'.

To return to *The Anathemata* whose theme is the simultaneity and unity of all human life in the eternal presence of God. The simultaneity of all those *signa* that David Jones found 'down the history-paths' is true not only of all that the mind brings together from past and future and near and far; it is also true for the Catholic Christian because the Mass is not only a memorial of the Sacrifice of the Cross, but an actual perpetual entering into the timeless event, at which all mankind is present; from the Quaternary down to the British Tommies on the Somme, and down to ourselves. Of God the centre is everywhere and the circumference nowhere. In amassing his 'heap of all that I could find' David was not amassing what Blake calls 'a fortuitous concourse of memories accumulated and lost'—as all memories are, when seen as belonging to a sequence of temporal events external to ourselves; rather he is gathering up Clio's fragments into 'the artifice of eternity'—to quote Yeats; a poet, incidentally, never I think mentioned by David, and in most ways his opposite—Platonic and mythological where David is Aristotelian and historical; cold where David is warm; majestic where David is homely. But all history is, for David, sacred history; it is the supreme myth because history is God at work in human existence, from our pre-human, pre-animate beginnings to the Incarnation. The centre which is everywhere is, in *The Anathemata*, situated in David Jones, hearing Mass said, probably at the Carmelite Church in Kensington, some time before 1952, when the book was published. From this point in time, place and person, the perspectives are created; but what is seen is the single indivisible human experience common to us all. This remains true whether or not we are professing Christians; for him—as for whoever understands the Mass aright—the Mass is a sign and enactment of the central human mystery, universal by virtue of our very existence and nature. If for other religions there are other rites this in no way diminishes the all-embracing universality of what the Mass signifies for Christendom. One does not have to be a Catholic in order to share the experience offered in *The Anathemata*: one has merely to be human.

One other very beautiful aspect of David Jones's 'actually loved and known' is the natural creation; above all the animals 'who praised God with growl and cry' but also the kingdom of Flora Dea, and indeed the rock strata themselves, the forms of hill and mountain, the 'creature of water' or 'hearthstone creature of fire'. For him man is not dissolved into the cosmic but the cosmos subsumed into the human. I remember his once remarking, about a picture he was painting at the time, on the difficulty of raising every element in a painting to the same degree of transmutation. His sense of the sacred extended to all the elements of the real world. It was a cow, I seem to remember, that was giving him trouble. Unless he could transubstantiate, consecrate, 'make over' every flower, bird and beast as at once itself and significant of the sacred (and for David as for Blake everything that lives is holy because it is the signature of God) he would not be satisfied. He loved the words of St Irenaeus, *nihil vacuum neque sine signum apud deus*. We are 'at one with that creaturely world inherited from our remote beginnings'. Others have pointed out the great delicacy of the extremities of the limbs of animal or human in his work; paw, or hoof, or the slender fingers of the Blessed Virgin in her Welsh wattle enclosure. It is as if he wishes to indicate to us that every creature is filled to its very claws and fingertips with its essential being. Although the animals cannot know God they in a sense 'are God'. Those fine fingertips of the Mother of God are akin to the innocent paws and claws and hooves he painted with no less reverence and delicacy for they are her kindred, her ancestors, she their flower. Of

133

the animals he writes always with a wonderful perceptive warmth. From *In Parenthesis* (after a reveille and the departure of troops on their way to the front): 'Only some animal's hoof against her wooden stall made a muted knocking breaking, from time to time upon the kindly creature's breathing.' Or the unloved rat:

> you can hear the rat of no-man's-land
> rut-out intricacies,
> weasel-out his patient workings.
> scrut, scrut, sscrut,
> harrow out-earthly, trowel his cunning paw;
> redeem the time of our uncharity, to sap his own amphibious
> paradise

'Creaturely' was one of David's favourite words; nature even at its most despoiled and bare is 'creaturely'; in contrast to machines of destruction:

> Field-battery flashing showed the nature of the place the kindlier night had hid: the tufted avenue denuded, lopt, deprived of height; stripped stumps for flowering limbs—this discontent makes winter's rasure creaturely and kind.

Man too is 'creaturely', sharing with the animals our bodily being and earth as our home. David would have liked to, but could not, find the machines and chemicals typical of our present culture 'creaturely and kind'. These perhaps bear too clearly the signature not of God but of man's destructive will to seem any longer part of nature. In the Introduction to *In Parenthesis* he writes:

> We who are of the same world of sense with hairy ass and furry wolf and who presume to other and more radiant affinities, are finding it difficult, as yet, to recognise these creatures of chemicals as extensions of ourselves, that we may feel for them a native affection, which alone can make them magical for us.

Knowledge without love cannot make them ours. Yet man makes himself somehow at home even in the trenches, as in this section of 'King Pellam's Launde', finding there creatures, however humble, to which his love can hold.

A man, seemingly native to the place, a little thick man, swathed with

134

sacking, a limp, saturated bandolier thrown over one shoulder and with no other accoutrements, gorgeted in woolled Balaclava, groped out from between two tottering corrugated uprights, his great moustaches beaded with condensation under his nose. Thickly greaved with mud so that his boots and puttees and sandbag tie-ons were become one whole of trickling ochre. His minute pipe had its smoking bowl turned inversely. He spoke slowly. He told the corporal that this was where shovels were usually drawn for any fatigue in the supports. He slipped back quickly, with a certain animal caution, into his hole; to almost immediately poke out his wool-work head, to ask if anyone had the time of day or could spare him some dark shag or a picture-paper. Further, should they meet a white dog in the trench her name was Belle, and he would like to catch any bastard giving this Belle the boot.

> John Ball told him the time of day.
> No-one had any shag.
> No-one had a picture-paper.

They certainly would be kind to the bitch, Belle. They'd give her half their iron rations—Jesus—they'd let her bite their backsides without a murmur.

Among those treasured things David kept in his room—his mother's scissors, a postcard of the New Grange spirals, certain china teacups and a silver teaspoon, a nail in a glass chalice (signifying for him the nails of the Cross)—there was a photograph of the little dog, Leica, sent up by the Russians in their first sputnik; a relation of Belle's.

And so with Flora Dea's kingdom, kindly to the dead who return to Mother Earth at the end of the story:

> The Queen of the Woods has cut bright boughs of various flowering.
>   These knew her influential eyes. Her awarding hands can pluck for each their fragile prize . . .
>   Some she gives white berries
>   Some she gives brown
> Emil has a curious crown it's
>   made of gold saxifrage.
> Fatty wears sweet-briar,
> he will reign with her for a thousand years.
> For Balder she reaches high to fetch his.
> Ulrich smiles for his myrtle wand.
> That swine Lillywhite has daisies to his chain—you'd hardly credit it.
> She plaits torques of equal splendour for Mr. Jenkins and Billy Crower.
> Hansel and Gronwy share dog-violets for a palm, where they lie in serious embrace beneath the twisted tripod.

In this sleep of the dead the Mother is still the kindly guardian, not an indifferent cosmic principle. Her 'influential eyes' give her a human face, and surely suggest the Blessed Virgin Mary as the 'gracious advocate' who turns her 'merciful eyes' towards mankind. As the Tutelar of the Place (in the poem of that name), she is 'but one mother of us all' . . . 'Gathering all things in, twining each bruised stem to the swaying trellis of the dance, the dance about the sawn lode-stake on the hill where the hidden stillness is at the core of struggle.' The Blessed Virgin in David's painting *The Annunciation in a Welsh Hill Setting* carries a foxglove for her lily and is enthroned surrounded with animals, birds and flowers. The painter would indicate that in the Incarnation all these are humanized, all become participants in the consubstantiality of Heaven and Earth. While so many moderns re-dissolve man into the cosmos, with David Jones it is quite the contrary; for him the whole cosmos is 'made man' when God puts on our human flesh, which is of one substance with the bear and the 'thick-felled cave fauna' and the older and less creaturely dinosaur and 'unabiding rock' and the 'terra-marl' from all which we are made. 'Incarnational' was perhaps for him the most significant word of all. What is 'capable of being loved and known' is God incarnate.

8

Cecil Collins, Painter of Paradise

IN writing about the imaginative world of Cecil Collins my difficulty is not that I know his work too little, but rather that after a friendship of more than thirty years I find it difficult to detach myself sufficiently from works which have become so much a part of my life, which have perhaps changed my own consciousness. The visitor often sees more of a country than the old inhabitant, and in Cecil Collins's world I am an old inhabitant.

That way of putting it seems the most natural because, above all else, the work of Cecil Collins is the revelation of a total world. It is a world of Imagination, but not 'imaginary'—on the contrary, since the world of Imagination is the supremely, specifically human universe, the 'kingdom' proper and peculiar to humankind, which we alone inhabit, it is the most real of all worlds. The human world is above all an invisible world of thoughts, feelings and imaginings, experienced not by the body but by the soul. That world does not belong to nature, nor can it be known or measured in natural terms, being of another order, differing from the natural order not in degree but in kind. The inner kingdom has laws of its own, forms of its own, communicated only through the reflected images of painting, music and poetry; which Blake called man's three ways of 'conversing with Paradise'. It is of the very nature of human art to make perceptible the invisible world of the Imagination; for from the beginnings of human prehistory the forms of art have been not copies of natural appearances (although these have necessarily served as the language of art) but, on the contrary, the expression of that inner order, of the structures, the energies, the living presences within the psyche. Yet so far has the modern West departed from that human norm that for many the work of Cecil Collins, not being naturalistic, seems strange: not as the avant-garde is strange through novelty, but because his work stands outside the 'movement' of modern art altogether. For him that movement is irrelevant; his work is a return to the age-old tradition of sacred art. As Cecil himself once remarked, apropos the 'modern movement' (he can be very witty at times), 'He who is not "with it" is against it'. Cecil Collins is 'against' all that is 'with it'.

Cecil Collins's world, then, is the interior country of the human Imagination, where rivers and mountains and stars, sun and moon and seas, trees and birds, exist not as natural objects but as imaginative experiences. It is a world of correspondences, not arbitrary but intrinsic; for in the Paradisal state meaning and being are indivisible, are the same thing. In that country, strange only to our outward selves but familiar to our dreams and imaginings, the inhabitants likewise are spiritual beings, whose faces are not faces of clay, who clothe themselves not in bodily garments but in the joyous adornments and regalia of their inner states—crowns, wands, robes, fantastic shoes not made for walking this earth, head-dresses of mountains, stars, crests; the dress of fancy worn by those joyous, bodiless beings who inhabit our worlds of thought. The aspects they assume are whatever we imagine, incarnating our fantasies, as naturally as an exotic bird adorns itself in its plumage. By our standards, but not by theirs, they are fantastic—are indeed pure fantasy. Swedenborg in his accounts of the spirit-worlds tells how the discarnate spirits imagine into existence gardens, landscapes, houses, and change their garments and appearance at a thought; with every change of mood these surroundings and aspects correspondingly change also; for in the inner worlds (as in our own dreams) appearances correspond to thoughts. So are the heavens and hells created.

Even in this world the aspect of things changes according to our mood. I remember Stanley Spencer once describing how he had looked at a certain painting of Cookham, and thought, 'That is the very essence of Cookham'. He had then gone out to look at the barn he had painted, but, he said, he could not find it again, for the aspect it had when he painted it was no longer to be found, being a place of the Imagination. Thus the imagination uses the outer world as the mirror of its moods. But in the paintings of Cecil Collins the inner landscapes are not seen in the mirror of nature. His living figures are vested in bodies purely imaginary, situated in places created by their thoughts as in dreams. And, as in dream nothing is vague or drifting but of a minute precision, so Cecil Collins's Angels and Fools, Oracles and Brides, together with their surroundings, are minutely articulated. Few readers of Blake have believed him when he affirms, in his *Descriptive Catalogue*:

A Spirit and a Vision are not, as the modern philosophy supposes, a cloudy vapour, or a nothing: they are organized and minutely articulated

138

beyond all that the mortal and perishing nature can produce. He who
does not imagine in stronger and better lineaments, and in stronger and
better light than his perishing and mortal eye can see, does not imagine at
all. The painter of this work asserts that all his imaginations appear to
him infinitely more perfect and more minutely organized than anything
seen by his mortal eye. Spirits are organized men. (K576–7)

—or again in *A Vision of the Last Judgement*:

In Eternity one Thing never Changes into another Thing. Each Identity is
Eternal . . . Eternal Identity is one thing & Corporeal Vegetation is
another thing . . . (K607)

In the work of Cecil Collins there is no possibility of confusion: we
are among eternal identities, never of corporeal vegetation. His work
is the expression of such minutely articulated visions as Blake
describes. Consider his *Procession of Fools* (1940), where each Fool is
the expression of the delight of his own fantasy, robed, capped,
beribboned, having no bodies other than their garments, their heads
and limbs by natural standards disproportionate but each the expression of some state of being.

His work is at the farthest remove from impressionism, whether
figurative or abstract, for the forms are clearly delineated. I showed
him once some work sent to me by a young woman who, attempting
'religious' art, had drawn those vague forms in which abstract impressionists express themselves. Cecil's comments were interesting:
'They are visceral forms,' he said; 'she is still in the womb; the image
has not been born.' Such depictions express not the artist's vision but a
failure to discover those 'ever existent images' which are, as Blake
knew, clear, minutely articulated, recognizable by all, since they
represent an imaginative order all share. They are not blurs into which
the spectator can project his own fantasies; not the nightmares of
subjectivity, but an order, albeit invisible, no less real, universal,
objective and recognizable, than the order of nature. Cecil Collins is
gifted with the rare gift of clear imagining which, as Blake also wrote,
is 'very little known'. He would agree with Blake that in copying
nature the artist does not discover but, on the contrary, loses the
clarity of visionary form. To quote again from Blake's *Descriptive
Catalogue*:

Men think they can Copy Nature as Correctly as I copy Imagination; this

139

they will find Impossible, & all the Copiers or Pretended Copiers of Nature, from Rembrandt to Reynolds, Prove that Nature becomes to its Victim nothing but Blots & Blurs. Why are Copiers of Nature Incorrect while Copiers of Imagination are Correct? This is manifest to all. (K5945)

As to blots and blurs Blake himself could hardly have foreseen—or perhaps only Blake could have foreseen—that a school of blots and blurs would actually and literally come into being, at the end of the cycle of materialism, and that the canvases of Jackson Pollock and his school would be hung in places of honour in museums of modern art. The genuflections of spiritual ignorance before this naked monarch have been amazing to behold; but not less amazing is the widespread inability even to recognize, when these are shown to us in such work as that of Cecil Collins, the true lineaments of our own inner worlds; shared by all, though lost by many and replaced by those rags and scraps, blots and blurs and old tin cans which litter our spacious, costly and pretentious galleries of modern art.

Cecil Collins is not of course the sole exception to this general decline. Stanley Spencer told me that he had in his mind all the pictures he hoped to paint; he did not live to paint all these, but had he done so, he said, all he needed to do was to put on canvas images clear in every imagined detail. That his paintings seem more realistic than those of Collins need not deceive us: the painter's imagination had totally transformed such memories as a soldier pulling a shirt over his head, or the tombstones of a Turkish burial-ground. Like the barn in Cookham these are imaginative experiences not to be found again. Or we think of David Jones, whose vision transposes nature into sacrament, transparent to the informing Imagination. For Stanley Spencer and David Jones this world is Paradise; for Cecil Collins the soul's country is not this world. Yet though his images are more remote from natural appearances than are Spencer's or David Jones's, this does not at all mean that they are more 'abstract': only that they are, like the images of our dreams, more autonomous. Free from the weight and opacity of whatever exists in time and space, the anatomy of his figures is not corporeal. Like the mermaid and the sphinx, the four-headed many-armed gods of India, or the masks of African magic, they express other human possibilities than those of nature.

The first work by Cecil Collins that I remember having seen was in the studio of our mutual friend the painter Julian Trevelyan. It was a small oil-painting of magical beauty. In the glade of a forest of dark trees a woman, robed and crowned as the beloved of some troubadour of the Church of Love, contemplates a cup, a chalice, of an unusual, squared shape; while on the ground a flock of birds, all turned one way (as real birds turn one way while feeding in the furrows), seem like thoughts come to rest. The lyrical, one might say musical, quality of this painting is in the tradition of Palmer and Calvert; deeply English, or rather Celtic, for Cecil Collins is a Cornishman from the land of Avalon—a lost land that continues to haunt our legends of the Grail, of the Sleeping Lord, of Merlin, of the Apples of eternal youth. This land is itself an expression of the Imagination and not to be found by taking a train to Cornwall. We recognize the painter as an English, a Celtic, perhaps specifically as a Cornish painter, not, therefore, by the scenery he likes to paint, but because of the quality of his imagination, which belongs to the semi-mythical land of Avalon; not by the forms, or the light (though these also have their affinities with that native country of the Grail) but by an unmistakeable imaginative atmosphere, at once local and interior. In *The Gatherers of the Fruit* (1955), the tree is formalised and symbolic as the Tree of the Hesperides, yet it has about it a tincture of the West Country; or rather of the West-Country race which created the mythological world of Avalon and the Grail.

In about 1940 I saw in the collection of Helen Sutherland a pencil-drawing of a landscape, with clouds and sea and trees and stream and descending rain, formalized and calligraphic. The technique was different but the country was the same as in Julian Trevelyan's oil-painting, the same clarity of image reached by a different method. In that country I found myself indescribably at home. Among Helen Sutherland's, Ben and Winifred Nicholsons, David Joneses and Christopher Woods the one Cecil Collins struck a different note. To Helen herself that note was never quite audible; but I, a generation younger than she and therefore more familiar with a whole rediscovered world of the psyche in the writings of C. G. Jung and through my own work on Blake, recognized Cecil Collins as belonging to the tradition not of 'religious' art (which Helen Sutherland could accept in David Jones) but of mystical vision. Once indeed that world had been familiar country within Christendom, but since Cecil Collins did not approach it through traditional symbols, but from within, that ancient holy land seemed strange and unfamiliar to an earlier generation whose expectations were attached to a specific iconography. I believe Helen even felt herself in some way threatened by these gentle beings who might be Angels but were not called so; and the nameless demands of us a recognition not all are prepared to give.

141

Cecil Collins is a painter of the sacred but not a religious painter, generally avoiding—evading—keeping himself out of reach of the orthodox religious, official and unofficial. Sacred art mediates the spiritual visions and intuitions of humankind; religious art illustrates the symbols of some cult. In the course of time the cult images become external copies of copies; spiritual art never copies copies but returns always to the source, to the Imagination, that holy land where abide the originals of which the cult-images are remote copies. Those originals are in themselves sacred, and to experience them is to experience that awe and wonder which belongs to holy things. There has been no greater loss to modern Western civilization than the loss of access to the sense of the numinous, the holy, which necessarily results from the loss of access to the inner worlds and the exclusive concentration—often for ideological reasons, as with the Marxist school of social realism—on the external, natural world. The sacred is no part of that world, held to be external to the human imagination and to possess, therefore, though it can be weighed and measured, neither qualities nor values. And yet the sense of the sacred is perhaps not only the deepest but the most specifically and characteristically human experience. When, as at the present time, cult-images fail to evoke these spiritual realities which once inspired them, it falls to such artists as Cecil Collins to renew our access to the source through unnamed forms, freed from all those rationalizations and misrepresentations which have made most religious art of this time banal and trivial. He believes that it is no longer possible to find a canonic entry into the eternal world, and his work is a lyrical penetration of that world.

The inner worlds are none the less real in our own than in any other age. By closing ourselves to those inner worlds we shut ourselves off from the possibility of experiencing the sacred. In religious terms the sacred is something imputed; in spiritual terms it is inherent within a certain order of experience. The sense of awe, of overwhelming wonder and love which we experience in the presence of the sacred mysteries is the sole and sufficient proof of their reality. Unless we experience these things at first hand we do not, in fact, stand in the presence of the sacred but outside the door of the holy of holies, which is within ourselves. Sacred art, whether Christian, Buddhist, primitive or, as in the case of Cecil Collins, an art of lyrical inspiration, is always a witness to the spiritual reality inherent in our very nature. There seems no longer the possibility of a collective experience mediated through the symbols of any cult; but in our age of confusion

142

and change the sacred can still inform the work of individuals who have access to the source. Such work can still serve to remind us, to reawaken us to a lost knowledge, a lost self-knowledge. From first to last the art of Cecil Collins is, in this sense, sacred art; as perhaps the work of Chagall may be so described, while the work of Rouault is religious art, a modern reinterpretation of traditional symbols rather than the spontaneous birth of living symbols from within.

I have heard Cecil Collins criticised on the grounds that his vision is not more fully incarnated; but at this time his task, as I see it, is to remind us of the source, of the reality of the inner worlds and of those living mental existences, those powers and intellections, which have their whole existence in the psyche. Only by removing the screen of 'nature' can this world be seen in its purity, rather than as it is reflected in the mirror of nature. This is not to say that Cecil Collins's art is an abstract art. Cubism is an analytical art and, seen in terms of imagination, comes to nothing, reveals nothing; it does not create images of the imaginative world but rather dismantles those forms of the natural world which have traditionally, in Western civilization, reflected the imaginative. So understood, its purpose is anti-imaginative, the reduction of order to chaos rather than some new insight into the Imagination. The work of the abstract impressionists, by contrast, is a kind of limbo between two worlds, neither of which is real. It would be impossible to take Cecil Collins's forms to pieces, as the cubists dismantled the human body, for their sole reality is that they are imagined; they are therefore totally and irreducibly real in their own terms, in their own order. Nature can be dismantled and taken to pieces, but not Imagination, whose forms are indivisible wholes.

My own response to the world of Cecil Collins was of entering a world infinitely familiar; a sense of homecoming. I felt no need of having this world explained to me, nor could any art critic have added significantly to my experience of it. It was a world I knew, which I entered less with the excitement of discovery than with the thankfulness of a return, of a confirmation of something once and for ever known, familiar and congenial. It is an art of *anamnesis*, inviting the spectator to remember regions within ourselves whose very existence we had forgotten, visiting them only in our dreams. I have since seen that Cecil Collins's work divides those who confront it into two groups; those who feel, as I did myself, an instant recognition; and those who say, 'I am afraid I don't *understand* these paintings, can you *explain* them to me?' To explain to those who need such explanation is probably impossible; one can but say, they *are*. This is in fact what Cecil himself said to a hostile critic who complained to him that the landscape and figures he painted didn't exist. 'They exist *now*,' was the artist's reply.

Much could be said about the painter's technique that could draw attention to the mastery of means, the variety of skills at his command. I once heard Alex Comfort describe such refinements of technique; and have heard Cecil himself explain how in his oil-paintings on board he obtains that luminous depth, reminiscent of Orthodox Christian icons, by varnishing over a base of gold, over which the colours are laid, and re-varnished in successive layers to give a luminosity found in the work of no other modern painter known to me. As with the icon Cecil Collins's paintings are not made for instant effect, but for contemplation, for yielding not all at once but little by little their rich content. Both the calligraphic delicacy and the depth of the luminous icon-like oils are beautifully brought out in the film *The Eye of the Heart*, made for the Arts Council by Stephen Cross in 1978. But to say that Cecil Collins is a highly professional painter and a master of his art is to describe what he would himself call the 'how' of his art but not the 'what'; from which indeed the 'how' proceeds, as ends must always determine means. He has described to me also how some of his best images have come unsought; like a very beautiful lithograph head which, as it were, designed itself upon the plate as the artist worked; designed itself, to be sure, in terms of the artist's skill to respond in terms of the lithographer's technique. Inspiration and technique must always go together, and every great artist will find his own technique in terms of the realization of his particular ends. To fix and capture forms of the Imagination is a painful labour; 'Only bad painters enjoy painting,' Cecil says, laughing his mischievous Fool's laugh and making a harlequin gesture reminiscent of Marcel Marceau's mime; which, by the way, he never misses when Marceau comes to London.

Speaking of Marceau, Cecil loves also certain French films—Cocteau's *Orphée*, and *La Belle et la Bête*, and perhaps above all *Les Enfants du Paradis*, he being himself a child of Paradise, understood by other inhabitants of that happy country, not understood by those who have forgotten. Once at a lecture in which he had been highly critical of the English contemporary scene (as he always is, quietly but unremittingly speaking his mind) a member of the audience asked, 'Mr Collins, if you have such a low opinion of us here in England, with what country are you comparing us?' The answer was unhesitating:

'Paradise.' His best paintings are all scenes in Paradise, depictions of the children of Paradise: Fools, Angels, feminine figures of the Soul, the Muse. Blake calls himself an inhabitant of 'that happy country'; for the soul's native country, its native state, is one of beatitude; perhaps that felicity which Plotinus says belongs to any life which attains its proper term of fulfilment, since in the fulfilment of our nature happiness consists. Mankind being a spiritual being, human fulfilment cannot be discovered in the natural order, but only in the life of the Imagination. Of that place or state symbol and legend name Eden, or Paradise, Cecil Collins's work reminds us. If it be objected that to depict a world of felicity is to 'escape' from 'reality' it could be answered that such felicity is the supreme human state, attainable only at certain moments in which we transcend our ordinary selves. In this sense the Paradisal vision is more 'real' than the drab or the bitter commonplace; whose drabness and bitterness indeed arise only from the sense we have of our absence, our remoteness from our human fulfilment; to remind us of whose possibilities the arts indeed exist. Only the Imagination knows that 'other' country. I have heard Cecil speak of what he calls 'the great happiness'—the title of a very beautiful lithograph—by which he means not the natural happiness of this world, but the supreme joy of the Spirit. The painter of Paradise must with pain and labour raise himself into that state of being, by definition lost to us with the Fall, hard of access, hard to hold, hardest of all to bring down into Shelley's 'atmosphere of human thought',

> . . . dim and dank and grey
> Like a storm-extinguished day.

It may be for some such reason that Cecil Collins has undergone, in the course of his life, many arid and unproductive periods, between brief but rich bursts of inspiration. Such painting as his cannot be done without an expansion of consciousness beyond the common level of awareness.

Not that he cannot create strong and terrible images of the contrast between the two worlds, of Paradise and the fallen world. His *Christ before the Judge* (1954) stands, in all the vulnerability of the spirit before the powers of this world, the Judge encarapaced in the armour of those who have forgotten Paradise; machine more than man, invulnerable because such cannot love. More often he works rather through a certain grave pathos than through the dramatic confrontations of tragedy. The beautiful gentle face of the soul looks out (in a

145

lithograph head) from what seems an encrustation of earthly clay, superficial and adventitious, since the Soul's true face is always beautiful. In another lithograph head of the Sun (of creativity) the mouth bleeds; since (Cecil quotes the words from Bunyan) 'God enters through a wound', and he explains this by the fact that as the Spirit enters this world it must contract, causing the wound of pain. In an early and seminal work, the severed head of Orpheus floating singing on the waves expresses a similar recognition that in 'descending' into this world the soul that does not forget Paradise must suffer; only those who have forgotten can be 'well adjusted' to the world as it is in its present 'fallen' state.

Yet, more characteristically, Cecil Collins's Fools, his Angels and his figures of the Soul walk inviolate in their own innocence, unharmed because 'the soul is its own place', as Plotinus says. So these gentle spirits are in some sense invulnerable. Contemplating them we recognize with shame how petty are our defences or weapons of defensive attack, the armour of self-preservation we habitually wear; for these wear none.

In his earliest work Cecil Collins was classed among those in his country influenced by surrealism; a surrealist in the proper sense he never was; not only because he was never, like Breton and Aragon and Magritte, concerned with the politics of revolution; but also because, in a movement more or less inspired by the materialist psychology of Freud, members of this movement were mainly concerned with images from the personal unconscious. For such images Cecil Collins has no use at all; he finds them merely boring. This was never the world from which Cecil Collins drew his inspiration. He is closer to Jung, and there are distinguished Jungians who appreciate and admire his work, as an expression of those archetypal forms which Jung discerned as figures of the transpersonal mental worlds. But, although he was well read in the main currents of contemporary thought on these matters, his inspiration owes little to such reading; still less to those psychiatric probings whose results are, in general, works rather of pathology than of vision. Nor has he anything in common with those enthusiastic 'counter-culture' artists who construct their 'mandalas' and other symbols from their readings in the fields of psychology and anthropology but who do not themselves see with the eye of the Imagination. In this respect Cecil Collins is closer to the French Symbolists, especially Odilon Redon (whom he admires) or to Gustave Moreau. Another comparison that comes to mind only to be dismissed is with Paul Klee. The atmosphere of

Collins's romantic symbolism is very different from Klee's fantasies, in which little spirits seem to look through the bars and barriers between this world and some sort of limbo where they are trapped like displaced persons in a concentration camp. They rise up (so Cecil put it to me) from below the threshold of consciousness like gnomes and earth-spirits of German folklore. This is not to say that in technical virtuosity and invention Cecil Collins is a better artist than Klee; but it can be said that his inspiration comes from a greater depth, from a source in qualitative terms higher than that of either the Surrealist or the Bauhaus schools.

Cecil Collins is a symbolist painter, but not a 'literary' painter, constructing 'symbols' from naturalistic images juxtaposed in the manner of Magritte and other surrealist painters, whose 'meanings' we read off like words in a sentence: a canon points at a screen composed of pieces of sky, a tree, a torso, as realistic as a coloured picture-postcard, and the 'message' is self-evident to the most unimaginative; as indeed Magritte, whose motive was in great part political, doubtless intended. As images these pictures are banal and once the meaning is grasped have nothing more to give; whereas the true imaginative image remains always itself, communicating not information but its inherent and mysterious beauty, which because it has being in itself is inexhaustible. Cecil Collins is in no sense a 'literary' painter because his world is created, down to the lightest touch of pen or brush, in its own visual language. His transposition is total, whether into his characteristic calligraphic rhythms, or into his no less subtle gouaches or luminous oil-painted icons. We cannot even say that he distorts or adapts natural forms when he paints (for example) a Fool whose head is larger than his body, or whose face is made up of stars and mountains, or whose arms and legs are wands and rivers, bows of ribbon or fragile magic boots: for these forms are not naturalistic at all, do not belong to nature in any sense.

It is not my purpose to give a technical or a chronological account of Cecil's work; this will no doubt be done by those qualified to write on these matters. I wish, rather, to situate this artist of genius within the context of the rediscovery, in this century, of the inner worlds, 'the eternal worlds' which Blake had declared it his prophetic task to 'open'. The prestige of materialist ideologies notwithstanding, the great change which Blake himself, Yeats, and now a whole generation heralds as a 'New Age' seems to be characterised, rather, by a rediscovery of mental worlds than by anything likely to be discovered in outer space. To this rediscovery

147

Cecil Collins's work is a significant and beautiful contribution.

Although in technique we may discover significant changes in the course of his work, the imaginative elements are all present from the beginning, though in different degrees. In the earlier works we find above all symbols of cosmic life, with human and angelic forms coming in later. In many of his earliest painting we find cells or embryonic larval forms hidden in the earth, but radiant with germinal potentiality; free-floating stars, 'centres of the birth of life', in the phrase of Jakob Boehme; forms of potency, latency, purity. In the painting in the Tate Gallery entitled *Hymn* (1953) we see the souls asleep in their earthly graves like seeds sown in the garden of this world. Even in these embryonic forms we are aware of the latency of what can only be called the sacred.

Many of these earliest paintings are landscapes, but landscapes of the country within. Yet they are the work of an artist who has been deeply moved by natural landscape, by birds, flowers, cloud-forms, wave-forms. But all these are in his work transmuted, musically transposed into another key. Thus in natural forms he shows us not natural appearances but the inner life that circulates in clouds and streams, ascends into trees and flowers, embodies itself in the figures of birds or Fools or Angels, a rhythm flowing through all these as the one life in all. We see *Angels Dancing with the Sun and Moon* (1950), whose cosmic rhythm is answered by the waves of a living ocean; or in *The Joy of the Fool* (1944) the Fool's heart (his love) hangs on a little tree beside him. In another of the same series of Fools, mountains and rivers full of fish crown the Fool, who in one hand holds a flower, in the other a living fish. Perhaps his best-known painting, *The Sleeping Fool* (1943) in the Tate Gallery, depicts a Fool asleep beneath a flowering tree, which extends a branch like a sheltering arm over the sleeper, while a feminine figure watches over him.

Each landscape is a lyrical expression in its own mode or key; yet each one gives us, at the same time, the knowledge that it is but one place or moment within a single universe within which inner landscapes and imagined inhabitants 'live, and move, and have their being'. Some of the landscapes painted in the 1940s are large paintings, rich and detailed and of great power; all are minutely articulated, self-born, visionary realities.

These landscapes are not made for the sensual or the sensible (using the word in its English, not in its French sense). They exist for—exist in—the inhabitants of our inner worlds: in Cecil Collins's terms, Fools, Angels and the Soul. There are occasionally other figures of the world of the Imagination: Kings (in the sacred, not the political sense, as fulfilled spirit of man, the crowned consciousness), Oracles, occasionally children, who are the new souls of those who have experienced the second birth, besides magical birds, flowers, trees. All these are concerned in the work of Paradise; they are the inhabitants of the Kingdom.

One might say that the Fool is the living spirit who enters this world bent upon some quest, in order to carry out some task or action, to make a journey or a pilgrimage, a quest whose secret nature totally engrosses him. Because those who act from instructions received from the spiritual world cannot be understood by those who behave according to the laws of the world of generation, the Fool's quest or pilgrimage, the Fool's errand on which he travels, is seen as folly, meaningless in terms of natural survival and natural desires. Like the Fool of Pamela Coleman Smith's illustration of A. E. Waite's Tarot (designed, it is said, in consultation with Yeats himself) the living spirit enters the world in magical invulnerability of innocence, guided, in its journey through this world, by the Spirit, by inspiration. The Fool does not possess wisdom, since the wisdom by which he is moved is the divine wisdom itself; he is possessed by wisdom but does not possess it. Yet the invulnerability of innocence is only a spiritual invulnerability: the Fool is poignantly, totally vulnerable; as easy to crush and destroy as a glittering dragon-fly. But though the Fools might be destroyed (by their total fragility, their defenceless gentleness, so the painter suggests) they walk in their own inner worlds, in the light of eternity; they never leave Paradise.

Cecil Collins himself has written his own beautiful apologia, *The Vision of the Fool* (1947). Pamela Travers has compared his Fools to those despised third brothers who in fairy-tales succeed in performing magical tasks where two elder brothers have failed. Intellectual analysis of fairy-tales, like that of Dr Marie von Franz, could no doubt situate Cecil Collins's Fools within some psychological category. But to explain the fairy-tale is not to create it; and to classify these living ephemerids can neither explain, nor explain away, their life. In any case, like Pierrot and Harlequin and Columbine their only existence is in their masks, expressive of some mood; they have no other existence than the part they play, as they enact our dreams for us. Petroushka is a figure of the fool that Cecil finds deeply touching. All these, being the likenesses of our imagined selves, are more real than our natural selves who can classify, but not create these people more real than our unperfected, indefinite selves.

149

If you ask Cecil what he 'means' by some composition he will never answer but is inclined to turn the question back to the querist: 'What do you find in it?' In doing this I believe he seeks confirmation, wants to know that his vision is shared. It saddens him, I think, to discover that to so many his invisible country seems strange or puzzling. He is far from affecting 'obscurity' which places him above the understanding of the uninitiated; on the contrary, he suffers at times from a deep loneliness in 'this land of unbelief and fear'. He knows that his universe of imaginative images is not a world of private fantasy, but a distant vision of the homeland of every soul. In the same way Blake appealed in vain 'to the public' in the catalogue of an exhibition scarcely anyone attended. Neither Blake nor Cecil Collins see themselves as working for an esoteric group with a secret language. In the long run the vision of the Fool will surely be understood because of its truth to the reality of the human soul. This in itself distinguishes Cecil Collins's vision from the private nightmares of surrealism or the drug-inspired 'trips' of uninspired and unenlightened subjectivity.

If the Fool is the human spirit, the Fool's companioning feminine figure is the Soul, the Muse, the *anima*. If the Fool is identified with his quest, his pilgrimage, the woman, always, in Collins's work, represents love. Her still, dreaming face (nearly always in profile) looks on, regards in uncritical wise compassion. The self-absorbed figure of the Fool is intent on the action he is carrying out, the quest, that which he must do. The feminine figure does not act, but is. She accepts, and loves. She is never maternal; her existence is in relation to the figure of the Fool, even when she creates about her some apple-garden or Paradise, or builds round herself a room where her lamp, her sewing, the bread and wine on her table, express her nature as the guardian of the sanctuary of homecoming. While the Fool is, typically, departing on a journey, travelling, she waits; or rather, she awaits. The place she creates will always be the expression of her love. A feminine being who does not love is, spiritually speaking, non-existent, inconceivable. Sometimes the woman accompanies the traveller; but more often she spreads her sacramental bread and wine on the table of participation; as do the painter and his wife in an early painting where the painter's wife is herself that sacred figure. Even here the beautiful portrait of Elizabeth is not naturalistic; it is a portrait of an inner likeness. Hers is not the sensuous beauty of Renoir's or Bonnard's voluptuous women. Cecil Collins sees the woman rather in those ceremonious terms created by the Church of Love. Crowned, robed, veiled, she fulfils some sacred rite by tree or fountain, lamp or grail; for woman, spiritually, is sacred in her nature, as man is, whether in his role of the Fool on his pilgrimage, or, as the fulfilled spirit of man, as King. There can be no confusion of these roles; no 'unisex', or even sex, which is of the natural body, whereas love is of the spiritual world. In Eden Adam and Eve had not divided themselves into multitude through generation; in that world men and women delight only in contemplating, in knowing one another in an eternal mode, without past or future, ancestry or progeny. 'Liberated' from love's secret places, sacred tasks, woman has all to lose; silence, tenderness, her own world created about herself where, with table and lamp, cup and bread, she awaits the beloved.

The third group of figures who inhabit Cecil Collins's Paradise—as they visited Adam before the Fall into the unconsciousness of generated life—are the Angels. These appear in his early paintings as cosmic powers, dancing with the sun, generating the rhythms of cosmic life. Later the Angels seem rather to be intellections, mysterious knowledge entering the human mind from higher worlds, concerned less with the energies of creation than with their traditional role as messengers, mediators between the human worlds and the inner worlds of the Spirit. As the Fool knows nothing but lives in total obedience to his unknowing; and as the woman knows only love, so the Angels are embodiments of wisdom. Since the Renaissance there have been virtually no serious attempts to depict angelic beings in the Christian West; this is an inevitable consequence of the closing of the inner worlds and the extraversion of consciousness into an ever-increasing concentration upon material nature. We may perhaps compare them with Rilke's Angels; certainly with no others of the modern West. Blake's Cherubim, and his Recording Angel of the Presence in his Dante illustrations, and the Angels illustrating the text of the Book of Enoch, are rather adopted from the texts he is illustrating than typical of his own imaginative creations; for Blake was a Swedenborgian, and according to Swedenborg all Angels are discarnate human spirits—his system had no place for the Celestial Hierarchies. Thus, while Blake's paintings abound in weightless spiritual beings, these are human spirits rather than angelic beings in the traditional sense, as these are known to Islam, and indeed to pre-Renaissance Christianity. The psychology of Jung indeed recognises archetypes which are objective to the human ego, and resemble the angelic messengers and divinities of the revealed religions. Cecil Collins restores in all their range and splendour the celestial hierarchies of the Angels. There are, he says, many hierarchies of Angels.

Speaking of his painting *A Wounded Angel* (1967), which represents an Angel, prone on the ground, enfolded in its wings, he said: 'This world is a graveyard of small angels; the great angels they can do nothing with—they cannot kill. There are many hierarchies of angels, and the small angels are not protected by the great power; the small angels are continually betrayed.'

Cecil Collins's Angels cannot be mistaken for human spirits; they have a grandeur, a solemnity, a remoteness, bringing from great interior distances that knowledge which informs them. In one superb lithograph three Angels approach, so distanced as to evoke the sense of their arrival from their far worlds, the foremost Angel rushing towards us, the farthest just becoming visible in its great distance. An oil-painting, *The Landscape of the Threshold* (1962), shows, again, three angelic figures, guarding three doors, the gateways between the worlds. Beyond these doors is the divine sun, pouring out the river of light. From that world all that is impure is turned back by the swords of the Angels. *The Angel of the Flowing Light* (1968) depicts a single monumental being whose eyes express at once knowledge, sorrow and judgement, but in a mode utterly remote from the human. Such a figure, too powerful for any secular art gallery, should be in a shrine dedicated to St Michael and All Angels, were there any such church, whose dedication to the Angels was more than nominal.

Another category of Angels summon worlds into being. Sometimes it is the woman who performs this act, as in *Dawn* (1964) we see a woman between two hills, summoning the dawn. Cecil Collins is supremely a painter of dawn; in the same sense as Swedenborg says that for the Angels the sun is always in the East, and the East always before their faces, let them turn which way they will. It is in this sense that Blake wrote that

> Those who catch the joy as it flies
> Live in eternity's sunrise.

As guardian Angels they may appear as travelling companions, like the Angel who accompanies the Fool in *Fool and Angel entering into the City* (1969); here the Angel is present in the role of initiator. In *An Angel comforting a Fool* (1957), the Angel represents the presence of another world to the Fool who suffers in this. In *A Wounded Angel* the Angel who has descended to struggle in this world has been wounded, and returns to rest on the ground of Paradise, bruised and broken in

152

its defeat in its combat with the mortal world. The Angels, in their mysterious grandeur, are Cecil Collins's crowning achievement; although it is of course impossible to separate the elements of his single universe.

Another group of figures, feminine, though not figures of the soul, or of love, are Sibyls, or Oracles. These may be of stately grandeur, as in *The Oracle* (1940), a pen and ink drawing. They are figures of power, some terrible as they communicate sacred truth—the judgement of the eternal on the temporal world. They are not malevolent, not witches, who are merely human beings with ill intent, and not instruments of higher powers, as the Sibyls and Oracles are. Like the Delphic or Cumaean Sibyls they seem to rave their god-inspired utterances, messages overheard by none.

Seldom, and with reluctance, does Cecil Collins work within the symbolic terms of the Church; but inevitably commissions of this kind sometimes come to England's sole mystical painter. Blake would have liked to paint great temperas in Westminster Abbey, for Jesus and his Disciples were his constant theme; but he was never invited to do so. Cecil Collins cannot be called, even in Blake's sense, a Christian painter. Yet his *Christ before the Judge* is one of his finest works. His Crucifixion with a procession of Fools is impressive but leaves with the spectator some of the unease that the painter seems to have felt with his subject; it lacks that total sense of authenticity, of inner freedom that characterizes his landscapes with Angels or with Oracles. A head of the Virgin Mary (1974) is beautiful and quite unmistakeably the Madonna of Western Catholicism; but again the artist seems stiff and inhibited, uneasy within the traditional iconography. Only in the altarpiece painted for a chapel in Chichester Cathedral of the spiritual Sun surrounded by the multitude of the stars (*The Icon of the Divine Light*, 1973) has he better succeeded in coming to terms with his commission without losing anything of his own vision.

I have done no more than indicate, in simple terms, what one might call the mythology of Cecil Collins's visionary paintings. Of his characteristic technical accomplishment, too delicate and too subtle to evoke the instant response (soon followed by instant forgetfulness) which captures the vacant mind of a public conditioned by the advertisement-hoarding and the television screen, I have said very little; this can await the notice of those who possess the expertise to write on such things. But to this visionary painter technique is a means, not an end in itself. Blake cut through the jargon of his day when he wrote 'one thing alone makes a poet—Imagination, the

153

Divine Vision'. Cecil Collins, whose techniques are not at all like Blake's, shares with him the rare gift of embodying imaginative forms which owe nothing to nature. At the present time, when historic traditions no longer mediate those visions which inspired their originators, it is perhaps only through such works as his that we can again experience the freshness, the numinous, awe-inspiring reality of the sacred. Those for whom nothing is numinous, awe-inspiring or sacred are less than human; since these experiences are of the very essence of the world of the Imagination, grounded in the human nature in which all partake.

9

The Chamber of Maiden Thought

WHILE I was still at school Keats was for me the supreme poet, in whose vision I felt I could wholly participate, an experience I am sure many of us have shared; for his poetry perfectly expresses youth's vision—it is 'a vision in the form of Youth', as he himself phrases it. But that is not at all to say that this vision is in any way partial or immature: rather that Keats had retained for long enough to embody it in his poetry that paradisal recollection of the radiant beauty of the world whose loss is called experience. Moneta, or Mnemosyne, Keats's own figure of Platonic recollection of some anterior perfection, is the goddess who in *Hyperion* initiates Apollo, the lyre-bearer, symbolic image of Keats's own poetic genius. I do not share the view that Keats had not yet found the range of that genius or that, had he lived, he would have written greater poetry. He might indeed have developed in ways unforeseen; but that he failed to give complete expression to the young poet's dream I do not believe. True, life teaches us more about imperfection, but do we ever see perfection more clearly than we do at the outset? I believe that those who seek to defend Keats by speaking not of his achievement but of his promise do him a disservice. Some have sought to defend him on the grounds that he would, had he lived, have abandoned the 'deliberate happiness' of his imagination to write about the sufferings of the world; as in his life he did indeed assume his share of human responsibility, in caring for his dying brother, his younger sister, and generously concerning himself with the problems of his friends. But such pleas could never reconcile social realist critics to the poetry he actually wrote. When I was at Cambridge in the early thirties Keats was rated low by the school of I. A. Richards, F. R. Leavis, and William Empson. That so-called 'scientific criticism' was grounded in the positivist ideologies then current; the very terms of such criticism discounted the Imagination. Speaking as his poetry does immediately to the imagination and not at all to the discursive reason, Keats was easily demolished by standards that left out of account all that was valuable in his work. By such standards he became invisible, like the magic

palace of his Lamia. Keats himself knew that mentality; and his aged
Apollonius is Blake's Urizen to the life, 'Aged Ignorance' whose
wisdom of experience clips the visionary wings of youth:

> . . . Do not all charms fly
> At the mere touch of cold philosophy?
> There was an awful rainbow once in heaven:
> We know her woof, her texture; she is given
> In the dull catalogue of common things.
> Philosophy will clip an Angel's wings,
> Conquer all mysteries by rule and line,
> Empty the haunted air, the gnomed mine—
> Unweave a rainbow . . .
>
> (*Lamia*)

There has been much clipping of wings and unweaving of rainbows
in our time, and soul's butterfly with her 'deep-damasked
wings'—Keats's goddess Psyche—taught to know itself a presumptu-
ous caterpillar. Imagination reverses the unweaving operation by
means of an alchemy which transmutes common things into gold. It
depends on which we choose to consider as more 'real', the perfection
we lack, and fail, in greater or less degree, to realize; or the archetype
of that never-realized inner reality by whose measure we see and feel
and know the actuality of common things always to fall short. No
social improvement—and this Keats knew only too well, young as he
was—can change the nature of the mutable world:

> Here, where men sit and hear each other groan;
> Where palsy shakes a few, sad, last gray hairs,
> Where youth grows pale, and spectre-thin, and dies;
> Where but to think is to be full of sorrow
> And leaden-eyed despairs,
> Where Beauty cannot keep her lustrous eyes,
> Or new Love pine at them beyond to-morrow.
>
> (*Ode to The Nightingale*)

Sickness, old age, and death; Keats had seen them, and looked
elsewhere than to natural life for Psyche's house; he found it—and
built it—in art. Indeed, for what else does poetry exist but to create
for us these 'gardens where the soul's at ease' (so Yeats, who understood Keats so well, phrased it), a 'rest for the people of God' not to be
found in the world of generation and death. And if poor flesh and

blood will always cry out that 'The fancy cannot cheat so well/As she is fam'd to do', yet Keats also knew that his Grecian Urn is 'a friend to man' just because it stands as an affirmation—an epiphany—of a perfection unattainable in natural terms, but real in the world of Imagination.

Throughout European history every reaffirmation of the truth and value of the soul and her universe, the Imagination, the *mundus imaginalis*, has been accompanied by a revival of the Platonic philosophy, whose ground is not, as for modern materialism, matter, but mind. The Romantic Revival is no exception. All the English Romantic poets were, in their various ways, Platonists. Coleridge and Shelley studied their Plato in the original Greek, Blake in Thomas Taylor's translations of Plato and the neo-Platonists into English. And what of Keats? Is the Platonic caste of his thought only a reflection of ideas 'in the air' at the time of the Greek revival, between 1780 and 1821 (the year of Keats's death), or was he something more than a poet whose aesthetic sense was acute to the point of re-creating his imagined Greece from the Elgin Marbles and the Portland Vase? The Greek revival was at one time considered chiefly in terms of the visual arts—Flaxman and the Wedgwood replicas, the housing of the Parthenon Frieze in the British Museum built for its reception, the publication of Stuart and Revett's *Antiquities of Athens*, and so on. What has until recently tended to be overlooked—I would even put it more strongly, and say deliberately dismissed—by a critical school that reflects current 'secular materialism is the accompanying revival of the Platonic theology. I say theology rather than philosophy because an early essay by Thomas Taylor—an essay that is at once a manifesto and a programme—is entitled 'On the Restoration of the Platonic Theology by the Late Platonists'. In that essay (included in the second volume of his translation of Proclus's Commentaries on Euclid) Taylor pours scorn alike on Deist Christianity and materialist science as lacking philosophic grounds and unworthy of serious consideration by a true philosopher. Taylor called for a new restoration of that great Western formulation of the *sophia perennis* to replace the vapid Deism of the day, and the no less naive materialism which was already its successful rival. Fighting as he did on two fronts, Taylor found few supporters; but his call to the young men of the new age to enlist themselves under the banner of Plotinus and Plato was certainly heard by the poets. From Taylor's translations and commentaries came that great influx of Platonic thought which transformed English poetry from the rationalist mode of the Augustans to the imaginative flowering of the Romantic movement. Taylor was an acquaintance of Blake, to whom he even gave some lessons on Euclid; and he had given a course on the Platonic theology in the house of Blake's friend 'Flaxman the statuary'—probably the basis of the essay already mentioned. Coleridge was reading the works of 'the English Pagan' at school. It seems unlikely that Shelley's misadventure in Oxford only coincidentally took the form of a rejection of the Christian in the name of the Platonic theology; and Shelley may well have met Taylor through their mutual friend Thomas Love Peacock who put Taylor in his novel *Melincourt* as 'Mr. Mystic'. Could Keats, anticlerical as he was (yet believing in the soul's immortality), and in love with all things Greek, have failed to discover Taylor, whose translations and commentaries were the only ones at that time available?

It is true that Keats nourished his imagination above all on the visual arts. In his book *Keats and the Mirror of Art* Dr Ian Jack has shown us many of the actual paintings Keats had seen (often in the form of engravings) in the collections of his friends Leigh Hunt and Benjamin Robert Haydon. Most of these, certainly, were the Greek myths as transmitted and transmuted through Ovid into Renaissance Italian painting, and so to Claude, Poussin, Canova and the rest. Dr Jack also paints for us the picture of Keats, in Haydon's company, strolling by candlelight among the Elgin marbles, not yet on view to the public but stored in a shed in Park Lane. The closeness of Keats's visual descriptions to these pictorial and sculptural originals is abundantly demonstrated in that fascinating book. Although Keats's Greece is at many removes from classical Greece, we may see his genius at work, penetrating, through so many intervening veils, to the imaginative essence of that great seminal tradition within which he himself stands in a manner no less authentic than do the Italian and French painters of themes from Greek mythology, all alike inspired by the Platonic philosophy of the beautiful.

Bernard Blackstone, whose book *The Consecrated Urn* is the best critical and scholarly assessment of Keats's poetry known to me, believes that Keats read Taylor's translation of the *Timaeus* in 1817, at the time he was writing *Endymion* during his stay at Magdalen College, Oxford, with William Bailey. Which if any of Taylor's other books Keats had read we can only surmise. Professor Blackstone thinks possibly Porphyry's treatise *On the Cave of the Nymphs*, which is included in Taylor's essay 'On the restoration of the Platonic Theology'. It is possible that he knew Taylor's *Mystical Hymns of Orpheus*, which include a hymn to Demeter listing many of the symbolic attributes of his own goddess of Autumn, and an essay on the Orphic theogonies which might have suggested some elements of *Hyperion*; though from internal evidence this is no more than conjectural.

The *Timaeus* is a dialogue on the theme of nature; with which Keats was doubly concerned as a student of medicine and as a poet for whom nature was a mirror of imaginative life and meaning, 'full of gods' as for the Greeks. Professor Blackstone has perceptively written that of all the Romantic poets Keats stands closest to Blake—a view by no means self-evident in style or temperament, but certainly so in the view they shared of the natural world as a living being and not, as the experimental scientists and their Deist followers held, as a material mechanism.

> I'll . . . shew you all alive
> The world, where every particle of dust breathes forth its joy

Blake wrote. And so with Keats, whose oreads and nymphs and spirits of the elements are not at all (as for the Augustan poets, or as for that interesting nature-poet Erasmus Darwin) natural substances personified by the simple device of a capital letter. As for Blake, so for Keats, Nature is living:

> A thousand Powers keep religious state,
> In water, fiery realm, and airy bourne

If both poets were familiar with the *Timaeus*, where Plato calls the world 'a blessed god', informed with life from a divine source; and also perhaps with the tradition, which preserved in Alchemical and Rosicrucian writings, the lovely living figure of the soul of the world, the *anima mundi* (as she appears, for example in Robert Fludd's *Mosaicall Philosophy*), the resemblance between Keats and Blake in this respect is not coincidental. Not indeed that Keats resembles Blake as a poet who fought a lifelong battle with Bacon, Newton and Locke, using all the weapons and arguments of powerful discursive thought: rather, perhaps, he was fortunate in never having lost the experience native to childhood of a living earth. He perhaps discovered in time, in the *Timaeus*, a philosophic vindication of something we all, in childhood, know without the assistance of philosophy.

The 'four elements' as described by Plato have little to do with the elements of matter as analysed and defined by chemists. These states

159

of matter have indeed more to do with poetry than with the scientific way of speculating about our world. This has been revealingly demonstrated in the writings of the French phenomenologist, Gaston Bachelard. Bachelard, as a scientific historian, set out to purge the language of science from all such animistic implications as gender, or of such phrases as acids 'attacking' bases, and the like. But in so doing he perceived, as in a flash of revelation, that the very terms he was seeking to eliminate from pure scientific discourse constituted no mere residue of inaccuracy but a whole poetic vocabulary expressing our living *experience* of nature. And basic in this poetic, qualitative experience—no less a mode of knowing our world than is scientific measurement—he discovered earth, air, fire and water to be elements not of material science but of poetic experience. He later wrote his famous books on the poetics of the four elements—of Shelley's use of the element of air; of the sombre stagnant water-imagery in which Edgar Allen Poe discovered the objective correlative of his dark vision; or Blake's mythological characters seeking to break out of the constrictions of a world of 'rocks and solids'. In Keats's *Endymion*, had he known this poem, Bachelard would have found in their poetic purity the four elemental worlds of imaginative experience through which Endymion travels: the jewelled caverns of the earth; the land-under-wave of Glaucus and Scylla; the airy ascent of the hero to attain immortality in his union with the divine beloved, as

> . . . into her face there came
> Light, as reflected from a silver flame . . .

As in the *Timaeus* the ascent from the lowest to the highest of the four elemental worlds is at the same time a qualitative ascent. Endymion must 'by some unlook'd for change/Be spiritualiz'd', as in an alchemichal transmutation.

In 'Song of the Four Fairies' the elements are charmingly personified (as so often they are throughout the whole European alchemical tradition) in a play of love; while in 'Hyperion' we see them at strife:

> . . . earth, water, air, and fire,—
> At war, at peace, or inter-quarreling
> One against one, or two, or three, or all
> Each several one against the other three,

As fire with air loud warring when rain-floods
Drown both, and press them both against earth's face,
Where, finding sulphur, a quadruple wrath
Unhinges the poor world . . .

From that elemental world the poet may learn 'strange lore, and read it deep', Keats writes. As against our scientifically oriented knowledge of nature, he knew nature imaginatively, yet in a detailed and intimate manner in which nature is not merely cognized but experienced; not observed, but lived.

There are indeed poets who observe and describe natural appearances as an external object of knowledge, as it is to science. Keats uneasily felt that this was true of Wordsworth and refused to be 'bullied into a certain philosophy' by the great elder poet. Nature was for Keats much nearer to Blake's definition of body as 'a portion of Soul discern'd by the five Senses'. Keats is the 'chamelion Poet', 'continually informing and filling some other Body —The Sun, the Moon, the Sea and Men and Women'. He pours himself into whatever he beholds—'if a Sparrow come before my Window I take part in its existence and pick about the Gravel'. This imaginative apprehension, this flowing out of the soul into nature, sets Keats apart from the descriptive school of English poetry. Indeed we might say that for him the natural world does not belong to the physical order at all, but is, rather, his experience of that 'great dream' of which he wrote in *Endymion*

> . . . I have clung
> To nothing, lov'd a nothing, nothing seen
> Or felt but a great dream! . . .

In a letter to Bailey he wrote more explicitly, more Platonically, of the *mundus imaginalis*, 'The Imagination may be compared to Adam's dream—he awoke and found it truth.' The archetypes of that world of Imagination (in the words of Coleridge) 'already and for ever exist' in mind, which discovers in the panorama of nature the correspondences of an inner world.

Like Spenser, whose work he loved, Keats had the gift of entering imaginative times and spaces which open into a boundless inner universe, which he adorns with all the minute particulars of the sensible world that eye has observed. We do not enter Endymion's forests as we set foot on Wordworth's dales and fells by looking outwards but by opening the eye of Imagination into a spacious and changeless world within the mind, of which external nature serves as a mirror which reflects back to the poet those archetypal forms which already and for ever exist not in physical nature but in the Imagination itself; without which, indeed, we would be unable to recognize and distinguish them; or (to use Keats's own image of Adam's dream) to 'name' them, and know what they signify.

This is a quality of all mythological stories, all fairy tales from time immemorial to Tolkien; and what are *Lamia*, and *The Eve of St Agnes* and *La Belle Dame Sans Merci* and *Endymion* but fairy-tales?—and so is that light-hearted satirical fairy-tale *The Cap and Bells*. In this scope and spaciousness Keats saw the very essence of poetic imagination. He liked poems to be long, and wrote (of *Endymion*):

> I must make 4,000 lines of one bare circumstance and fill them with Poetry'—and he adds, 'God forbid that I should be without such a task! I have heard Hunt say and may be asked—why endeavour after a long Poem? To which I should answer—Do not the Lovers of Poetry like to have a little Region to wander in where they may pick and choose, and in which the images are so numerous that many are forgotten and found new in a second Reading: which may be food for a Week's stroll in the Summer?

He understood Imagination as a region to be entered—the 'realms of Gold' with its many states and goodly kingdoms, Plato's 'garden of the Muses', which is Psyche's inner kingdom:

> Now it appears to me that almost any Man may like the spider spin from his own inwards his own airy Citadel—the points of the leaves and twigs on which the spider begins her work are few, and she fills the air with a beautiful circuiting. Man should be content with as few points to top with the fine Web of his Soul, and weave a tapestry empyrean full of symbols for his spiritual eye, of softness for his spiritual touch, of space for his wandering, of distinctness for his luxury.

He held 'That if Poetry comes not as naturally as the Leaves to a tree it had better not come at all'; a statement that may be compared with Blake's words that 'He who does not imagine in stronger and better lineaments, and in stronger and better light than his perishing mortal eye can see, does not imagine at all'. Both poets knew the way to

162

Plato's Garden of the Muses which can be reached only by flying there—'on the viewless wings of poesy', in Keats's words. That Garden is Adam's Paradise, the soul's native country. In his poetry Keats transports us there, and how familiar, how native to us it seems. For it resembles earth in all but its imperfection and mutability, the weight of body and years and distances.

Keats knew very well the regions of his own inner universe, and wrote of this in one of his wonderful letters:

> I compare human life to a large Mansion of Many Apartments, two of which I can only describe, the doors of the rest being as yet shut upon me. The first we step into we call the infant or thoughtless Chamber, in which we remain as long as we do not think . . . we no sooner get into the second Chamber, which I shall call the Chamber of Maiden-Thought, than we become intoxicated with the light and the atmosphere, we see nothing but pleasant wonders, and think of delaying there for ever in delight . . .

But beyond that point the poet perceives

> that the world is full of Misery and Heartbreak, Pain, Sickness and oppression—whereby this Chamber of Maiden Thought becomes gradually darken'd and at the same time on all sides of it many doors are set open—but all dark—all leading to dark passages—We see not the ballance of good and evil. We are in a Mist. *We* are now in that state—We feel 'the burden of the Mystery'.

To this point, Keats goes on to say, Wordsworth had come; and we remember Wordsworth's sense of the fading of the Paradisal vision. We may think also of Blake's Thel, the virgin soul, who is shown the 'grave-plot' of the earthly life that awaits her. She sees, as Keats saw those dark passages,

> . . . the secrets of the land unknown.
> She saw the couches of the dead, & where the fibrous roots
> Of every heart on earth infixes deep its restless twists:
> A land of sorrows & of tears where never smile was seen.

Keat's soul, like Thel, was never destined to make that descent; rather his genius was to give expression to the light and the atmosphere of the Chamber of Maiden Thought; not, as for Wordsworth, the world of childhood, but that dream of beauty and love that unveils itself to adolescence and ends with the descent into sexuality. Yet it is not true that Keats as a poet did not reach his prime: his prime *was* his youth, ' "a Vision in the form of Youth," a Shadow of reality to come'. Endymion is the lover not of mortal woman but of the archetype, the virgin goddess within the soul. Although he tries to argue that in loving the goddess Endymion had deprived his natural love (the Indian girl) of her due, and that it is necessary to discover the immortal love in and through the mortal, he fails to convince us. The passages on natural and sensual love are (to use his own words) 'mawkish' and uninspired. They lie outside that universe of Adam's dream in which the poet beholds the vision of the goddess, in an unfallen world, over whose dream-landscape there hangs

An orbed drop of light, and that is love.

John Keats the man was to experience the bitterness and anguish of the 'descent' of Adam from Paradise, from the dream of the beloved to the reality of a very different relationship with 'the girl next door'. The poet sought to discover the image of his soul in Fanny Brawne; who could never be that goddess, not because she was the wrong woman but because the soul-image inhabits the Imagination, not this world. Let us not make moral judgements about the necessity of 'coming to terms' with this world's reality: let us rather be grateful to the poet who holds before us the soul's first vision of love in all its intensity and purity. In a letter to his Platonic friend Bailey, Keats declares his faith in that ideal vision: 'That the Prototype must be here after—that delicious face you will see.' For the prototype dwelling in the recesses of the soul is the reality of which no earthly love is more than the shadow. The moon-goddess is ever virgin, though she kisses the lips of Endymion in dreams.

Lamia too, with her house built of lovers' dreams, is a fairy-bride whose rainbow fades in 'the dull catalogue of common things'. And the enchantment of those exquisite poems of first love, *The Eve of St Agnes* and *Isabella*, distilled from the world of Romeo and Juliet, depict a love that is total, in which each sees in the beloved not (as in mortal life—how all too well Byron understood this) one among many possibilities, but the only beloved, the one and all. *The Eve of St Agnes* celebrates the dreamed-of consummation of the first embrace; and although the lovers depart towards a future of which the narrative seems to imply that they 'lived happily ever after', what the symbolism of the images themselves tells us is quite otherwise. As they depart the magic has faded; the arras

> Flutter'd in the besieging wind's uproar;
> And the long carpets rose along the gusty floor.

The lovers have no future:

> And they are gone: aye, ages long ago
> Those lovers fled away into the storm.

As long ago as Eden; and the poem ends as the lovers go out into the storm through an 'iron porch' whose 'door upon its hinges groans', more suggestive of Adam and Eve's departure from Eden than of a happy future. The castle that had held the lovers' jewelled chamber is now 'be-nightmared' with forms of woe and mortality—

> Of witch, demon, and large coffin-worm.

The future of the young lovers is foreshadowed in the images of old age and death with which the poem ends. Angela the nurse 'died palsy-twitch'd, with meagre face deform' and

> The Beadsman, after thousand aves told,
> For aye unsought for slept among his ashes cold.

Dust and ashes; and how significant that the ballad Porphyro sings to Madeleine as he is about to bestow on her that mortal kiss in which the Paradisal dream enters corporeality is *La Belle Dame sans Merci,* telling of a world of post-coital sadness where

> The sedge is wither'd from the lake,
> And no birds sing.

Only in the archetypal world does beauty abide in her own universe; and it is of this inner world that music speaks, and poetry, and the imagined figures on the Grecian urn; itself virginal, the 'still unravish'd bride of quietness'. And it was this imaginal world inaccessible to flesh and blood, that Keats chose:

> Fair youth, beneath the trees, thou canst not leave
> Thy song, nor ever can those trees be bare;
> Bold Lover, never, never canst thou kiss,
> Though winning near the goal—yet, do not grieve;
> She cannot fade, though thou hast not thy bliss,
> For ever wilt thou love, and she be fair!

Body cannot enter that native country of the soul,

> All breathing human passion far above,
> That leaves a heart high-sorrowful and cloy'd,
> A burning forehead, and a parching tongue.

But for Keats Paradise was not unreality but reality itself. He asks his friend Bailey:

> —Have you never by being Surprised with an old Melody—in a delicious place— by a delicious voice, felt over again your very Speculations and Surmises at the time it first operated on your Soul—do you not remember forming to yourself the singer's face more beautiful than it was possible and yet with the elevation of the Moment you did not think so—even then you were mounted on the Wings of Imagination so high— that the Prototype must be here after— that delicious face you will see.

In the story of Cupid and Psyche Keats discerned something more than a fable of sexual love; for Psyche is the soul itself, and Keats, addressing her (in his *Ode to Psyche*) as 'goddess', did so of intent, for he believed the soul to be immortal. She is winged, too, wings being symbolic of her spiritual nature. His very voluptuousness is of the Imagination. In Canova's statue of the embracing lovers (known to Keats, according to Dr Jack) the sculptor has caught that timeless moment between dream and carnality, whose atmosphere is reflected in Keat's poem:

> They lay, calm-breathing on the bedded grass;
> Their arms embraced, and their pinions too;
> Their lips touch'd not, but had not bade adieu . . .

The poet vows to be the priest of Psyche and her love:

> Yes, I will be thy priest, and build a fane
> In some untrodden region of my mind.

Psyche's house will be raised into being by the same magic that built
Lamia's palace:

> A rosy sanctuary will I dress
> With the wreath'd trellis of a working brain,
>   With buds and bells and stars without a name,
> With all the gardener Fancy e'er could feign,
>   Who breeding flowers, will never breed the same;
> And there shall be for thee all soft delight
>   That shadowy thought can win,
> A bright torch, and a casement ope at night,
>   To let the warm Love in!

It is the country of the soul, not that of the body, which is 'holy land'.
Madeleine in her chamber too is depicted as a being of that world:

> Rose-bloom fell on her hands, together prest,
> And on her silver cross soft amethyst,
> And on her hair a glory, like a saint:
> She seem'd a splendid angel, newly drest,
> Save wings, for heaven . . .

(St Agnes)

And we remember how the anti-clerical Keats took a love-letter from
Fanny Brawne into Winchester Cathedral in order to read in a holy
place words that for him were sacred.

Although it is impossible to say with certainty which, if any, of
Thomas Taylor's Platonic writings Keats had read, there is one which
I would venture to guess that he knew. Taylor's paraphrase translation
of Plotinus's *Concerning the Beautiful,* which in 1792 you could have
bought for half-a-crown, was one of the most widely read of Taylor's
works, going into a second edition. Did this little volume play a part
in the formation of Keats's religion of the beautiful—the authentic
religion, so he must have believed, of the ancient Greeks of whom his
own consecrated urn is the symbol? Keats's declaration of faith,
'beauty is truth, truth beauty', signifies in terms of the Platonic
philosophy infinitely more than to the unphilosophic reader; and in
the concluding section of this paper I shall try to bring the light of
Plotinus's thought to bear on Keats's words and what they meant for
him. Plotinus in his Tractate equates the beautiful not with 'truth'
but with 'the Good'; but in Platonic terms the Good signifies the real,
or what is, source of being, the creative and ordering principle rather

than moral goodness in the modern sense of the word as the contrary of 'evil'; a fact which may have determined Keats's identification of beauty with truth rather than 'the good'. On the title-page of Proclus's *Commentaries on Euclid* Taylor has himself inscribed a phrase from Plotinus, 'There is nothing higher than the truth'; and in this sense there is no difference between the Good, the Truth, and real being. We need not, therefore, make any distinction between the Good (in the Platonic sense) and Truth (in Keats's sense). Taylor in a footnote to his annotated paraphrase translation says:

> It is necessary to inform the Platonical reader, that the Beautiful, in the present discourse, is considered according to its most general acceptation, as the same with the Good: though, according to a more accurate distinction, as Plotinus himself informs us, the Good is considered as the fountain and principle of the Beautiful.

In Keats's letter to his Platonic friend Bailey, already quoted, in which we find the poet's fullest affirmation of his thought on 'the authenticity of the Imagination' he also wrote:

> . . . what the Imagination seizes as Beauty must be truth—whether it existed before or not—for I have the same Idea of all our Passions as of Love—they are all in their sublime, creative of essential Beauty.

The whole context of the letter is Platonic, and seems to be taking up themes the two young men had already discussed in terms that are here assumed rather than argued.

Some may here object that, far from speaking of a Platonic ideal world, Keats here goes on to proclaim his faith in sensations and his scepticism about philosophizing; such readers would like to present Keats as a thoroughly down-to-earth poet; for he writes:

> I have never yet been able to perceive how any thing can be known for truth by consequitive reasoning . . . O for a Life of Sensations rather than of Thoughts! It is 'a Vision in the form of Youth' . . .

Yet the sentence continues in specifically Platonic terms, for this life of sensations is

> a Shadow of reality to come—and this consideration has further convinced me for it has come as auxiliary to another favourite Speculation of mine, that we shall enjoy ourselves here after by having what we called happi-

ness on Earth repeated in a finer tone and so repeated—And yet such a fate can only befall those who delight in Sensation rather than hunger as you do after Truth. Adam's dream will do here and seems to be a conviction that Imagination and its empyreal reflection is the same as human Life and its Spiritual repetition.

'Beauty *is* truth' could well be Keats's clinching of this running argument with Bailey, the abstract thinker for whom truth was an abstraction. What then are we to make of the apparent paradox of this poet who delights in sensation yet relates the experience of the senses to an empyrean and spiritual order? We may compare Keats here again with Blake, who wrote that sense is 'the Eye of Imagination'. Commenting on a passage from Berkeley's *Siris* in which the philosopher argues that 'all beings are in the soul' and that it is 'the soul that imparteth forms to matter', Blake wrote in the margin:

This is my Opinion, but Forms must be apprehended by Sense or the Eye of Imagination.

Blake then goes on to write of 'the Heathen or Platonic Philosophy, which blinds the Eye of Imagination, The Real Man'. Unjust as Blake's words are to the Platonists, we catch an echo here of Keats's disagreement with Bailey, who tried (as Blake implies the philosophers also tried) to reach truth by abstract thought. Elsewhere Blake wrote that the inspired poets (Homer, Virgil, Milton and the Bible) addressed their writings to the Imagination, 'which is Spiritual Sensation & but mediately to the Understanding or Reason'. For Keats, as for Blake, this sensible world is 'one continued vision of the Imagination', and 'Nature is Imagination itself'. The parallel is so striking that we are inclined to look for some common source; which was, I believe, Plotinus, who argues that the perception of the beautiful is unmediate through sense. Such is the opening theme of his Tractate:

Beauty, for the most part, consists in objects of sight: but it is also received through the ears, by the skilful composition of words, and the consonant proportions of sounds; for in every species of harmony, beauty is to be found. And if we rise from sense into the regions of the soul, we shall there perceive studies and offices, actions and habits, sciences and virtues, invested with a much larger proportion of beauty. But whether there is, above these, a still higher beauty, will appear in its investigation.

169

And Plotinus goes on to consider

What is it then, which causes bodies to appear fair to the sight, sounds beautiful to the ear, and science and virtue lovely to the mind? May we not enquire after what manner they all partake of beauty?

Keats wrote of sensation 'repeated in a finer tone'; and Blake wrote on the same theme—the Imagination:

There Exist in that Eternal World the Permanent Realities of Every Thing which we see reflected in this Vegetable Glass of Nature.

Blake, for all his denunciation of the Heathen Philosophers is here writing pure Platonism; and so is Keats when he speaks of his 'speculation'. Keats wrote in playful mood of this archetypal paradise of the Platonic 'eternal forms' whose imperfect reflections we meet in nature; there the poets are

Seated on Elysian lawns
Brows'd by none but Dian's fawns;
Underneath large blue-bells tented,
Where the daisies are rose-scented,
And the rose herself has got
Perfume which on earth is not;
Where the nightingale doth sing
Not a senseless, tranced thing,
But divine melodious truth;
Philosophic numbers smooth;
Tales and golden histories
Of heaven and its mysteries.

(Ode)

But that the poet could play with the idea is not to say that 'happiness on Earth repeated in a finer tone' was not therefore an idea to which he had given more serious thought; in Ode to a Nightingale the bird does indeed sing 'divine melodious truth'; it sings with the voice of Imagination itself. And for his speculation Keats can claim the support of Plotinus himself. It is not reason but sense that perceives the beautiful; about which indeed reason can tell us nothing, as Keats and Blake both understood. So far from placing him among the down-to-earth poets we see that Keats's words 'O for a life of Sensation rather than thoughts!' place him among the Platonic lovers, whom

170

Plato in the *Phaedo* describes as proceeding from the love of earthly to the love of heavenly beauty. Sense, not thought, is the organ which first perceives that beauty 'repeated in a finer tone'. How important this idea was to Keats we know from those lines in his *Ode on a Grecian Urn*:

> Heard melodies are sweet, but those unheard
>   Are sweeter; therefore, ye soft pipes, play on;
> Not to the sensual ear, but, more endear'd,
>   Pipe to the spirit ditties of no tone.

The unheard melody is not a faint overtone of sense but, as Plotinus taught, the higher reality of which the lower is an echo or reflection inviting the lover of beauty to ascend:

> . . . He ne'er is crown'd
> With immortality, who fears to follow
> Where airy voices lead . . .

And we remember also the singer of the 'old melody' that awakened in the poet the imaginative certainty 'that the Prototype must be here after—that delicious face you will see'.

Plato has written in the *Phaedrus* of the three ways to knowledge, that of the philosophers, of the musical souls, and of the lovers. Keats was, surely, of all English poets the one who most closely conforms to the type of the lover who, from the adoration of mortal beauty, ascends to the discernment of 'the beautiful itself'. For beauty is perceptible only by love; it is the object of love; and Plotinus is true to Plato's teaching when he writes of the awakening of the affections which

> ought to be excited about true beauty, as admiration and sweet astonishment; desire, also; and love, and a pleasant trepidation.

So it was with Keats; and it ill becomes those less sensitive to the divine essence of beauty to reproach him with the excess of his love for Fanny Brawne. All souls, Plotinus says (in Taylor's paraphrase), are indeed affected by beauty,

> but those the most who have the strongest propensity to their love; as it likewise happens about corporeal beauty: for all equally perceive beautiful corporeal forms, yet all are not equally excited, but lovers in the greatest degree.

171

A religion of beauty is alien alike to Christian puritanism and positivist materialism; but Keats had in this respect rediscovered the very essence of the Greek vision of the holy quality inherent in beauty; the religion that made Helen the daughter of Zeus a goddess, on account of her beauty alone.

For Keats, as for the Greeks, the lover's vision of the beauty of the beloved is a mode of spiritual knowledge and leads to the perception of 'the good itself'.

Plotinus seeks to penetrate to the mystery of sensible beauty, asking the question 'What is the beauty of bodies?', and he answers:

> It is something, which, at first view, presents itself to sense; and which the soul familiarly apprehends, and eagerly embraces, as if it were allied to itself. But when it meets with the deformed, it hastily starts from the view, and retires abhorrent from its discordant nature.

Those who insist that we ought to look squarely at the far from beautiful 'reality' of the world of sickness, old age and death, who in nature see above all conflict and decay, seek to make the doctrine of beauty seem trivial. These ideologies deny the soul and its universe, the *mundus imaginalis*. But the Platonists see beauty otherwise, as the principle which leads the soul to self-knowledge by discovering through sense, the eye of Imagination, its own nature, and the nature of the Good. In the words of Plotinus

> . . . since the soul in its proper state ranks according to the most excellent essence in the order of things, when it perceives any object related to itself, or the mere vestige of a relation, it congratulates itself on the pleasing event, and is astonished with the striking resemblance, enters deep into its essence, and, by rousing its dormant powers, at length perfectly recollects its kindred and allies.

Psyche was for the Greeks, as for Keats, a divine being. Because body, as Plotinus writes, 'becomes beautiful through the communion supernally proceeding from divinity', he supports with his authority Keats's leap in the dark, his trust in the immediate perception of sensation; for

> . . . the soul, by her innate power, than which nothing is more powerful, in judging its proper concerns . . . acknowledges the beauty of forms. And, perhaps, its knowledge in this case arises from its accommodating its internal ray of beauty to form, and trusting to this in its judgment . . .

No rational process is required, only the immediate discernment of beauty.

Keats's lovers, too perfect in every feature for the warty world—lovers thrice distilled, as Dr Jack has shown us, through the world of art—do nevertheless conform to his 'Vision in the form of Youth'; and here again Plotinus is with Keats in praising the beauty of youth. Against those who in youth have seen only its transience, Keats, with Plotinus, saw in the beauty of youth an image of soul's immortal lineaments; writing that

> . . . virtue shining forth in youth is lovely, because consonant to the true virtue, which lies deep in the soul.

Why else do we love fairy-tales, those archetypal stories of the soul, let the proponents of anti-heroes and anti-art say what they will? Yeats, whose own writings are so full of echoes of Keats—and of Plotinus also—understood that a beautiful body is the likeness of the soul:

> All thought becomes an image and the soul
> Becomes a body: that body and that soul
> Too perfect at the full to lie in a cradle
> Too lonely for the traffic of the world:
> Body and soul cast out and cast away
> Beyond the visible world.
>
> (*The Phases of the Moon*)

Plotinus concludes of the beauties of sense that they 'like images and shadows flowing into matter, adorn with spectacles of beauty its formless being, and strike the respective senses with wonder and delight'. How much more philosophical, how much more profoundly true to our human nature, is Keats, poet of sensible beauty, than are those arrogant detractors who have never looked so high.

For the soul is, according to the Platonic tradition, in its nature beautiful, belonging as it does to the order of forms, of which bodies are more or less perfect copies or imprints. It is immersion in matter that obscures the inherent beauty of its lovely forms:

> And as the gold is deformed by the adherence of earthly clods, which are no sooner removed than on a sudden the gold shines forth in its native purity; and then becomes beautiful when separated from natures foreign from its own

—so the soul, when separated from the 'base stains' of its immersion in a material world will 'shine forth in its native beauty'.

The soul, according to Plotinus, in its true nature, 'wholly participates of that divine nature which is the fountain of loveliness, and of whatever is allied to the beautiful and fair' and 'the beautiful itself is that which is called beings; and turpitude is of a different nature, and participates more in non-entity than being'. Of what value is an art that shows us only the absence of the unifying and illuminating life of the soul of whom Spenser wrote 'For soul is form and doth the body make'? What young girl, reading the story of Cinderella, identifies herself with the ugly sisters?

But every Platonic school of art, whether the sculptors of Parthenon Frieze Keats with his friend Haydon studied in such detail, or the Renaissance painters, or the English Romantic poets and painters—Keats and Shelley and Blake, Calvert and Samuel Palmer—show the soul its own obscured features. And what higher function has art than to show us our deepest reality?

> Thou, silent form, dost tease us out of thought
> As doth eternity: Cold Pastoral!
> When old age shall this generation waste,
> Thou shalt remain, in midst of other woe
> Than ours, a friend of man, to whom thou say'st,
> 'Beauty is truth, truth beauty,—that is all
> Ye know on earth, and all ye need to know.'

Plotinus's Tractate ends with an eloquent passage describing how the divine principle, the 'fountain of Good', 'everywhere widely diffusing around the streams of beauty', is called 'the beautiful itself because beauty is its immediate offspring'. Therefore it is not either necessary or possible to separate beauty from its principle, and 'you may place the first beautiful and the good in the same principle'. The aspect—beauty—is inseparable from its principle—the Good. If Keats had not read Plotinus's *Concerning the Beautiful* the conformity of his own view of the supreme character of the beautiful to the philosophy of Plotinus would be nothing short of miraculous; and I therefore believe that he had both read and loved this book.

Taylor adds a long footnote in which he attacks 'materialism and its attendant sensuality' as the philosophy in vogue, then as now. Keats, who proclaimed the truth of beauty, was not ignorant of the alternative ideologies; he had, on the contrary, too much reason to know the

174

discrepancy between the archetypal perfection and the so-called 'reality' of the world. For many reasons—and among them, I believe, the specific character of his own genius—Keats was to die young. But, whatever he might have become, it remains true that he gave perfect and complete expression to his 'Vision in the form of Youth', in all its scope and depth. His work lacks nothing of completeness; to what he knew of the imaginal and its beauty experience could have added nothing—could only have misted and obscured that bright Chamber of Maiden Thought. For, as Yeats writes,

> What portion of the world can the artist have
> Who has awakened from the common dream
> But dissipation and despair?

—and Yeats goes on to write of Keats, whose work he had so deeply loved and so well understood:

Hic　　　　　　　　　　　　　　　　　　　　　　And yet
　　　　No one denies to Keats love of the world;
　　　　Remember his deliberate happiness.
Ille　　His art is happy, but who knows his mind?
　　　　I see a schoolboy when I think of him,
　　　　With face and nose pressed to a sweet-shop window,
　　　　For certainly he sank into his grave
　　　　His senses and his heart unsatisfied,
　　　　And made—being poor, ailing and ignorant,
　　　　Shut out from all the luxury of the world,
　　　　The coarse-bred son of a livery-stable keeper—
　　　　Luxuriant song . . .

　　　　　　　　　　　　　　　　　　　　　　(Ego Dominus Tuus)

10

The Beautiful and the Holy

W HEN I was invited to take part in this conference whose theme is 'Beauty and Psyche' I decided—since I had already written on the idea of the beautiful according to the neo-Platonic tradition which has been the inspiration of so much English poetry—to talk about William Blake; not merely because he is the poet whose work I know most intimately, but because Blake, more than any other English poet, proclaims and illustrates a vision in which the world is transformed, transfigured in that radiance in which we recognise the aspect of 'the beautiful'. But, although Blake's text gives so strong an impression of that transfiguration, radiance and Paradisal perfection which we call beauty, he seldom uses the word 'beauty' or 'the beautiful' and then only in a limited sense. This is all the more strange because Blake was, through the writings and translations of his contemporary and acquaintance, Thomas Taylor the Platonist, familiar with the Platonic literature in which the idea of the beautiful is developed; and in particular with Plotinus's *Concerning the Beautiful*, in Taylor's paraphrase translation. Blake borrowed much from the neo-Platonists and it is therefore all the more striking that he did not borrow the Platonic concept of the beautiful. The word that resounds through Blake's writings as his epithet for the highest glory of the visible world is, instead, the 'holy'. The words, 'Everything that lives is holy' carry the power, and contain the essence of, his whole teaching. They derive not from sentimental enthusiasm nor from strong emotion, but from a total metaphysical vision of the nature of 'life'.

When many years ago I wrote a paper entitled 'The Use of the Beautiful' I took as my starting-point Plotinus's conception of the beautiful as whatever is congruous with forms inherent not in nature but in the soul itself. Works of art are embodiments of those inherent forms, whether in paintings or music or architecture or any of the other arts. When Yeats wrote that line which so troubles the 'young in one another's arms'—

> Once out of nature I will never take
> My bodily form from any natural thing

—he was affirming the function of the arts as the embodiment of an invisible order. This order he saw exemplified in those works of Byzantine architects and goldsmiths of whom he wrote that their vision made 'the work of many seem the work of one', made 'building, picture, pattern, metalwork of rail and lamp, seem but a single image; and this vision, this proclamation of their invisible master had the Greek nobility'; for it was an expression of the Greek view that the true function of the arts is to embody and reflect that inner order. The intelligible order we recognize as beautiful corresponds, according to the Platonic philosophers—and their thought still lived on in Byzantine Greece—to originals 'laid up in heaven', as Plato says. This universal harmony orders the whole universe, and its reflection may be discovered, as in a mirror, in the object of knowledge we call nature.

This universal harmony, be it in the mind or in the mind's object, nature, resolves itself, for the Greeks, into number; not, indeed, numbers considered in a merely quantitative sense, as by modern science, but as principles whose interplay is expressed in forms, visible or invisible. The Pythagorean 'gods' are numbers, so understood as the universal ordering powers. The Greek concept of beauty relates above all to whatever has form; it is, in the final analysis, those aspects assumed by the gods of number.

Blake was certainly thinking of this Pythagorean and Platonic tradition when he wrote 'the Gods of Greece & Egypt were Mathematical Diagrams—see Plato's works'. Blake's God is not a mathematical diagram, although he is most certainly an 'invisible master' in Yeats's sense. The terms of Blake's equation are not, as for the Greeks, number and beauty, but 'life' and the 'holy'.

Both terms—the beautiful and the holy—denote some supreme excellence that satisfies the beholder in an ineffable manner; neither term can be quantified, both exist only in being experienced. To the beautiful we give an assent which goes far beyond conscious judgement. We experience beauty as satisfying something innate in us which assents to some painted form or piece of music as if we had known it always. Some image, seen or heard, corresponds to an idea latent in ourselves.

But in neither term of Blake's equation, 'everything that lives' and the 'holy', is there any implication of form. We are no longer in the paradigmatic Platonic universe, in which the creatures of time are the 'moving images' of an eternal perfection; that which moves in time is, relatively to the unity of the Platonic eternal paradigm, imperfect, a

177

fleeting shadow of the changeless order of the number and proportion, of what Yeats calls 'unageing intellect'.

From the outset Blake, his knowledge and extensive borrowings from the Platonists notwithstanding, placed himself in another tradition: biblical rather than classical, prophetic rather than philosophic; a tradition in which not form but energy is the ground—being itself, the I AM of the God of Moses. Blake's essence of 'life' is close to the *sat-chit-ananda*, the 'being-consciousness-bliss' of Vedanta. Indeed the three terms of this Vedantic definition of the ultimate ground are all to be found in Blake's definition of the essence of life, which for him also is 'bliss' in the same ultimate sense as the Vedantic *ananda*, the essence of being itself, in the very nature of what he calls life. Blake's words are the conclusion of an eloquent passage in which he has invoked the themes of 'bliss' and 'eternal joy':

> 'And trees & birds & beasts & men behold their eternal joy.
> 'Arise, you little glancing wings, and sing your infant joy!
> Arise, and drink your bliss, for everything that lives is holy!' (K195)

Beauty is a word Blake uses mostly in an adjectival sense; the four functions of the human psyche—Blake's 'four Zoas'—'in beautiful Paradises expand'. These 'paradises' are four respective 'worlds' apprehended by reason, sense, feeling and intuition. The appearances of the earth thus apprehended are woven by the 'daughters of Albion'

> 'As a beautiful Veil, so these Females shall fold & unfold,
> 'According to their will, the outside surface of the Earth,
> 'An outside shadowy Surface superadded to the real Surface
> 'Which is unchangeable for ever & ever . . .' (K728)

The 'outside shadowy surface' is the 'veil' of sensible appearances, here called by Blake 'beautiful'. Beauty is itself a veil of appearances; those paradises created by the Four Zoas as a *maya*. In Blake's description of his painting of the three Britons who escaped alive in the last battle of King Arthur—'the Strongest Man, the Beautifullest Man, and the Ugliest Man'—the 'Beautiful Man represents the human pathetic, which was in the wars of Eden divided into male and female'. It is in the world of generation that the souls assume their male or female 'garments' and thus beauty is above all something perceived by the senses, it resides in bodily form. Blake does not forget Plato when he writes of the same painting:

178

The Beauty proper for sublime art is lineaments, or forms and features that are capable of being the receptacles of intellect; accordingly the Painter has given in his beautiful man, his own idea of intellectual Beauty. (K579-80)

The concept of intellectual beauty is Platonic, and so is Blake's meaning.

But the holy is not definable in terms of form. It is, as Blake uses the term, prior to beauty, which is the 'receptacle', the form taken by the play of life. Beauty is delightful, but life is delight itself, not a paradigm of eternal perfection but an energy. 'Energy is eternal delight', and the boundless creativity of this energy is of the nature of life. Energy is also called 'desire'; and in his earliest Illuminated Book, *There is No Natural Religion*, Blake writes that without desire reason would have no ideas to build on; no Platonic archetypes or paradigms; for these are the creation of life itself, as 'life delights in life'. Desire, in *The Marriage of Heaven and Hell*, is identified with the Holy Spirit, the divine creative principle, and in Blake's sense of these words holy is not an attribute of spirit—or of one kind of spirit amongst others—spirit is in its nature holy because it is life, bliss, energy, the desire to be of the creative principle.

Blake affirms the unity of the creative energy of life with that which it creates:

The Vegetative Universe opens like a flower from the Earth's center
In which is Eternity. It expands in Stars to the Mundane Shell
And there it meets Eternity again, both within and without . . . (K633)

The circumference of the 'mundane shell'—the boundaries of the universe—brings us back to Plato's sphere of the soul and of the universe; but Blake relates this sphere or egg to the creative energy from which it springs, the 'infinite centre' of the 'birth of life'. All creation springs from a living source of desire and delight, a creative principle which not merely 'is', but is living. That is, Blake's creative principle is a Person, since life, desire, energy, eternal delight are attributes which belong to a Person: not to the 'it is' but to the I AM of the biblical tradition of the living God.

The aspect of beauty is thereby altered but not removed, by situating it in the context of a universe somewhat different from Plato's and very different from Aristotle's. The Alchemists whose works Blake read—Boehme, Paracelsus, Agrippa, Fludd, Thomas

179

Vaughan, the 'Mosaicall' philosophers—had constructed this alternative view of the universe; and within this tradition Blake placed himself, acknowledging Boehme and Paracelsus rather than Plato and Plotinus (whom he had also read, which makes his choice the more striking) as his masters. Common to all these is the conception of the universe not as a paradigm but as an energy, not as a physical object made up of the four elements, but as the ephiphany of a living God experienced in four modes. I have already suggested that beauty can only be experienced, not measured; and yet a beautiful object can be experienced in an objective manner; we can be aware of beauty coldly, as if external to ourselves. In the experience of the holy this is not possible: the sense of the numinous that word describes transforms and includes at once the object and the beholder. We cannot know the holy otherwise than as an experience of our own deepest being; as an external object of knowledge the holy has no existence.

In *The Marriage of Heaven and Hell* Blake places himself within the Prophetic tradition of Israel:

> The philosophy of the east taught the first principles of human perception: some nations held one principle for the origin, & some another: we of Israel taught that the Poetic Genius (as you now call it) was the first principle and all the others merely derivative, which was the cause of our despising the Priests & Philosophers of other countries, and prophecying that all Gods would at last be proved to originate in ours & to be the tributaries of the Poetic Genius. (K153)

Later Blake used, rather than 'the poetic genius', the word 'Imagination'; and this he identified with Jesus—'Jesus the Imagination' who is the 'divine body', the divine Person, in every man. 'Imagination is the human existence itself', at once the creator and the 'place' of the universe each inhabits.

Blake affirms, as against the universe as an object of knowledge, the Aristotelian universe, as transmitted through the Scholastic philosophers and throughout the scientific centuries from Descartes, Bacon, Newton and Locke to our own time, the universal being of a Person. To the modern mentality the concept of a personal God is automatically dismissed as 'anthropomorphism', a primitive mode of thought which attributes to imaginary personal agents called 'gods' causality which really resides in natural forces of a totally impersonal and mechanistic nature. According to this view ideas of 'God' or 'the gods' are a primitive and ignorant misconception of scientific laws, and those poor primitives who imagine themselves to be within a living universe to be pitied, despised, and taught otherwise. Science claims to give the true explanation of all once attributed to living agents. Blake understood that, by mechanizing creation, what has been eliminated from our world by the alleged explanations of science is the concept of life itself, which becomes superfluous, dissolved into the laws of biochemistry or biophysics, electrical waves and whatnot. Life, as defined by materialist science, is an attribute of inanimate matter, is conceivably measurable; but such definitions omit the most evident thing of all, that life is something experienced: it may be deduced by measurement but can be known only by a living being. Life, so understood, is immeasurable. For the Mosaic tradition—indeed for all Tradition (using the word in the sense of the primordial tradition of the *Sophia Perennis*)—life is the I AM, is the experience of being itself.

We find confirmation of Blake's thought in the writings of the great Persian scholar Henri Corbin apropos those Persian mystics he studied in his book *Corps Spirituel et Terre Céleste* (2nd edn, Paris 1979): 'with the loss of the *Imagino vera* and the *mundus imaginalis* begins nihilism and agnosticism'. This is why we say that 'it is here necessary to forget everything the Aristotelian and related philosophers have to say about the Imagination, considering it as a corporeal faculty'.

For Blake the universe is alive; the I AM is not 'a' person in the ordinary sense, but the supreme Person of the universe. In calling the world the creation of a 'living God' prophets and primitives alike are but affirming the primacy of life over the object of knowledge we call nature. To say, at the present time, that there can be no creation without a creator would seem meaningless; meaningless above all because the term 'creator' came, through Deism, to be associated with some sort of transcendent engineer who constructed the mechanism of the universe as science has described it. But to say that without a knower there cannot be a known is not perhaps any longer meaningless within the terms of modern knowledge. For Blake the universe is not a mechanism but an experience, and neither separate from nor separable from the Person who knows, experiences, and thereby brings into existence, the world. That Person Blake calls the Imagination; and 'Jesus the Imagination'. Blake reverses the positivist view to affirm that the universe has its existence from, and within, a living mind whose organs we are; therefore the world lives with the life of the beholder. Not only in its whole but in its parts the world lives in and by the creative power of the Imagination. 'Everything that Lives

181

is Holy' because life is the attribute of the Person of the universe within whose whole all parts, all the 'minute particulars', are contained. 'All things are comprehended . . . in The Human Imagination'. And answering the question of where that Imagination or divine Person is to be discovered, Blake replies, 'God only Exists and Is in created beings and in Man.' Knower and known, creator and creation, are not two universes but one and indivisible.

Thus we see that holiness is not attributed by Blake to 'everything that lives' in the enthusiasm of emotion: in his equation of the living and the holy he is making a metaphysical affirmation. Since the only life is the divine Person, the living Imagination which perpetually bodies forth all that is, holiness is inherent in being; it is not something attributed, as we might consecrate some temple-site or statue designed to serve some religious function. On the contrary, Imagination is anterior to all existence, anterior even to Plato's intelligible world of eternal forms. Blake, supreme poet of the Imagination, speaks therefore rather of the holy than of the beautiful because life is anterior to form, the energy of creative desire anterior to the beauty whose lineaments are its receptacles. In this sense we could say that 'the beautiful' in the Platonic sense is the formal aspect of 'the Holy' (in Plato's terms, 'the Good'), as Blake implies in his definition of those lineaments which are the 'receptacles' of 'intellectual beauty'. Blake is in this definition paying his tribute to Plato; but these are not the terms he habitually uses, being himself constantly aware of the universe as above all alive and in a state of continuous 'formation, transformation', as Goethe wrote, who stands also within the tradition of Alchemy. So to experience the world as a living being is not, we discover, a primitive notion which science has made obsolete, but the supreme understanding of mystic and metaphysician alike. To Blake the experience of the universe as a Person was not an opinion held but a daily experience; and to him the glory of the natural world lay in its being alive within his own imaginative experience of it; as it is alive within the imaginative experience of everyone who is awake to this awareness.

His work is full of examples; his paintings are full of depictions of flowers, insects, clouds, trees and streams in human form. To the spirit of a flower whom the poet overheard mocking 'the cavern'd man' who has, like the prisoners of Plato's cave, shut himself off from the Imaginative life within the philosophy of the five senses, Blake addresses the question which to him was all-important:

'Then tell me, what is the material world, and is it dead?'
He, laughing, answer'd: 'I will write a book on leaves of flowers,
'If you will feed me on love-thoughts & give me now and then
'A cup of sparkling poetic fancies; so, when I am tipsie,
'I'll sing to you to this soft lute, and shew you all alive
'The world, when every particle of dust breathes forth its joy.' (K237)

Blake is being playful but means what he says: poetic intoxication and love can reveal more than the five senses; which is, of course, a truth we have all experienced at one time or another; and, to quote Blake again (he is here comparing poetic inspiration with rational knowledge), 'pray is an inferior kind to be call'd Knowing?'—the inferior kind being the rational. Those who are in love do not need to be told—and will laugh at those who would persuade us otherwise—that, for the time of rapture, we are seeing more, not less; and so with that divine poetic intoxication which, under the symbolism of wine and drunkenness, Rumi and the other Sufi poets never tire of proclaiming as the vision of the divine Person and the way of supreme understanding.

In a letter to his friend Thomas Butts he describes such a moment of divine intoxication in which every mote in the sunbeams appeared as

> . . . a Man
> Human-form'd. Swift I ran
> For they beckon'd to me
> Remote by the Sea,
> Saying: Each grain of Sand,
> Every Stone on the Land,
> Each rock & each hill,
> Each fountain & rill,
> Each herb & each tree,
> Mountain, hill, earth & sea,
> Cloud, Meteor & Star,
> Are Men Seen Afar.

—and, as Blake's vision continued, all these

> Heavenly Men beaming bright,
> Appear'd as One Man (K804–5)

—the all-embracing 'divine body' of the human Imagination. The concept of the holy is inconceivable—is totally meaningless—within the terms of natural science, for love goes only to the living, not to an inanimate object. The holy is an experience in its nature inaccessible to natural reason, with its universe of lifeless matter external to mind or thought.

> Think of a white cloud as being holy, you cannot love it; but think of a
> holy man within the cloud, love springs up in your thoughts, for to think
> of holiness distinct from man is impossible to the affections. (K90)

We must not suppose that Blake was attributing to a wreath of water-vapour a being, in human terms, which clouds do not possess: he is, on the contrary, affirming what Henry Corbin has more recently told us in his books on Iranian mysticism: that 'the Earth is an Angel'.

We must understand that quantitative investigation of the object will never discover to us this other, living earth, Blake's Imagination, named also by Corbin the *mundus imaginalis*. Blake and Corbin alike knew that this different aspect of the world is discoverable only by a change in the consciousness of the beholder. Blake, in the passage quoted, playfully names love and the intoxication of the poetic imagination; elsewhere he writes constantly of the 'imaginative vision' of the 'man of Imagination' who beholds the 'eternal' aspect of the earth which reason can never discover. Neither atom-splitting nor space-travel can ever remove us to 'other' worlds, since we take with us everywhere our limited consciousness. His admonition to Western man is to awake, to stop looking for the infinite and the eternal in the 'void outside existence' of the material universe and to discover infinity and eternity in existence itself—the Imaginative vision. The change is not in the objects but in ourselves.

Corbin, in the book from which we have already quoted, writes that to encounter Earth in the person of its Angel is essentially a psychic event which cannot 'take place' either in the world of abstract impersonal concepts or on the plane of simple sense-impressions. The perception of the Angel of the Earth, according to Corbin, takes place in an intermediate universe which is neither that of those essences considered by philosophy nor of those sense-data upon which positivist science works, but a universe of 'imaginal' forms, the *mundus imaginalis* experienced as so many personal presences. This imaginal world is the 'place' in which the earth, with its mountains and trees, 'cloud meteor and star' are encountered not as things but as persons—angels. This is precisely the world in which Blake encountered the sand-grains 'all alive'. In another of his letters to Thomas Butts Blake wrote of 'Angels planted in Hawthorn bowers'; and again we find an exact parallel in Corbin's Mazdean mystics, of whom he wrote that, in the encounter with the earth in its person, as an 'Angel', the question is not (as for positivist science) *What* is it?' but 'Who is the Earth, who are the waters, the plants, the mountains, or *to whom* do they correspond? (See 'Towards a Living Universe' p. 21 *ff.*)

Of this mode of experience Blake's holy man in a white cloud, his angels planted in hawthorn bowers, are perfect examples.

The experience of the 'imaginal form', Corbin writes, 'corresponds on every occasion to the presence of a certain state of mind'; and this is the state of mind in which Blake experienced the holy man in the cloud, or the angels in the sun:

> I assert for My Self that I do not behold the outward Creation & that to me it is hindrance & not Action; it is as the Dirt upon my feet, No part of Me. 'What,' it will be Question'd, 'When the Sun rises, do you not see a round disk of fire somewhat like a Guinea?' O no, no, I see an Innumerable company of the Heavenly host crying 'Holy, Holy, Holy is the Lord God Almighty.' (K617)

I hope it is by now clear that Blake's 'visions' were not of another order of things, or another world, but of this world, experienced imaginatively. All that we see is vision, he said; and 'This World Is a World of imagination & Vision. I see Every thing I paint In This World.' His 'Visions of Eternity' were of the sun that rises every morning, of the vine in his garden, 'the tree which moves some to tears of joy' and 'is in the Eyes of others only a Green thing that stands in the way. Some See Nature all Ridicule & Deformity & by these I shall not regulate my proportions; & Some Scarce see Nature at all. But to the Eyes of the Man of Imagination, Nature is Imagination itself' (K793). In all these passages the concept of the holy is as it were an intrinsic attribute of the vision of the creation in personal and living form. To the natural vision of the cloud or of the sun holiness neither could, nor indeed should, be attributed, for this would only be fanciful make-believe. In the imaginative vision holiness is inseparable from the experience itself. The perception of the living, the personal (as contrasted with personified) nature of these necessitates a certain state of mind, the Imaginative vision. So seen there is no question of imputing attributes to sun, cloud, hawthorn-tree, 'cloud, meteor and star'; the angels in the sun who sing 'Holy, Holy, Holy is the Lord God Almighty' could sing nothing else, being themselves the proclamation and manifestation of the Divine life. The

'Heavenly Men, beaming bright' of Blake's vision by the sea merge into the single holy Person of the Divine Body, whose Person is also the 'place' of the Imaginal world (to use the term Corbin introduced, in order to make a clear distinction from the 'imaginary' in the sense of a make-believe); this Person is at the same time the living universe and the 'holy land' itself.

But it was above all from Swedenborg's visionary writings that Blake derived his grand conception of the Divine Humanity or Divine Body who is at once the Person and the region of the Imagination. The description of the 'men seen afar' in his letter to Butts is little more than a paraphrase of passages in Swedenborg's *Divine Love and Wisdom*, a book Blake had carefully annotated.

It is clear from those contexts in which Blake writes of the holy that for him, as for those Iranian mystics of whom Corbin writes, the experience itself is the authentication of the 'angelic', the living, the numinous character of the earth of the Imagination, which he calls the eternal world. This is for Blake—as for the Iranian mystics—the 'real' world of human experience; mankind is not a natural species, but a 'kingdom'; and that kingdom, the kingdom of Christ, 'not of this world', the Imagination, which Blake constantly seeks to tell us is not in time or in space but in living consciousness. It is anterior to time and space:

> Many suppose that before the Creation All was Solitude & Chaos. This is the most pernicious Idea that can enter the Mind, as it . . . Limits All Existence to Creation & to Chaos. To the Time & Space fixed by the Corporeal Vegetative Eye, & leaves the Man who entertains such an Idea the habitation of Unbelieving demons. Eternity Exists, and All things in Eternity, Independent of Creation . . . (K614)

This universe, existing in independence of corporeal time and space, is not subject to change, death and decay; and Blake writes of it (as does Corbin) as the celestial world into which the spiritual body is resurrected in a 'second birth'.

> The world of Imagination is the world of Eternity; it is the divine bosom into which we shall all go after the death of the Vegetated body. This World of Imagination is Infinite & Eternal, whereas the World of Generation, or Vegetation, is Finite & Temporal. There Exist in that Eternal World the Permanent Realities of Every Thing which we see reflected in this Vegetable Glass of Nature. All Things are comprehended in their Eternal Forms in the divine body of the Saviour, the True Vine of

186

Eternity, The Human Imagination, who appear'd to Me as Coming to Judgement among his Saints & throwing off the Temporal that the Eternal might be Establish'd. (K605–6)

The Imagination is called the saviour because it rescues humankind from the temporal predicament, enabling us to enter the eternal mode of experience proper to the human kingdom. Corbin also understood that the resurrection of the spiritual man—Blake's 'true man', who is intellect, or Imagination—is into the *mundus imaginalis*; for both Blake and the Sufi mystics, that is the real world, and Corbin writes in words similar to Blake's of this transcendental Imagination, or soul of the world:

> All realities exist there in the state of *imaginal forms*, and these images are *a priori*, or archetypal, that is to say they are themselves as it were *pre-meditant* in the meditation of the soul, whose world they are, because, since they are the soul's world, that is to say the activity proper to that soul, they 'give the measure' of each soul, expressing its structure and its energies.

I hope that it is now clear that the world of the Imagination is, for Blake as for Corbin, not only real, but reality itself, the world of transfiguration and of resurrection; the Paradise for which man was created and from which, through a darkening of consciousness, through that 'forgetfulness' of which the Platonists wrote, the 'sleep' into which, according to the Biblical myth, Adam fell in Paradise, we have fallen. Since for Blake experience is itself knowledge, the ultimate inadequacy of the materialist mentality must lie in the fact that this mentality precludes certain experiences native to the human soul and Imagination. He has depicted Urizen, 'the mind of the natural frame', as 'aged ignorance', blind, joyless, the eternal doubter, the 'idiot Questioner who is always questioning/But never capable of answering' . . .

> Who publishes doubt & calls it knowledge, whose Science is Despair. (K533)

It is in the nature of this mentality to

> Charge Visionaries with deceiving
> And call Men wise for not Believing . . . (K756)

187

But a philosophy which precludes experiences which are native to our humanity—as of awe, wonder, the sense of the holy, for which we are naturally equipped, as a bird is equipped with wings—cannot, for Blake (nor indeed for Corbin), lay claim to a higher degree of truth than that which these experiences mediate. The transfigured vision of the *mundus imaginalis* speaks for itself; it expresses, as Corbin writes, the 'measure' of the soul, its structures and its energies. If we take as our measure of reality not a material structure external to consciousness but living experience, the soul's capacity becomes the measure.

How, then, is the 'holy', as conceived by Blake as the transfigured vision of the Imagination, related to the Greek concept of 'the beautiful'? Perhaps this has already become clear. Since the holy is an attribute of the divine ground of the human Imagination itself it is for Blake the supreme value. It is primary, it is the Holy Land. Blake situates the beautiful on the plane of forms which 'contain' by their 'lineaments' the beauty of 'intellect'. How close Blake's conception of the Imagination is to Plato's 'intellect' may be seen from his description of the 'Treasures of Heaven' as 'Realities of Intellect', 'the Eternal Births of Intellect from the Divine Humanity'. Blake's world of the Imagination is, like Plato's Intellect, a world filled with forms; and the 'births of Intellect' are the 'little glancing wings', 'each grain of sand/Every stone on the land', the minute particulars of existence which are themselves, seen with that transfigured vision, the 'ideas of Imagination', whose creativity is boundless, generating as many worlds as there are living individuals,

Creating Space, Creating Time, according to the wonders Divine
Of Human Imagination throughout all the Three Regions immense
Of Childhood, Manhood & Old Age . . . (K746)

Blake forewarned us of the profane violation of the world of life that must inevitably follow from the materialist ideologies which have come to dominate the West and are now spreading over the whole world. Now it seems that humankind is coming to be seen, by the behaviourist sciences of America no less than by the Marxist materialist political regimes, as a mere complex mechanism. Men and women have become enslaved to the machines we have invented, the willing servants of a mechanised world, easily replaceable spare parts in a great network of machinery. 'Intelligence' (so I heard recently on the radio) can now be 'measured' by little gadgets fixed to the head. So much for man, made in the image of God; so much for Blake's 'eternal delight' and the 'sports of wisdom in the human Imagination'. To say that 'nothing is sacred' is the merest truism; what meaning, in such a world, can Blake's words have, 'everything that Lives is Holy'? There must be great numbers of people living in our Western cities who have been prevented by the current ideologies from ever experiencing the sense of the holy; who perhaps have never allowed themselves to experience the beautiful, so painful is it to be reminded of an order of things so far removed from the world habit has induced us to accept. All those fantasies about 'other worlds' in 'outer space' are pathetic and futile attempts to discover a lost holy land that Blake beheld whenever he saw the sun rise, or a hawthorn tree in blossom.

11

Towards a Living Universe

EVERY civilization is grounded in certain premises but it is precisely of these that we are least aware. Yet those who find meaning in Plato's fable of the alternation of ages of gold and iron, or in 'The Great Year of the Ancients', see in the alternation or progression of historic 'ages' precisely a reversal or a change of premises. Some see in the precession of the equinox from the sign of Pisces to Aquarius such a reversal. Others without recourse to symbol have reached a similar conclusion; for when the implications of certain assumptions—in our own case those of the natural sciences—have been fully unfolded and explored, other assumptions, other premises become necessary. Many, not least among the scientists themselves, are now calling in question the basic premise of the natural sciences, that the universe is a self-contained material system acting autonomously as a mechanism, according to 'laws of nature'.

Yeats, one of the first great voices to proclaim, at the beginning of this century, a reversal of the age, described the centuries of science, on which those who see in human history a steady progression from ignorance to knowledge, a 'conquest' of nature and the ascent of man to the top of the tree of natural evolution so pride themselves, the 'three provincial centuries', a mere deviation from a human norm whose premises—and whose fruits therefore—are of quite another kind.

Technology and its products is to the mass of mankind the obvious and incontrovertible vindication of science. But there is a growing realization that the naive premises of materialism are applicable within certain limits only. The pursuit of 'matter' into its ultimate origins has resulted only in the discovery that what to the senses seems so solid is in reality something intangible, one might say immaterial. The end of the history of scientific investigation would seem to be a dematerialization of matter itself.

So our New Age seems likely to begin with a reversal of premises, a return to metaphysical orthodoxy: that is, the assumption that not matter but mind is the ground of our universe, and that, in consequence, the natural universe can no longer be seen as a mechanism (however complex) but, as Plato called the world, an immortal and blessed God, a living being.

The fruits of these two views of reality will be as different as their premises. The fruits of materialist science are utilities; those of the spirit are the qualities and values of life. It is the great merit of scientific thought that the laws of the natural order are respected throughout the whole field of natural science. The coherence, the ordered harmony of the scientific world-picture is truly a wonderful speculation of nature. What is in question—as Owen Barfield many years ago set forth in his book *Saving the Appearances*—is the nature and context of that speculation. The implications of an account of the universe which excludes mind, or soul, or spirit—excludes whatever is not of a material order—have in the long run proved disastrous. Naive materialism nevertheless remains the irreligion of the masses in this world of material wealth and spiritual indigence. For the price paid for our prestigious material civilization is that we are, in comparison with many backward races, spiritual savages. Blake himself pointed to the American Indians as a race who have more in common with Homer's world than have the scholars who study 'the classics'; and that the Brahmans of India are 'naked civilized men' whose inner culture is in marked contrast with that of our own 'trousered apes' who have rejected as primitive ignorance that dream of divine descent which haunts every mythological—that is to say imaginative—account of our origin and nature. The field of the arts, religion and moral values, and metaphysics have become debased in proportion to the incursions of scientific standards and assumptions into their respective fields. Since scientific standards of measurement are inapplicable to whatever is not of a material order, there have ceased to be any standards at all in whatever belongs to what is (pejoratively) called the 'subjective'. And yet other civilizations have recognised the laws of mind as the most real, the most universal of all things. In the arts and in criticism of the arts (not to mention behavioural psychology and other bastard sciences) the distinction between the significant and the meaningless and even of the pathological has been virtually lost. Our age can gape at the great works of the past—megalithic circles, the pyramids, the Parthenon, Chartres, the Alhambra, or comparable works of poetry, music or painting. But with our vast technical skill we ourselves do not possess the knowledge to create such works; for that knowledge was a spiritual knowledge. Do we even possess the knowledge necessary to understand these 'monuments of unageing intellect'? Perhaps science is itself the one significant work of imagination our spiritually forgetful culture has produced.

If a New Age means anything it means a change of premises, and the consequent recovery of a whole body of knowledge excluded by materialist science as irrelevant: a knowledge no less exact, no less extensive, structured and objective than the laws of nature; knowledge of man's inner worlds, of the imagination. Many are now turning to the Far East, to those philosophies based upon the premise that mind or spirit is the ground. But the West has its own tradition, of Greek philosophy, united in Christian theology with the Jewish prophetic affirmation of a 'living God'. From this norm post-Cartesian thought has deviated; but the threads of tradition are never quite lost. I myself discovered this knowledge, excluded as irrelevant by materialist humanism, in the course of my studies of William Blake, who is a key figure in the reaffirmation and recovery of the perennial wisdom. His prophetic voice was unheard by his contemporaries, but speaks eloquently to our own, better able than the nineteenth century to appreciate the force of his arguments, the truth of his vision, and the reality of those inner worlds it was his prophetic mission to reopen.

Blake was not an 'original' thinker, nor would he have wished to be so in the modern sense. Rather he gathered up the threads of the excluded knowledge—gnosticism, alchemy, the mythologies of many races. He was in principle eclectic, believing as he did that the human Imagination is itself the source of all religions and all mythologies. In these he found traces of what he regarded as the universal religion of mankind, which he called the Everlasting Gospel or 'the religion of Jesus' (by which he did not necessarily mean the religion of the Christian Church), who is, in Blake's terms, the Imagination itself. But two of his principal sources were neo-Platonism and the writings of Swedenborg; and these we shall presently consider.

Blake's fundamental objection to the scientific philosophy, 'natural religion'—and the objection is still valid—is that the universe of material science is devoid of life. It is located outside the perceiving mind in 'a void outside existence' (that is, outside living consciousness), in 'non-entity's dark void', 'a soul-shuddering vacuum' filled with 'voids and solids'. This lifeless universe outside the human Imagination is created by the 'wrenching apart' of the 'eternal mind' resulting, on the one hand, in an externalized 'nature' devoid of life, and on the other in a 'shrinking' of humanity from the boundless being of Imagination into the 'mortal worm' of 'sixty winters' and 'seventy inches long', an insignificant part of the externalized nature this wrenching apart has created. In this fall from the infinity and expansiveness of the Imagination into a world of matter man becomes 'a little grovelling root outside of himself'; for the human imagination is not contained by a material universe, but contains and is coextensive with whatever it perceives and experiences. Thus Blake held the materialist view of nature to be both false and destructive to humanity. Nature, no longer within the human imagination, has an existence merely quantitative, and becomes a spiritual desert, 'a wondrous rocky World of cruel destiny,/Rocks piled on rocks reaching the stars', which Blake calls

A building of eternal death, whose proportions are eternal despair. (K702)

With the 'shrinking' of eye and ear from imaginative to natural vision, the sun and moon are 'hurried afar into an unknown Night',

. . . the Sun is shrunk: the Heavens are shrunk
Away into the far remote, and the Trees & Mountains wither'd
Into indefinite cloudy shadows . . .
The Stars flee remote; the heaven is iron, the earth is sulphur,
And all the mountains & hills shrink up like a withering gourd. (K703)

Externalized nature becomes an 'unfathomable non-ens'. The rationalist thought of Bacon, Newton and Locke alienates man from his universe. All nature 'flees' from man into externality; the animals 'wander away' in 'sullen droves', and as with the natural world so with human cities:

The Cities & Villages of Albion become Rock & Sand Unhumanized. (K697)

The astonishing writings of Emanuel Swedenborg reopened in the eighteenth century those inner worlds which post-Cartesian science had thought dispensible. Blake and his wife were members of the Swedenborgian Society; and Blake's seemingly original 'system' is, in its essentials, that of Swedenborg's New Church—a fact which Blake scholars, including myself, have been slow to recognize. Indeed, the only interpreter of Blake who has not made this mistake is his first and greatest disciple, Yeats. Yet Swedenborg represents in its most pure form the alternative view of the world which in our own time can no longer be brushed aside.

Swedenborg was a geologist and assessor of minerals to the Swedish government, a distinguished and respected man of science; nevertheless, after the 'opening' of his inner perceptions, which took place in middle life, he saw the world as a purely mental phenomenon. There are, he says, three worlds: the celestial, the spiritual, and the world of 'uses', the natural world. These degrees correspond to the Platonic, Cabbalistic and other cosmologies and doubtless to the actual structure of the mental universe; and—again like other systems—the degrees are not a continuous gradation, but 'discrete'; a point on which Blake, and Yeats also, insists. In countless passages throughout his work Swedenborg insists that whereas all in the mental worlds is alive, all in 'nature', Blake's world 'outside existence', is 'fixed and dead'—a view, as we shall later see, shared by Plotinus and the neo-Platonists:

> . . . for all that is created, in itself is inanimate and dead but things are made alive by the fact that the Divine is in them, and that they are in the Divine. (*Divine Love and Wisdom* 53)

Of nature he writes that 'in herself she is dead, and no more contributes to produce these things [that is the appearances] than the instrument to produce the work of the artificer' (DLW.340). This divine artificer, called by Swedenborg, and Blake after him, the 'Divine Body', is present in humanity as the 'Divine Humanity', called by Swedenborg the Lord and by Blake the Imagination. God, according to Swedenborg, is life in itself two-fold aspects of love and wisdom.

Blake in the *Book of Los* describes in mythological symbol the creation of a 'dead' sun in the fixed and dead spaces of the 'deeps' of the Newtonian universe formed by the 'wrenching apart' of human consciousness. This natural sun, Blake says, gives 'no light'. In the same way he mythologizes the dry bones of a statement by Swedenborg that 'space in the natural world may also be called dead' in contrast with the imaginative spaces of the mental world, which are flexible according to thought. By this Blake by no means understands only the imagined spaces of dreams and inner reverie; for we also imaginatively perceive the outer world. His two mythological figures, Los (time)

194

and Enitharmon (space), create these imaginative extensions and durations we inhabit:

> For Los & Enitharmon walk'd forth on the dewy Earth
> Contracting or expanding their all flexible senses
> At will to murmur in the flowers small as the honey bee,
> At will to stretch across the heavens & step from star to star.

(K288)

We all possessed as children this imaginative faculty of entering imaginary caverns and burning mountains in the fire, or losing ourselves in a miniature forest of grass. That is imaginative space and cannot be measured. Blake mythologizes the effect of the 'wrenching apart' which separates the merely quantifiable spaces of nature from the Imagination, describing how Enitharmon becomes frozen into deadly rigidity:

> . . . Enitharmon stretched on the dreary Earth
> Felt her immortal limbs freeze, stiffening, pale, inflexible (K305)

So Los and Enitharmon are 'shrunk into fixed space' and

> Their senses unexpansive in one stedfast bulk remain (K305)

in externalized nature, whose state Blake follows Swedenborg in describing as 'eternal death'.

Into this externality sun and moon, mountains and fields and animals 'wander away into a distant night, separated from man'. So nature is externalized to become the 'dark Abyss' 'outside existence'. Thus both Blake and Swedenborg are concerned with the human consequences of abstracting a material universe from a living mind. Blake by no means calls in question Newton's mathematics; he depicts the human consequences of the abstraction of matter from mind in the portrait he paints of Urizen, the usurping rational faculty who builds for himself a hell of lifeless nature, a 'ruined world' where

> . . . A Rock, a Cloud, a Mountain
> Were now not Vocal as in Climes of happy Eternity
> Where the lamb replies to the infant voice, & the lion to the man of years,
> Giving them sweet instructions; where the Cloud, the River & the Field
> Talk with the husbandman & shepherd (K315)

Nature 'talks' to man in the sense that perception itself is experienced as meaning.

The separation of a universe of matter from the universe of life is for both these visionaries the tragedy of our civilization, dooming us to an existence in a world of inanimate objects devoid of qualities or meaning; René Guénon wrote a book entitled *The Reign of Quantity*, and this reign had already been foreseen by Blake who denounced as 'Satanic' the reverence paid to 'length bredth and highth' under the domination of the mind of the ratio. In the world of the Imagination 'everything that lives is Holy'. The rational mind can know nothing of the sacred, which is immeasurable and exists only as an experience.

Locke had argued—and his supposition remains the basis of behaviourist psychology and of naive materialism generally—that the human senses are passive recipients of stimuli from a 'real' material order exterior to us and to which our senses are merely a passive mirror, Flaubert's 'mirror dawdling down a lane'. For the imaginative tradition the reverse is true—'nature' is the mirror in which Imagination beholds herself.

Swedenborg also answered in detail Locke's view of the passive role of the senses before an externalized nature. In his pedantic way, Swedenborg insists, as Plotinus does, that the forms we perceive reside in the percipient and not in an external nature; and such is the importance of this point that I quote, without apology, Swedenborg's laboured argument:

A man has five external senses which are called touch, taste, smell, hearing, and sight. The subject of touch is in the skin with which a man is encompassed: the very substance and form of the skin cause it to feel the things applied to it: the sense of touch is not in the things which are applied, but it is the substance and form of the skin, which are the subject; this sense is merely an affection of the subject from the things applied. It is the same with taste; this sense is only an affection of the substance and form belonging to the tongue; the tongue is the subject. The same is the case with smell; it is well known that odour affects the nostrils, and that it is in the nostrils, and that it is an affection of them by odoriferous particles touching them. It is the same with the sense of hearing: it appears as if the hearing were in the place where the sound begins, but the hearing is in the ear, and is an affection of its substance and form; that the hearing is at a distance from the ear is an appearance. The same is the case with sight: when a man sees objects at a distance, it appears as if the sight were there; and yet it is the eye which is the subject, and is likewise an affection of the subject . . . It may appear from all this

196

that the affection of the substance and form which causes sense is not anything separate from the subject, but only causes a change in it, the subject remaining the subject then as before, and afterwards.

(DLW.41)

In other words whatever we behold as if an external universe is in reality subjective—within the consciousness of the beholder; a very obvious truth which Western scientific thought has continued to overlook. So Blake wrote: 'Forms must be apprehended by Sense or the Eye of the Imagination' (K775). The forms which we perceive as external nature are in reality within the perceiving mind. That mind cannot perceive otherwise than in accordance with its innate structure.

The Imagination or Divine Body—man's real body—is of an immaterial nature and the *mundus imaginalis* is man's proper world; not as an 'afterlife' (called by Blake 'an allegoric abode where existence has never come') but as the place where we actually are. Swedenborg wrote '. . . man is a spirit; from that he thinks and wills: wherefore the spiritual world is where man is, and in no way far from him . . . every man as to the interiors of his mind is in that world'. Swedenborg insists again and again that the divine body is neither large nor small since it exists otherwise than in natural space. Thus the Imagination is at once mind and its universe. The created world is itself an image of consciousness and Swedenborg argues that everything in nature—the dead world—is an image or reflection of this living world of consciousness. It is not mind but nature which is the mirror, in which objects have only an apparent existence. This view, shared within the whole Platonic tradition (of which Swedenborg is himself a remote recipient), is in total opposition to the view of causality which sees mind as an epiphenomenon of bodily organs and functions:

For the dead thing to act upon the living thing, or for the dead force to act upon the living force, or, what is the same, for the rational to act upon the spiritual, is entirely contrary to order . . . (166)

This world is, according to Swedenborg (again like the Platonic philosophers), the *ultimum opus* in which all things end and upon which they rest.

Blake writes of 'Eden, the land of life'; and mankind's exile from Eden is, quite specifically, exile from the *mundus imaginalis* in which 'all things exist in their eternal forms'. Thus the breaking of the

197

Platonic unity of being, the separation between knowledge and its object made by Aristotle as a convenience for discursive thought, ends in a dehumanization of the natural universe and, ultimately, of humanity also. Our positivist science (like a conquering army which brings devastation in its wake) seeks in our own time to quantify consciousness itself, equating mind with brain, and thought with a mechanical process which can be carried out by computers. As Blake long ago wrote of the English national being, 'his machines are woven with his life'. The thing itself, life, becomes an irrelevance within the vast, self-contained and perfectly functioning mechanism of an externalized nature.

Underlying all later affirmations (in the West) of a living universe is the Platonic tradition. With every return to a philosophy which gives primacy to mind comes a return to the Platonic succession. Blake's acquaintance and contemporary, Thomas Taylor the Platonist, played, through his many translations and commentaries on the neo-Platonic writers, and above all Plotinus, a part no less important than Blake's in establishing the ground for a return to the Platonic succession. His writings provided the basis of the American Transcendentalist movement, and were later an important element in the Theosophical movement and in the Irish renaissance. The Platonic philosophy, coherent and lucid, considers matter as the last effect of a descending chain of causes originating in a divine source, through the intelligible world of 'reason' by way of the 'seminal reasons' of individual souls of every species, which in turn inform the world of matter, itself devoid of form, but the mirror, as it were, in which the intelligible world beholds itself. Among Taylor's paraphrase translations of Plotinus is *On Nature, Contemplation, and The One* (*Ennead* III, book 8). Since it was through Taylor that both Blake and the American Transcendentalists received this sublime teaching of Plotinus, I shall use his version in presenting the Platonic view of the universe.

Like Swedenborg, Plotinus calls the material universe both 'dead' and without the power of causality, which belongs only to Intellect, the living principle. He calls matter a 'non-ens' whose existence is only equivocal. Matter can be said to exist only insofar as it is the recipient of forms (the 'seminal reasons'—*rationes seminales*) but (and modern physics would support Plotinus's argument) unknowable in its ultimate nature because by definition without form. And Plotinus summarizes his view of the forms we discover in the external world:

198

Reason, therefore, extrinsically produced according to a visible form, is the last reason, generated, as it were, in the shade of the first, destitute of life, and incapable of forming another reason; But reason endued with life, and which is as it were the sister of that which fabricates form, and possesses the same power, generates that reason which is the last in the effects. (*Five Books of Plotinus* 205)

That is to say, in matter. Blake, with his gift for grasping the essence, summarizes Plotinus's teaching—and indeed Swedenborg's also—in his own affirmation:

And every Natural Effect has a Spiritual Cause, and Not
A Natural; for a Natural Cause only seems; it is a Delusion
Of Ulro & a ratio of the perishing Vegetable Memory. (K513)

(Ulro is Blake's and Swedenborg's lifeless world 'outside existence'.)

According to Plotinus, 'Nature' is reason, is form, and the mother of the multitude of 'seminal reasons' of the diverse multitude of creatures—plants, animals and all the rest—which derive the inherent reasons responsible for the unfolding of their diverse forms from the overruling 'reason' of 'nature' considered as a whole. Thus the phrase 'mother nature'—or Spenser's Dame Nature—is by no means a personification of a mechanism but in the most literal sense true since Nature is 'endued with life' and in this sense not a thing but a Person. The parent-reason of 'Nature' generates her innumerable offspring while 'abiding in the mean time permanent in itself'.

The Darwinian scheme of evolution which we all learned at school as the very canon of scientific orthodoxy concluded from the serial unfolding and diversification of natural species in time that natural causality which the Platonists deny; but if time be merely relative to our own situation within it Plato may be nearer the truth when (in the *Timaeus*) he describes this world as a 'moving image of eternity, unfolding according to number of eternity abiding in one'. From a non-temporal point of view all is simultaneously present, effects already implicit in their 'seminal reasons'. Plotinus, developing this Platonic theme, sees Nature operating, not as the blind mechanism of 'natural selection' postulated by Darwin (a kind of hit-or-miss process whose beginning is in chaos and whose end is indeterminate); conceives the operation of Nature as 'contemplation' of what eternally exists. And he considers what is the speculation of earth, and trees, and plants, and after what manner we may be able to reduce that which is produced in these into the energy of speculation; and lastly, how nature, which is said to be void of imagination and reason, possesses contemplation in herself, and yet operates from contemplation she does not possess. (201)

(The word 'speculation' is here not used in the modern sense, as more or less synonymous with a reasonable guess, but in its literal sense, of looking into a mirror—*speculum*—in which reality is contemplated.) Plotinus concludes that Nature contemplates herself in an endless reverie of her innate 'reason':

> But does nature operate from contemplation? From contemplation entirely. But what if after a certain manner she contemplates herself? For she is the effect of contemplation, and is contemplative of something . . . such as she is, such she fabricates. (206–7)

Nature is said to contemplate 'a soul more powerful and vivid' which does not operate in matter but resides in the intelligible world. Nature is not fully conscious, as intellect is, and in a beautiful image Plotinus describes Nature as a dreamer, whose dream is the 'spectacle' of natural forms:

> And if any one is desirous of assigning to nature a certain apprehension or sensation, he ought not to attribute to her a knowledge of the same kind as that of other beings, but in the same manner as if the knowledge of a man dreaming should be compared with the perceptions of the vigilant: for contemplating her spectacle she reposes; a spectacle produced in herself, because she abides in and with herself and becomes her own spectacle and a quiet contemplation, though more debile and obscure; for the soul from which she is produced is endued with a more efficacious perception, and nature is only the image of another's contemplation. (210)

Thus the image of nature as a mirror—Jakob Boehme's 'vegetable glass', Blake's 'looking-glass of Enitharmon'—goes back to the Platonic tradition. Plotinus develops the myth of Narcissus, who falls in love with his image reflected in water, as the soul which falls in love with its bodily image and is in consequence turned into what Blake calls a 'human vegetable'—losing his humanity. Yeats summarizes the doctrine in his line

Mirror on mirror mirrored is all the show.

That which Nature contemplates in order to produce her 'spectacle' is soul, which is 'full of speculative forms'. Thus:

> Indeed all things proceed in a beautiful and quiet order . . . The intellectual soul of the world contemplates indeed a sublime spectacle, and that which she thus contemplates, because it rises higher than soul, generates that which is posterior to itself, and thus contemplation begets contemplation, so that neither has speculation or spectacle any bound, and on this account they proceed through all things; (215)

This dreaming figure of Nature (generative and therefore feminine) survives or re-emerges in the *anima mundi* of the alchemical and Rosicrucian tradition, *natura naturans*. Robert Fludd, in his *Mosaicall Philosophy*, wrote,

> . . . The Platonists did call the generall vertue, which did engender and preserve all things, the *Anima Mundi*, or *the soul of the world*. And to this their opinions, the *Arabic Astrologians* do seem to adhere: forasmuch as they did maintain, that every particular thing in the world hath his distinct and peculiar soul from this vivifying spirit. (II.I.IV.)

—and Fludd quotes the Greek saying that the world is 'full of Gods'. This allusion to the 'Arabic Astrologians' points forward to Henry Corbin's work in our own time on Iranian mystical theology; and Fludd enumerates the sources of the tradition he represented in his generation:

> . . . Mercurius Trismegistus [that is the Hermetica] Theophrastus, Avicenna, Algazel, as well all the Stoiks, and Peripatetiks, . . . Zoroaster and Heraclitus the Ephesian, conclude that the soul of the world is that catholick invisible fire, of which and by the action whereof, all things are generated and brought forth from puissance into act. (II.I.IV.)

The soul of the world Fludd equates with the angel Metatron and with the Divine Wisdom of the Scriptures:

> The Cabalist's tenent is, that the great Angell whom they term Mitattron . . . is that very same catholick Spirit, which doth animate the whole world, and thereupon *Rabbi Moses* does averre it to be *Intellectus agens, or the general intellectuall agent, from which all particular forms do flow*. And they say, that from this universall angelicall Spirit, all singular vertues as well animall, as vitall and naturall, do proceed, which also they call Angells, whereof there are an infinite number in respect of our capacity. (II.I.IV.)

201

Fludd goes on to equate the soul of the world with the Wisdom of the Scriptures, whose 'spirit filleth the whole world' and indeed (being in this respect close to Blake, who would have read the *Mosaicall Philosophy* and may have been directly indebted to Fludd) with

> *that Christ which filleth all things, who is all in all*, as the Apostle sayeth, who *in the beginning made the earth, and the heavens were the work of his hands*; And after his creation of all things he doth (as St. Paul telleth us Heb.i.) *bear up, suffer and sustain all things by the vivifying virtue of this Word.*

And Fludd continues:

> But each Philosopher cannot but acknowledge that *Anima* is nothing else, but that which doth animate or vivifie a body or spirit. Why then should not the catholick divine spirit which filleth all, and operateth all, and in all, be tearmed the fountain of the worlds life, by which it liveth, moveth, and hath its being, and consequently the essentiall life, and Centrall or mental soul of the world, moving the created humid spirit thereof, no otherwise, then the spirit which God breathed into *Adam*, did move and operate, in and by the Organ of the created aire? (II.I.IV.)

Plotinus also says that 'in every soul there is the same spectacle'. There is no question of 'subjectivity' in the modern sense. If the view of Locke, continued in our own time by the behaviourist schools, that all knowledge comes through the senses and refers to an externalised world, of which every individual is a passive mirror, were true, then subjectivity would indeed be, in Blake's words, 'a fortuitous concourse of memorys accumulated and lost'. But if, on the contrary, the 'seminal reasons' of all creatures individually 'speculate' the universal 'reason' of Nature, then it is the 'latent reasons' residing in the soul which unfold in energy and action. Self-knowledge is the soul's desire—to behold her latent reasons externally and 'as if different from herself'. This is the root of her speculation; but she 'cannot produce what she has not received' and she 'perceives what she possesses'. But in so doing—so Plotinus puts it—she has 'relinquished part of herself' into externality, as that 'spectacle' in which soul sees itself in generated beings.

Again Blake has summarized this philosophy—which reached him indeed also through Swedenborg—with his inimitable aphoristic clarity:

. . . in your own Bosom you bear your Heaven
And Earth & all you behold; tho' it appears Without, it is Within,
In your Imagination, of which this World of Mortality is but a Shadow.
(K709)

This might be—perhaps in fact is—Blake's summary of Plotinus's *On Nature, Contemplation and the One*.

Thus Plotinus presents us with a living universe in which there is neither distinction nor separation between knowing and being: since 'in intellect essence is the same as intellection. For it cannot be any longer said that *this* is one and *that* another.' Coleridge, great philosopher of the Imagination, for whom also Plotinus was supreme, wrote of 'the adorable I AM' in which knowledge and being are one and indistinguishable. Thus the *unus mundus* is restored, in whose unity of being Blake's 'wrenching apart' of the natural universe and the mind which beholds it is healed.

To conclude this summary of Plotinus's teaching concerning Nature, we see him in the following passage reaching the affirmation characteristic of Christian, Jewish and Islamic thought, that the universal living mind or spirit the Greeks call Intellect must be considered as a Person—the only and supreme Person of the universe. For what constitutes a 'person' if not life, knowledge, and that unity of being which belongs by definition to 'the Good Itself' and which is, for the Platonists, also 'the One':

Intellect indeed is beautiful, and the most beautiful of all things, being situated in a pure light and in a pure splendour, and comprehending in itself the nature of beings, of which indeed this our beautiful material world is but a shadow and image; but intellect, that true intelligible world, is situated in universal splendour, living in itself a blessed life, and containing nothing unintelligible, nothing dark, nothing without measure; which divine world whoever perceives will be immediately astonished, if, as is requisite, he profoundly and intimately merges himself into its inmost recesses and becomes one with its all beauteous nature. And as he who diligently surveys the heavens, and contemplates the splendor of the stars, should immediately think upon and search after their artificer, so it is requisite that he who beholds and admires the intelligible world, should diligently inquire after its author, investigating who he is, where he resides, and how he produced such an offspring as intellect, a son beautiful and pure, and full of ineffable fire. But his father is neither intellect nor a son, but superior to both; for intellect has a posterior subsistence, and is indigent of nourishment and intelligence, being situated the next in order to that nature which is superior to every kind of want. Intellect, however, possesses true plenitude and intelligence, because it possesses the first of all things; but that which is prior to intellect is neither indigent nor possesses; for if this were the case, it would not be *the good itself*. (245)

Thus Intellect, as the 'son' of 'the good itself', is the same as the Johannine Logos, called alike by Blake and Swedenborg the Divine Body, and the Divine Human. In the Christian creed also it is said that it is 'the Son' 'by whom all things were made'; in Blake's terms 'Jesus, the Imagination'; a concept which goes far to restore Christendom's garbled and distorted version of the teaching of the philosophers. 'All things exist in the Human Imagination', which Blake calls 'the Divine Image':

The Eternal Body of Man is The Imagination, that is

God himself   ⎱ יש[ו]ע, Jesus. we are
The Divine Body ⎰   his members.

(K776)

The fact that Blake and Swedenborg from whom he derives his Christian theology have nothing to say (as Plotinus and Plato have) of that which is the 'father' of Intellect or Imagination does nothing to lessen the truth or the value of what both these visionaries have to say about the 'son'—the *mundus imaginalis*—even though this is in fact the one epithet Blake never does apply to his 'Jesus the Imagination' who for him is, simply, 'God'.

Attempts have been made by natural scientists to restore the wholeness and unity of the *unus mundus* in their own terms; but because, as we have seen, this attempt implies the exclusion of those meanings and values proper to inner experience, and which alone call into play the whole gamut of our innate potentiality, these attempts must fail. The solutions offered by behavioural psychology and the like would be laughable were they not also tragic. But, whereas the lesser cannot include the greater, the imaginative universe by no means excludes that of science, which becomes, as we have seen from Plotinus, the mirror of intellect itself. Quantity itself becomes what Blake calls 'humanized'. In its return to Imagination '. . . the all tremendous unfathomable Non-Ens Of Death was seen in regenerations terrific' (K746). By 'death' Blake means of course the 'dead' universe of matter; his use of Plotinus's word 'non-ens' indicates his source.

Thus the nature of the experience is itself determined by our view of it; and those who conceive themselves to be obsolescent parts in a material universe devoid of life forgo the whole range of those unquantifiable values which constitute the universe of Imagination:

> . . . What seems to Be, Is, To those to whom
> It seems to Be, & is productive of the most dreadful
> Consequences to those to whom it seems to Be, even of
> Torments, Despair, Eternal Death . . . (K663)

Blake in no way exaggerates the human consequences of those ideologies which reduce all to mechanistic terms: love to biochemistry, the moral sense to imprinted behaviour patterns, and so on, the higher being in every case reduced to the lower, a value to a material cause. The end is the spiritual *nihil* which those who subscribe to such ideologies avoid only by allowing themselves blind-spots, areas of illogicality or unawareness, pain-killers and palliatives, that way of life T. S. Eliot describes as 'distracted from distraction by distraction' or lives of 'quiet desperation'. I do not wish to underrate the intellectual satisfaction many find in contemplating the ordered complexity of the physical universe; but history seems to bear out Blake's judgement that 'the same dull round, even of a universe, would soon become a mill with complicated wheels' (K97).

Plotinus, like Blake and like the Vedas, equates felicity—'bliss'—with 'life', which has in all creatures, so he argues, 'a certain end' in which, when accomplished, 'nature makes a stop, as having accomplished the whole of their existence, and filled it with all that is wanting from beginning to end' (*Enn*. I.4.). The 'seminal reasons' of animals and plants find their fulfilment within the terms of their simpler states of consciousness; but human beings, precluded by some ideology from experiencing whatever lies within our capacity, can never experience the 'felicity' or 'bliss' proper to human existence. 'More! More! is the cry of the mistaken soul,' Blake writes; 'less than All cannot satisfy Man' (K97). It is science which asks for 'more' while 'All' is the capacity of mankind's boundless Imagination.

Ruskin, a man of the nineteenth century, wrote of the 'pathetic fallacy', by which he meant the arbitrary attribution to inanimate objects or phenomena—storms, rainbows, the sun and so forth—of conscious feelings which are merely 'projected' (as we would say) upon them by the experiencer. And doubtless a writer who does regard nature as an inanimate system and then proceeds to pretend that it is alive is being doubly dishonest and is likely to be a bad writer. But in the *unus mundus* of the Imagination 'nature is one continued vision of the Imagination'. Man and his universe cannot be separated. Cloud and mountain do really 'talk' to the husbandman and the shepherd, for they communicate meaning.

I have entitled this paper 'Towards a Living Universe' but have spoken rather of a departure from than an advance towards such a universe, once normal to humankind, and still envisaged and experienced by the Eastern theologies of Hinduism, Buddhism and Sufism, for all of which the primacy of life and of the *mundus imaginalis* over 'matter' is self-evident. It is therefore not surprising that growing numbers in the West are turning towards those ancient treasuries of spiritual knowledge. But truth belongs neither to the past nor to the future, but is always itself. The nature of things does not change with our ideologies; tradition does not reach us from some golden age, neither does it concern itself with any future Utopia; it teaches what is eternal in the human imagination; its relevance is at all times immediate.

Henry Corbin has performed for Iranian mysticism a service comparable to that of Thomas Taylor for the Platonic philosophers at the turn of the eighteenth century. He understood the relevance, the timeliness of the thought of the Mazdean and Sufi mystics in a West forced to reconsider the premises of naive materialism. I remember his describing Swedenborg as 'the Buddha of the West'; and Swedenborg's radical calling in question of the premises of materialism justified the comparison. Corbin was a friend of C. G. Jung and a member of the Eranos Circle; and it is in the context of the contemporary re-opening of the world of psyche (with a consequent re-examination of metaphysical premises) that Corbin has re-presented the Iranian mystical tradition relating to the *mundus imaginalis*, the world of *hurqalya*. Like Blake, like Swedenborg, like Plotinus, this tradition teaches that man's body is a mental body and his universe a mental universe. Like these also the Iranian tradition (whose roots also are of course in Platonism) understands the world to be informed with life.

Robert Fludd had long before quoted Alguzel (Lib. i Chris.) in his own *Mosaicall Philosophy*, in which is embodied the counter-tradition to Aristotelian naturalism:

Some say that whatsoever filleth the Heaven, the Aire, the Earth, and wide Seas, is stirred up by a soul, through the vertue whereof all things in the world do live; and also that the world itself doth exist by it. But because there is not any bodily substance that is void of a soul, and that the world and every particular thereof doth consist of a body, therefore there is an intermediate spirit betwixt this soul and body, which they neither call a soul or a body, but a mean substance, participating of them both to reduce both extreames together into one. (II. I. IV)

Islamic angelology considers not only natural but also mental orders of beings; and indeed this view follows from the understanding that not matter but life is the substance and place of the cosmos; the world, as the Greeks also held, is 'full of Gods'. A quotation from Corbin's *Corps Spirituelle et Terre Céleste* summarizes the view I have attempted to indicate in the title of this paper:

The encounter with the Earth not as a sum of physical facts but in the person of its Angel is essentially an event of the psyche; it cannot 'take place' either in the realm of impersonal abstract concepts nor on the level of simple sense-experience. The earth must be perceived not by the senses at all but by means of a primordial Image; and because that Image has the aspect of a personal countenance it will present itself as a 'symbolic correspondence' with the image proper to itself which the soul bears in its inmost ground. The Angel of the Earth is to be met within that intermediate universe which is neither that of the essences considered by philosophy, nor the sense-data with which material science busies itself; a universe of imaginal Forms, the *mundus imaginalis* experienced as so many personal presences.

If we are to grasp the meanings which constitute that universe in which Earth is figured, meditated, and encountered in the person of its Angel, we must understand that the questions to be answered concern not essences ('what is it?') but persons rather ('who is it?' or '*to whom* does it correspond?')—for example *who* is the Earth, *who* are the waters, plants, mountains, or *to whom* do they correspond? The answer to these questions renders present an imaginal Form, and that imaginal form invariably corresponds to some state of being. Therefore we must here understand the phenomenon of Earth as an angelophany or mental apparition of its Angel, within the totality of the fundamental Mazdean angelology, which imparts to its cosmology and its science alike a structure such that these constitute an answer to the question 'who?' (32)

—and Corbin comments that these angelic and archangelic forms correspond much more closely to the *Diis Angeli* of Proclus than they do to the angelic 'messengers' of the Bible and the Koran:

207

On this point I am convinced that the Neoplatonists (whom it has long been fashionable to deride) were much nearer to the Iranian angelology and understood better the theurgic and demiurgic rôle of these celestial entities than do those philosophic improvizations to which histories of religion are prone, lacking as they do the requisite categories. We must follow a precise tradition if we wish to understand, for example, what the Angels of the Earth represent to Mazdean piety. (33)

Such are Blake's 'angels stationed in hawthorn bowers' or his lark that is 'a mighty angel' or his sun which is 'an Innumerable company of the Heavenly host crying "Holy, Holy, Holy is the Lord God Almighty" ' (K617). To give Blake the last word I quote from his great poem on the living universe of the Imagination, *Milton*:

> Thou seest the Constellations in the deep & wondrous Night:
> They rise in order and continue their immortal courses
> Upon the mountain & in vales with harp & heavenly song,
> With flute & clarion, with cups & measures fill'd with foaming wine.
> Glitt'ring the streams reflect the Vision of beatitude,
> And the calm Ocean joys beneath & smooths his awful waves:
> These are the Sons of Los, & these the Labourers of the Vintage.
> Thou seest the gorgeous clothed Flies that dance & sport in summer
> Upon the sunny brooks & meadows: every one the dance
> Knows in its intricate mazes of delight artful to weave:
> Each one to sound his instruments of music in the dance,
> To touch each other & recede, to cross & change & return:
> These are the Children of Los; thou seest the Trees on mountains,
> The wind blows heavy, loud they thunder thro' the darksom sky,
> Uttering prophecies & speaking instructive words to the sons
> Of men: These are the Sons of Los: These the Visions of Eternity,
> But we see as it were only the hem of their garments
> When with our vegetable eyes we view these wondrous Visions.

>   (K511–12)